Lecture Notes in Computer Science 13216

More information about this series at https://link.springer.com/bookseries/558

Vincenzo Gervasi · Andreas Vogelsang (Eds.)

Requirements Engineering: Foundation for Software Quality

28th International Working Conference, REFSQ 2022
Birmingham, UK, March 21–24, 2022
Proceedings

Editors
Vincenzo Gervasi 🆔
University of Pisa
Pisa, Italy

Andreas Vogelsang 🆔
University of Cologne
Cologne, Germany

ISSN 0302-9743   ISSN 1611-3349 (electronic)
Lecture Notes in Computer Science
ISBN 978-3-030-98463-2   ISBN 978-3-030-98464-9 (eBook)
https://doi.org/10.1007/978-3-030-98464-9

This Springer imprint is published by the registered company Springer Nature Switzerland AG
The registered company address is: Gewerbestrasse 11, 6330 Cham, Switzerland

Preface

This volume contains the papers presented at REFSQ 2022, the 28th International Working Conference on Requirements Engineering: Foundation for Software Quality, held on March 21–24, 2022 in Aston, Birmingham, UK. As we write these lines, it seems highly likely that REFSQ 2022 will be held in-person as planned, for the first time after a two-year hiatus forced by the COVID-19 pandemic which has impacted so many aspects of our lives.

We, on behalf of the entire REFSQ community, would like to take this chance to thank the many colleagues who, in their various roles, have dedicated their time, energy, and ingenuity in the last two years to organizing REFSQ 2020 and 2021 in such difficult conditions and with so much uncertainty.

The REFSQ series was established in 1994, at first as a workshop series, and since 2010 in the "working conference" format, with ample time for presentations and substantial discussions of each contribution. It is often considered among the major international scientific events in Requirements Engineering, and the only one to be permanently located in Europe, with a special connection to European industry and academia. The need for ever-increasing levels of quality in requirements has not diminished in the 28 years since the first REFSQ; on the contrary, requirements are pervasive in the design, implementation, and operation of software systems and related services that impact the lives of billions.

The special theme for REFSQ 2022 was "Explainability in Requirements Engineering". As the impact of decisions taken by software systems increases, so does our duty, as requirements engineers, to investigate how such systems can be held accountable, and their operations made understandable to those affected by them, as part of our collective social responsibility.

The call for papers explicitly solicited contributions on how to elicit, specify and validate requirements for explainability in (and thus accountability of) software system, and how to design and implement systems whose behavior in specific instances is explainable, back to the requirements whose implementation caused the behavior, to the stakeholders expressing those requirements, and to their rationale for supporting those requirements. Among others, the special theme included issues such as:

- What is Explainability and who needs it
- How to elicit and specify Explainability
- How to check/assure Explainability
- Product vs. Process Explainability
- Consequences of low Explainability
- Self-Explainable Systems
- Explainability of Design Decisions

We were very happy to observe that the challenge was promptly taken up by the research community, with many submissions focusing on exactly those issues. Several of those contributions were accepted for presentation at the conference, and are now part of this volume.

In response to the Call for Papers, we received 50 abstracts, which resulted in 48 full papers. Three submissions were withdrawn by the authors prior to review, and each of the remaining 45 was reviewed by three program committee members, extensively discussed among the reviewers, and then brought for additional discussion if needed and final decision at the plenary program committee meeting that was held (online) on December 16, 2021. Six papers for which no consensus had been reached were discussed in special depth, with two of them accepted on the condition that certain improvements be made (those underwent an additional check by a PC member before final acceptance).

Overall, 19 papers were finally accepted for publication, and are now collected in this volume. In particular, based on paper category, the acceptance ratios are as follows:

- Scientific Evaluation (long): 20 submissions, 10 accepted (50%)
- Technical Design (long): 8 submissions, 2 accepted (25%)
- Vision (short): 5 submissions, 1 accepted (20%)
- Research Preview (short): 12 submissions, 6 accepted (50%)

The overall acceptance rate was thus 42% (19/45), almost identical for long and short papers.

As in previous years, the conference was organized as a three-day symposium (Tuesday to Thursday), with one day devoted to industrial presentations (in a single track), and two days of academic presentations (in two parallel tracks). In addition to paper presentations and related discussions, the program included keynote talks, a Poster & Tools sessions, and awards to recognize the best contributions in various categories. On the Monday before the conference, four co-located events were held: NLP4RE (5th Workshop on Natural Language Processing for Requirements Engineering) organized by Fabiano Dalpiaz, Davide Dell'Anna, Sylwia Kopczyńska and Lloyd Montgomery; RE4AI (3rd International Workshop on Requirements Engineering for Artificial Intelligence) organized by Renata Guizzardi, Jennifer Horkoff, Anna Perini and Angelo Susi; Design Thinking (International Workshop on Design Thinking, Design Fiction and Requirements Engineering) organized by Andrew Darby, Peter Sawyer, Wei Liu and Nelly Bencomo; and the REFSQ Doctoral Symposium, organized by Liliana Pasquale and Andrea Zisman. The proceedings of co-located events and the Poster & Tools track are published in a separate volume via CEUR.

We would like to thank all members of the Requirements Engineering community who prepared a contribution for REFSQ 2022: there would be no progress in our discipline without the talent, intelligence, and effort that so many brilliant researchers dedicated to the field. We would also like to thank members of the Program Committee and additional reviewers for their invaluable contribution to the selection process.

Special thanks are due to all the colleagues that served in various distinguished roles in the organization of REFSQ 2022 – your help in assembling a rich program has been invaluable. The REFSQ Steering Committee has provided excellent support and guidance throughout the process; we have found our path well marked by previous PC members who happily shared their experiences. Finally, we would like to thank the Local Organizers Nelly Bencomo and Pete Sawyer; the Steering Committee Chair Anna Perini and Vice-Chair Fabiano Dalpiaz, and the head of the Background Organization, Xavier Franch, for making our regular organizational meetings so enjoyable that we *almost* looked forward to each subsequent one with pleasurable anticipation.

Last but not least, we would like to thank you, the reader. You are the reason for this volume to exist. We hope you will find its contents interesting, useful, stimulating, and inspirational.

February 2022

Vincenzo Gervasi
Andreas Vogelsang

REFSQ 2022 Organization

Program Committee Chairs

Vincenzo Gervasi   University of Pisa, Italy
Andreas Vogelsang   University of Cologne, Germany

Local Organization Chairs

Nelly Bencomo   Durham University, UK
Peter Sawyer   Aston University, UK

Industry Chairs

Maria Chli   Aston University, UK
Amalinda Post   Robert Bosch GmbH, Germany

Workshop Chairs

Nelly Condori-Fernández   University of A Coruña, Spain/Vrije Universiteit
     Amsterdam, The Netherlands
Joerg Doerr   Fraunhofer IESE, Germany

Doctoral Symposium Chairs

Liliana Pasquale   University College Dublin/Lero, Ireland
Andrea Zisman   The Open University, UK

Posters and Tools Chairs

Marcela Ruiz   Zurich University of Applied Sciences (ZHAW),
     Switzerland
Jan-Philipp Steghöfer   Chalmers | University of Gothenburg, Sweden

Satellite Proceedings Chair

Jannik Fischbach   Qualicen GmbH/University of Cologne, Germany

Publicity Chair

Oliver Karras   TIB - Leibniz Information Centre for Science and
     Technology, Germany

Student Volunteer Chairs

Sara Hassan	Birmingham City University, UK
Huma Samin	Aston University, UK

Program Committee

Carina Alves	Universidade Federal de Pernambuco, Brazil
Daniel Amyot	University of Ottawa, Canada
Fatma Basak Aydemir	Boğaziçi University, Turkey
Richard Berntsson Svensson	Chalmers | University of Gothenburg, Sweden
Dan Berry	University of Waterloo, Canada
Sjaak Brinkkemper	Utrecht University, The Netherlands
Nelly Condori-Fernández	University of A Coruña, Spain/Vrije Universiteit Amsterdam, The Netherlands
Fabiano Dalpiaz	Utrecht University, The Netherlands
Jörg Dörr	Fraunhofer IESE, Germany
Alessio Ferrari	ISTI-CNR, Italy
Xavier Franch	Universitat Politècnica de Catalunya, Spain
Samuel Fricker	Blekinge Institute of Technology, Sweden
Matthias Galster	University of Canterbury, UK
Vincenzo Gervasi	University of Pisa, Italy
Martin Glinz	University of Zurich, Switzerland
Michael Goedicke	University of Duisburg-Essen, Germany
Paul Grünbacher	Johannes Kepler University Linz, Austria
Renata Guizzardi	Universidade Federal do Espirito Santo, Brazil
Andrea Herrmann	Free Software Engineering Trainer, Germany
Jennifer Horkoff	Chalmers | University of Gothenburg, Sweden
Fuyuki Ishikawa	National Institute of Informatics, Japan
Zhi Jin	Peking University, China
Erik Kamsties	University of Applied Sciences and Arts Dortmund, Germany
Eric Knauss	Chalmers | University of Gothenburg, Sweden
Kim Lauenroth	Adesso AG, Germany
Emmanuel Letier	University College London, UK
Grischa Liebel	Reykjavik University, Iceland
Nazim Madhavji	University of Western Ontario, Canada
Daniel Mendez	Blekinge Institute of Technology, Sweden, and fortiss, Germany
Luisa Mich	University of Trento, Italy
Gunter Mussbacher	McGill University, Canada
John Mylopoulos	University of Ottawa, Canada
Nan Niu	University of Cincinnati, USA

Andreas Opdahl	University of Bergen, Sweden
Barbara Paech	Universität Heidelberg, Germany
Elda Paja	IT University of Copenhagen, Denmark
Liliana Pasquale	University College Dublin, Ireland
Oscar Pastor	Universidad Politécnica de Valencia, Spain
Anna Perini	Fondazione Bruno Kessler Trento, Italy
Klaus Pohl	Paluno, University of Duisburg-Essen, Germany
Björn Regnell	Lund University, Sweden
Mehrdad Sabetzadeh	University of Luxembourg, Luxembourg
Klaus Schmid	University of Hildesheim, Germany
Kurt Schneider	Leibniz Universität Hannover, Germany
Laura Semini	University of Pisa, Italy
Norbert Seyff	FHNW University of Applied Sciences and Arts Northwestern Switzerland, Switzerland
Paola Spoletini	Kennesaw State University, USA
Jan-Philipp Steghöfer	Chalmers ǀ University of Gothenburg, Sweden
Angelo Susi	Fondazione Bruno Kessler - Irst, Italy
Michael Unterkalmsteiner	Blekinge Institute of Technology, Sweden
Michael Vierhauser	Johannes Kepler University Linz, Austria
Andreas Vogelsang	University of Cologne, Germany
Stefan Wagner	University of Stuttgart, Germany
Didar Zowghi	University of Technology, Sydney, Australia

Additional Reviewers

Anders, Michael
Habiba, Umm-E
Kobayashi, Tsutomu
Rohmann, Astrid

REFSQ Series Organization

Steering Committee

Anna Perini (Chair)	Fondazione Bruno Kessler, Trento, Italy
Fabiano Dalpiaz (Vice-chair)	Utrecht University, The Netherlands
Xavier Franch (Head of BO)	Universitat Politècnica de Catalunya, Spain
Klaus Pohl	University of Duisburg-Essen, Germany
Kurt Schneider	Universität Hannover, Germany
Paola Spoletini	Kennesaw State University, USA
Nazim Madhavji	Western University, Canada
Michael Goedicke	University of Duisburg-Essen, Germany
Eric Knauss	Chalmers ǀ University of Gothenburg, Sweden
Jennifer Horkoff	Chalmers ǀ University of Gothenburg, Sweden

Erik Kamsties   University of Applied Sciences and Arts
                            Dortmund, Germany
Vincenzo Gervasi   University of Pisa, Italy
Andreas Vogelsang   University of Cologne, Germany
Alessio Ferrari   CNR-ISTI, Pisa, Italy
Birgit Penzenstadler   Chalmers | University of Gothenburg, Sweden,
                            and Lappeenranta Lahti University of
                            Technology, Finland

Background Organization

Xavier Franch (Co-chair)   Universitat Politècnica de Catalunya, Spain
Carme Quer (Co-chair)   Universitat Politècnica de Catalunya, Spain
Carles Farré (Web Chair)   Universitat Politècnica de Catalunya, Spain
Quim Motger   Universitat Politècnica de Catalunya, Spain

Supporting Institutions, Companies and Groups

Organizers

Sponsors

Contents

Artificial Intelligence and Explainability

Transparency and Explainability of AI Systems: Ethical Guidelines in Practice

Nagadivya Balasubramaniam(✉), Marjo Kauppinen, Kari Hiekkanen, and Sari Kujala

Department of Computer Science, Aalto University, Espoo, Finland
{nagadivya.balasubramaniam,marjo.kauppinen,kari.hiekkanen,
sari.kujala}@aalto.fi

Abstract. **[Context and Motivation]** Recent studies have highlighted transparency and explainability as important quality requirements of AI systems. However, there are still relatively few case studies that describe the current state of defining these quality requirements in practice. **[Question]** The goal of our study was to explore what ethical guidelines organizations have defined for the development of transparent and explainable AI systems. We analyzed the ethical guidelines in 16 organizations representing different industries and public sector. **[Results]** In the ethical guidelines, the importance of transparency was highlighted by almost all of the organizations, and explainability was considered as an integral part of transparency. Building trust in AI systems was one of the key reasons for developing transparency and explainability, and customers and users were raised as the main target groups of the explanations. The organizations also mentioned developers, partners, and stakeholders as important groups needing explanations. The ethical guidelines contained the following aspects of the AI system that should be explained: the purpose, role of AI, inputs, behavior, data utilized, outputs, and limitations. The guidelines also pointed out that transparency and explainability relate to several other quality requirements, such as trustworthiness, understandability, traceability, privacy, auditability, and fairness. **[Contribution]** For researchers, this paper provides insights into what organizations consider important in the transparency and, in particular, explainability of AI systems. For practitioners, this study suggests a structured way to define explainability requirements of AI systems.

Keywords: Transparency · Explainability · Quality requirements · Ethical guidelines · AI systems

1 Introduction

The use of artificial intelligence (AI) is changing the world we live in [23]. Algorithmic decision-making is becoming ubiquitous in daily life. Moreover, machine learning is utilized in the crucial decision-making process, such as loan processing, criminal identification, and cancer detection [1, 18]. The number of organizations that are interested in developing AI systems are increasing. However, the black-box nature of AI systems has raised several ethical issues [3].

© Springer Nature Switzerland AG 2022
V. Gervasi and A. Vogelsang (Eds.): REFSQ 2022, LNCS 13216, pp. 3–18, 2022.
https://doi.org/10.1007/978-3-030-98464-9_1

To handle the ethical issues of AI and to develop responsible AI systems, various interest groups across the world (e.g., IEEE, ACM) have defined comprehensive ethical guidelines and principles to ensure responsible AI usage. The ethical guidelines of AI developed by three established expert groups [16, 20, 25] emphasized transparency and explainability for developing AI systems. In addition to that, organizations have defined their own ethical guidelines of AI that encompass the ethical issues which are prominent to the organization [3].

Organizations utilize different machine learning models and algorithms in the decision-making processes. Moreover, the outputs and the decisions of AI systems are usually difficult to understand and lack transparency [8]. Recent studies [6, 8] highlight explainability as a key requirement of AI systems that improves transparency. In addition, a study [2] on RE techniques and an industry guideline for building AI systems emphasized that explanations of AI systems enforced trust and improved the decision making of users when using AI systems.

Transparency and explainability are identified as key quality requirements of AI systems [6, 8, 13] and are portrayed as quality requirements that need more focus in the machine learning context [18]. Explainability can impact user needs, cultural values, laws, corporate values, and other quality aspects of AI systems [6]. The number of papers that deal with transparency and explainability requirements have recently increased. However, studies on how to define explainability and transparency requirements of AI systems in practice are still rare and at their early stage.

The goal of this study was to explore **what ethical guidelines organizations have defined for the development of transparent and explainable AI systems**. In this study, we analyzed the ethical guidelines of AI published by 16 organizations to understand what quality requirements these organizations have highlighted in their ethical guidelines. Then, we performed detailed study focusing especially on transparency and explainability guidelines to delineate the different components of explainability requirements of AI systems.

This paper is organized as follows. Section 2 describes the related work on transparency and explainability as quality requirements of AI systems. In Sect. 3, we present the research method used in this study. Section 4 describes the results from the analysis of the ethical guidelines and presents the components of explainability of AI. We discuss our results and their validity in Sect. 5. Finally, Sect. 6 concludes the paper.

2 Related Work

In what follows, we first emphasize the definition of ethical requirements of AI systems and the close association of ethical guidelines to requirement definition. Next, we focus on transparency and explainability which are emerging quality requirements of AI systems.

2.1 Ethical Requirements of AI Systems

Guizzardi et al. [17] introduced and defined ethical requirements of AI systems as *'Ethical requirements are requirements for AI systems derived from ethical principles or ethical codes (norms)'.* Besides, the authors highlighted that defining the ethical requirements at the beginning of AI system development helps in considering the ethical issues during the early phases of development. Generally, ethical requirements of AI constitute both functional and quality requirements derived from the stakeholder needs in accordance with ethical principles [17, 24]. The studies on ethical requirements depicted the close association of ethical guidelines to requirements definition.

2.2 Transparency as a Quality Requirement

Cysneiros [11] and Leite and Capelli [14]'s studies classified transparency as an impactful non-functional requirement (NFR) of the software system. Further, the authors delineated the interrelationship of transparency with other NFRs, such as trust, privacy, security, accuracy, etc. through softgoal interdependence graphs (SIGs).

In addition, the dependency between transparency and trust is a salient facet that needs to be considered in system development, such as self-driving cars [5, 13]. Kwan et al. [21] developed an NFR catalogue for trust, and the study reported that transparency positively impacted in achieving users' trust, which was portrayed as the key corporate social responsibility (CSR) principle.

The recent studies [12, 13, 18, 19] discussed transparency as a key NFR in machine learning and autonomous systems. Transparency in AI systems was identified as quintessential, but the black box nature of AI systems makes the definition of transparency requirements challenging [13, 19]. Horkoff [19] emphasized the real-world impact of machine learning and the crucial question *'how these results are derived?'*. Likewise, Chazette et al. [7] highlighted that transparency as an NFR is abstract and requires better understanding and supporting mechanisms to incorporate them into the system. Explanations of machine learning and AI results were proposed to mitigate the issues of transparency [7, 19]. The studies [7, 8] on the relationship between explanations and transparency of AI systems proposed explainability as an NFR.

Explainability suggested as an NFR had been linked to other NFRs such as transparency and trust by [6]. As Köhl et al. [22] link explainability to transparency, and Chazette et al. [7, 8] also report that explainability aims in achieving better transparency. Moreover, explanations of AI systems had been identified to contribute higher system transparency. For instance, receiving explanations about a system, its processes and decisions impact both understandability and transparency NFRs [6].

2.3 Explainability as a Quality Requirement

Köhl et al. [22] addressed the gap in ensuring explainability in system development and performed a conceptual analysis of systems that needs explanations (e.g., automated hiring system). The analysis aimed to elicit and specify the explainability requirements of the system. The authors proposed definitions for three questions: 1) to **who** are the 'explanations for' focusing on understandability, context, and target of the system, 2) **when** the system is considered explainable, and 3) **how** to define explainability requirements.

Köhl et al. [22] and Chazette et al. [6] proposed definitions to help understand what explainability means from a software engineering perspective (Table 1). The definition of the explainability requirement by Chazette et al. [6] is based on the definition proposed by Köhl et al. [22]. Both of these definitions have the following variables: a system, an addressee (i.e., target group), an aspect, and a context. In addition to these variables, Chazette et al. [6] have also included an explainer in their definition of explainability.

Table 1. Definitions of explainability requirement and explainability

Köhl et al. [22]	Chazette et al. [6]
A system S must be explainable for target group G in context C with respect to aspect Y of explanandum X.	A system S is explainable with respect to an aspect X of S relative to an addressee A in context C if and only if there is an entity E (the explainer) who, by giving a corpus of information I (the explanation of X), enables A to understand X of S in C.

Chazette et al. [7, 8] discussed explainability as an NFR and interlinked it with transparency. Further, explainability supports in defining the transparency requirements which impacts software quality. The authors also identified that end-users are more interested to get explanations during adverse situations, and they are least interested to know the inner working of the system i.e., how the system worked [7, 8]. In addition, [6, 8, 22] highlighted the tradeoffs between the explainability and other NFRs. Consequently, [6] indicated that when eliciting the explainability requirements, consideration of positive and negative impacts of explanations to the users could avoid conflict with transparency and understandability NFRs.

Subsequently, Chazette et al. [6] featured explainability as an emerging NFR and evaluated how explainability impacts other NFRs and qualities. Their study revealed that transparency, reliability, accountability, fairness, trustworthiness, etc. are positively impacted by explainability. However, the authors acknowledged that studies on incorporating explainability in the software development process are in its early stage and need more research [6].

3   Research Method

The goal of this study was to investigate *what ethical guidelines organizations have defined for the development of transparent and explainable AI systems*. In the analysis of the ethical guidelines, we used the following research questions:

- *What quality requirements do organizations highlight in their ethical guidelines?*
- *What components can explainability requirements of AI systems contain?*
- *How do transparency and explainability relate to other quality requirements?*

Our selection criterion was to find organizations that have defined and published their ethical guidelines for using AI. In late 2018, AI Finland, which is a steering group in-charge of AI programme, organized the 'Ethics Challenge'. The challenge invited enterprises in Finland to develop ethical guidelines of AI as a way to promote the ethical use of AI. We identified 16 organizations that have published their ethical guidelines. We gathered the documents from the organizations' websites and those documents contained data such as AI ethical guidelines and their explanations as simple texts, detailed PowerPoint slides set, and videos explaining the guidelines.

First, we classified the organizations that have published the ethical guidelines of AI into three categories: professional services and software, business-to-consumer (B2C), and public sector. Table 2 summarizes these categories. Category A includes seven professional services organizations that provide a broad range of services from consulting to service design, software development, and AI & analytics. The two software companies in Category A develop a large range of enterprise solutions and digital services. The five B2C organizations represent different domains: two telecommunication companies, a retailer, a banking group, and an electricity transmission operator. The public sector organizations represent tax administration and social security services. The six companies of Category A are Finnish and the other three are global. Furthermore, all the organizations of Category B and C are Finnish.

Table 2. Overview of the organizations of the study

Category	No. of Organizations	Identifications
Category A: Professional services and software	9	O1-O9
Category B: Business-to-Consumer (B2C)	5	O10-O14
Category C: Public sector	2	O15 and O16

We started the data analysis process by conceptual ordering [10] where the ethical guidelines of AI in 16 organizations were ordered based on their category name. Then, the categories which were also quality requirements of AI were identified by line-by-line coding process [4]. This process was performed by the first author and was reviewed by the second author. Next, we performed the word-by-word coding technique and we focused on transparency and explainability guidelines in this step. We used Charmaz's [4] grounded theory techniques on coding and code-comparison for the purpose of data analysis only.

The first two authors of this paper performed separately the initial word-by-word coding. The analysis was based on the variables used in the definition of explainability by Chazette et al. [6]. These variables were addressees of explanations, aspects of explanations, contexts of explanations, and explainers. We also analyzed reasons for transparency. Discrepancies in the codes were discussed and resolved during our multiple iterative meetings, and missing codes were added. Table 3 shows examples of ethical guidelines and codes from the initial word-by-word coding process. Next, in the axial coding process, the sub-categories from the initial coding process were combined or added under the relevant high-level categories. The quality requirements that are related to transparency and explainability were combined and the second author reviewed the axial coding process.

Table 3. Example codes of the initial word-by-word coding process

Example lines of ethical guidelines	Examples of codes
We tell our customers in a clear and understandable way where, why, and how AI has been utilized.	Addressees – Customers Relationships – Understandability
Their input, capabilities, intended purpose, and limitations will be communicated clearly to our customers.	Addressees – Customers Aspects – Input, Capabilities, Purpose, and Limitations
Ensure AI transparency. To build trust among employees and customers, develop explainable AI that is transparent across processes and functions.	Reasons for transparency – Trust Addressees – Employees and customers

4   Results

This section presents the results from the analysis of ethical AI guidelines of the sixteen organizations. First, we summarize what quality requirements the organizations have raised in their ethical guidelines of AI systems. In Sect. 4.2, we report the results of the analysis of transparency and explainability guidelines and describe the components for defining explainability requirements. We also propose a template for representing individual explainability requirements. In Sect. 4.3, we summarize the quality requirements that relate to transparency and explainability.

4.1   Overview of Ethical Guidelines of AI Systems

This section gives an overview of what quality requirements the organizations refer to in their ethical guidelines. In Table 4 and 5, we summarize the quality requirements of AI systems that have been emphasized in the ethical guidelines of the sixteen organizations.

In this study, 14 out of the 16 organizations have defined *transparency* ethical guidelines, and all the professional services and software companies have defined the transparency guidelines for developing AI systems. The key focus on the transparency guidelines encompassed the utilization of AI i.e., how the AI is used in the organizations (O2, O5, O6, O13). Moreover, openness or communicating openly (O4, O5, O11, O12, O14, O15) on how and where the AI is used in the system are indicated in the guidelines. Interestingly, *explainability* was always defined as a part of transparency guidelines in 13 out of the 14 organizations. The only exception was the organization O7 that did not cover explainability in their ethical guidelines of AI systems. A more detailed analysis of transparency and explainability guidelines is described in the following section.

Privacy ethical guidelines in organizations focused to protect and to avoid unethical usage of personal and sensitive data (O1, O2, O6). Moreover, compliance with privacy guidelines and the GDPR were emphasized in the privacy guidelines of the two organizations (O3, O4). Furthermore, Organization O6 highlighted that it is important to communicate how, why, when, and where user data is anonymized. Confidentiality of personal data and privacy of their customers are prioritized (O11, O16) and adherence to

Table 4. Quality requirements in ethical guidelines of Category A

Quality Requirements	Professional services and software								
	O1	O2	O3	O4	O5	O6	O7	O8	O9
Transparency	x	x	x	x	x	x	x	x	x
Explainability	x	x	x	x	x	x		x	x
Privacy	x	x	x	x	x	x	x		x
Security	x				x	x		x	x
Safety				x		x		x	
Fairness	x		x	x	x	x		x	x
Accountability			x	x	x		x		x
Reliability					x	x			

Table 5. Quality requirements in ethical guidelines of Category B and C

Quality Requirements	B2C					Public Sector	
	O10	O11	O12	O13	O14	O15	O16
Transparency		x	x	x	x	x	
Explainability		x	x	x	x	x	
Privacy		x		x	x	x	x
Security	x	x	x	x			x
Safety		x					x
Fairness	x	x	x	x			
Accountability		x			x		x
Reliability							x

data protection practices (O11, O12, O13 O14, O15) are covered in the privacy guidelines of B2C and public sector organizations.

Few of the professional services and software organizations (O1, O5, O6, O9) and B2C (O11, O13) organizations defined their *security* and privacy guidelines together. Ensuring the *safety* of the AI system and user data by preventing misuse and reducing risks, and compliance to safety principles were also highlighted in privacy and security guidelines (O4, O6, O8, O11, O16). The security guidelines portrayed the need to develop secure AI systems (O5, O6, O8) and to follow data security practices (O1, O10, O11, O13, O16).

Professional services and software organizations and B2C organizations developed ethical guidelines for *fairness* that aim to avoid bias and discrimination. According to the B2C organizations, AI and machine learning utilization should eliminate discrimination and prejudices when making decisions and should function equally and fairly to everyone (O10–O13). In professional services and software organizations, fairness is advocated by fostering equality, diversity, and inclusiveness. The algorithms and underlying data should be unbiased and are as representative and inclusive as possible (O1, O4, O6, O8). From the organizations' viewpoint, developing unbiased AI contributes to responsible AI development.

Accountability ethical guidelines focused on assigning humans who will be responsible for monitoring AI operations, such as AI learning, AI decision-making (O5, O11, O16). The objective of the organizations was to assign owners or parties who will be responsible for their AI operations and algorithms. The respective owners or parties will be contacted when concerns arise in the AI system, such as ethical questions and issues, harms, and risks (O4, O3, O11, O14, O16). Further, a couple of professional services organizations recommended establishing audit certifications, human oversight forums, or ethics communities to ensure accountability mechanisms throughout the system lifecycle and to support project teams (O7, O9). In organizations, the accountability guidelines are reckoned to closely relate to responsibility i.e., humans being responsible for the decisions and operations of the AI system.

Professional services and public sector organizations provide contrasting perspectives about *reliability* in AI development. For professional services and software organizations, reliability is coupled with safety and quality standards that help in assessing the risks, harms, and purpose of AI before its deployment (O5, O6). Whereas reliability in the public sector organization centered on the use of reliable data in AI. When the data or algorithms are unreliable or faulty, the organization corrects them to match the purpose of the AI system (O16).

4.2 From Ethical Guidelines to Explainability Requirements

In this section, we first report why the organizations emphasized transparency and explainability in their ethical guidelines. Then, we describe the four components of explainability we identified from the transparency guidelines of the organizations. These components are based on the explainability definition proposed by Chazette et al. [6]. Finally, we suggest a template for representing individual explainability requirements.

Reasons to be Transparent: The ethical guidelines of 10 organizations contained reasons why to incorporate transparency in AI systems. Five organizations (O1, O4, O5, O6, O11) portrayed building and maintaining users' *trust* as a prominent reason. Moreover, two organizations (O12, O13) highlighted that transparency supports *security* in AI systems. Organization O2 emphasized that being transparent helps in differentiating the actual AI decisions and AI recommendations. Furthermore, Organization O5 mentioned that transparency paves the way to mitigate *unfairness* and to gain more users' trust. The other reasons to develop transparent AI systems were to assess the *impact* of AI systems on society and to make AI systems available for assessment and scrutiny (O7, O14).

Figure 1 shows the components of explainability that can be used when defining explainability requirements of AI systems. The purpose of these components is to give a structured overview of what explainability can mean. The four components can also be summarized with the following questions:

- Addressees - To whom to explain?
- Aspects - What to explain?
- Contexts - In what kind of situation to explain?
- Explainers - Who explains?

Figure 1 also contains concrete examples what these explainability components can be in practice. These examples have been identified from the ethical guidelines of the organizations.

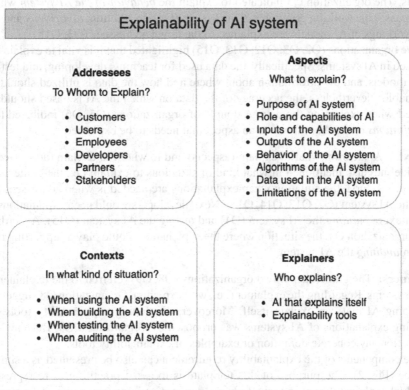

Fig. 1. A model of explainability components

Addressees: The transparency guidelines covered a wide range of addressees to whom the AI or the different aspects of AI should be explained. Seven organizations (O1, O2, O6, O7, O13, O14, O15) highlighted that their AI should be explained and clearly communicated to their *customers*. Likewise, the explanations of AI systems were targeted to their *users* in O3, O5, O6, O11. According to the transparency guidelines of the organization O14, *partners and stakeholders* are also addressees of their AI systems. Besides, Organization O1 mentioned *employees* as their addressees, and Organization O5 narrowed the addressees down to *developers* of the AI systems.

Aspects: The key aspect that needs to be explainable is the *purpose* of AI systems (O6, O11). The intended purpose of the system should be communicated to the people who could be directly or indirectly impacted by the system (O11). Particularly, the addressee(s) should know how and why the organization is utilizing AI (O5, O13). Further, the *role and capabilities of AI* (O2, O3, O6, O11) need to be explained, so that addressees can see when AI makes the actual decision and when it only supports people in making decisions with recommendations.

Further, four organizations (O4, O6, O11, O15) mentioned to explain the *inputs and outputs* of the systems, such as inputs and outputs of the algorithms, decisions of AI systems. The organization O5 indicated to explain the *behavior of the AI system* which encompasses the working principles of the system (O4). In addition, *algorithms* and the inner workings of AI models are explained to the target addressees (O3, O15).

Five organizations (O2, O3, O12, O13, O15) highlighted that it is vital to explain the *data* used in AI systems. Specifically, the data used for teaching, developing, and testing the AI models, and the information about where and how the data is utilized should be explainable. Nevertheless, the accuracy of the data on which the AI is based should be included when explaining the data. A couple of organizations (O5, O6) indicated that the *limitations* of the AI systems as an aspect that needs to be explained.

Contexts: Apart from what to explain (aspects) and to whom to explain (addressees), the guidelines also mentioned in what kind of situations to explain i.e., the contexts of explanations. First, the situation when explanations are needed is when addressees are *using* the AI system (O2, O13, O14, O15). Next, developers would need explanations in the context of *building* the AI system (O4) and *testing* the AI system (O15). According to the organization O4, the situation where the explanations could play a supporting role is when *auditing* the AI system.

Explainers: The guidelines of two organizations (O8, O9) referred to the explainer of the AI systems. Regarding the explainer (i.e., who explains), Organization O8 suggested developing AI that can explain itself. Moreover, developing explainability tools for providing explanations of AI systems was proposed by Organization O9. But they did not mention any concrete definition or examples of explainability tools.

The components of the explainability requirement can also be presented as a simple sentence (Fig. 2). The purpose of this template is to assist practitioners to represent individual explainability requirements in a structured and consistent way. This simple template is based on the template that is used for defining functional requirements as user stories in agile software development. The template suggested by Cohn [9] is the following: As a <type of user>, I want <capability> so that <business value>.

> As a **<type of addressee>**, I want to get explanation(s) on
> an **<aspect>** of a **<system>** from an **<explainer>** in a **<context>**.

Fig. 2. A template for representing individual explainability requirements

Here we give two high-level examples of explainability requirements based on Fig. 2.

- "As a user, I want to get understandable explanation(s) on the behavior of the AI system from the system, when I'm using it"
- "As a developer, I want to get explanation(s) on the algorithms of the AI system from an explainability tool, when I'm testing it"

These high-level examples of explainability requirements aim to show that different addressees may need different types and levels of explanations. For example, when debugging the system, developers are likely to need more detailed explanations of AI behavior than users. Users do not necessarily want to understand the exact underlying algorithm and inner workings of the AI model.

In their conceptual analysis of explainability, Köhl et al. also suggest that different addressees need different, context-sensitive explanations to be able to understand the relevant aspects of a particular system [22]. They also remark that an explanation for an engineer may not explain anything to a user. Furthermore, they mention that the explainer could be even a *human expert*.

4.3 Quality Requirements Related to Transparency and Explainability

The analysis of the ethical guidelines exhibited that transparency and explainability associates to several other quality requirements. Figure 3 presents the nine quality requirements that are related to transparency and explainability.

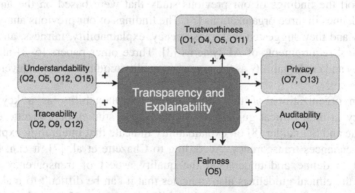

Fig. 3. Quality requirements related to transparency and explainability + Helps; – Conflicts

According to the organizations, *understandability* contributes to the development of transparency and explainability of AI systems. The transparency guidelines covered three details when addressing the importance of understandability, they are 1) to assure that people understand the methods of using AI and the behavior of the AI system (O5, O12), 2) to communicate in a clear and understandable way on where, why, and how AI has been utilized (O15), and 3) to ensure people understand the difference between actual

AI decisions and when AI only supports in making the decisions with recommendations (O2). Thus, understandability supports explainability and transparency by ensuring the utilization of AI is conveyed to people clearly and in necessary detail. *Traceability* in transparency guidelines accentuates the importance of tracing the decisions of the AI systems (O2, O12). Organization O12 also mentioned that it is important to trace the data used in the AI decision-making process to satisfy transparency.

The transparency and explainability of AI systems can also assist in building *trustworthiness* (O1, O4, O5, O11). Prioritizing transparency when designing and building AI systems, and explaining the system to those who are directly or indirectly affected is crucial in building and maintaining trust. Furthermore, two organizations (O7, O13) highlighted *privacy* in their transparency guidelines. Ensuring transparency can also raise potential tensions with privacy (O7). Moreover, *auditability* in the transparency guideline suggested that it is vital to build AI systems that are ready for auditing (O4). Organization O5 indicated that transparency also assists in ensuring *fairness* in AI systems. In addition to the relationships shown in Fig. 3, we identified *security*, *integrity*, *interpretability*, *intelligibility*, and *accuracy* in the transparency guidelines, but their relationship with transparency and explainability is not clearly stated in the guidelines.

5 Discussion

5.1 Transparency and Explainability Guidelines in Practice

Nearly all the organizations of this study pointed out the importance of transparency and explainability in their ethical guidelines of AI systems. There were only two organizations out of sixteen that did not emphasize transparency. The results of this paper support the findings of our previous study that were based on the analysis of ethical guidelines in three organizations [3]. The findings of our previous analysis were preliminary and they suggested that transparency, explainability, fairness, and privacy can be critical requirements of AI systems [3]. Three other papers [6–8] also report transparency and explainability as the important quality requirements for developing AI systems.

Thirteen organizations of this study defined explainability as a key part of transparency in their ethical guidelines. Similarly, the studies of Chazette et al. [7] and Chazette and Schneider [8] on explainability indicate that integrating explanations in systems enhances transparency. According to Chazette et al. [7], it can, however, be difficult to define and understand the quality aspect of transparency [7]. The analysis of the ethical guidelines also indicates that it can be difficult to make a clear distinction between transparency and explainability in practice. Nevertheless, providing explanations of AI systems supports fostering transparency.

The prime goal of the organizations to incorporate transparency and explainability in AI systems was to build and maintain trustworthiness. Two studies [6, 15] also report that explainability supports in developing transparent and trustworthy AI systems. Furthermore, Zieni and Heckel [26] suggest that delineating and implementing transparency requirements can support in gaining users' trust. According to the studies of Cysneiros et al. [13], and Habibullah and Horkoff [18], trust as a quality requirement plays a vital role in the development of autonomous systems [13] and machine learning systems [18].

Based on the definition of explainability proposed by Chazette et al. [6] and the analysis of the ethical guidelines, we suggest four important components to be covered in explainability requirements. These components of explainability are 1) to whom to explain (addressee), 2) what to explain (aspect), 3) in what kind of situation to explain (context), and 4) who explains (explainer). The ethical guidelines of the organizations included a considerable number of concrete examples what these components can be in practice. We believe that these components and concrete examples can support practitioners in understanding how to define explainability requirements in AI projects. Next, we discuss these concrete examples of addressees, aspects, contexts, and explainers.

The analysis of the ethical guidelines revealed that the organizations consider customers and users as key *addressees* that need explanations. Developers, partners, and stakeholders were also mentioned as addressees who require explanations of AI systems. According to Chazette et al. [6], understanding the addressees of the system was raised as a key factor that impacts the success of explainability.

The ethical guidelines of the organizations contained a rather large number of *aspects* that need to be explained to addressees. For example, the explanations should cover role, capabilities, and behavior of the AI system. In addition, inputs, outputs, algorithms, and data utilized in the AI system are aspects that need to be explained. Köhl et al. [22] point out that explaining aspects of AI system are beneficial for their addressees to understand the system. Subsequently, Chazette et al. [6] highlight aspects that need explanations are processes of reasoning, behavior, inner logic, decision, and intentions of the AI systems. Furthermore, the ethical guidelines of the organizations pointed out that it is important to describe the purpose and limitations of the AI system. It can be possible to identify positive impacts and negative consequences when explaining the purpose and limitations of the AI system.

The results show that the different *contexts of explanations* (i.e., in what kind of situations to explain) are: when using, building, testing, and auditing the AI system. Köhl et al. [22] and Chazette et al. [6] highlighted that the context-sensitive explanations support target groups receive intended explanations. Therefore, the context in which the explanations are provided can assist delineating what to explain (aspects). In our study, AI that explains itself was represented as the *explainer* of the system. Similarly, Chazette et al. [6] mentioned that explainers could be a system or parts of the system that provide information to their target groups.

One interesting result from the analysis of the ethical guidelines was the relationship of transparency and explainability with other quality requirements, such as understandability, trust, traceability, auditability, and fairness. For instance, the *understandability* quality aspect focused on explaining the AI utilization and behavior of the system transparently to the addressees. The addressees should also understand when the system makes a decision, and when it provides only recommendations. Chazette et al. [6] also report understandability as a crucial quality requirement that positively impacts explainability and transparency and enhances the user experience.

Further, the guidelines exhibited the association to *fairness*, where ensuring transparency and explainability helps in mitigating unfairness. Various studies [6, 18, 19] point out fairness as important quality requirement of machine learning [18, 19] and explainable systems [6]. In our study, *interpretability*, *integrity*, and *auditability* were also highlighted in the transparency and explainability guidelines. Similarly, Habibullah and Horkoff [18] identified interpretability and integrity as popular quality requirements of AI systems in industries, and Chazette et al. [6] report that explanations support the auditability requirement of the system. In addition, quality requirements such as, *accuracy*, *traceability*, *privacy* and *security* were emphasized in the ethical guidelines. In the literature [6, 18, 19], all these four quality requirements are considered to be essential when building AI systems.

5.2 Threats to Validity

Generalizability. Our study focused on the ethical guidelines of AI published by the 16 organizations. However, the ethical guidelines do not necessarily reflect what is happening in these organizations. Nevertheless, we think the guidelines contain important knowledge that should be considered when developing transparent and explainable AI systems. Therefore, we believe that organizations can utilize the results of this study to gain an overview and to understand the components that can help defining explainability in AI systems development.

Majority of the organizations of this study were Finnish or Finland-based international companies, and only three out of the sixteen organizations were global. When we compared the ethical guidelines of the global organizations with the ethical guidelines of the other organizations, there were no significant differences between them.

Reliability. Researcher bias might have influenced the data analysis process. To avoid misinterpretation and bias, the coding process was done by two researchers separately. The high-level categorization of the organizations was also reviewed by a third senior researcher who is also one of the authors of this paper.

The organizations selection strategy resulted in some limitations. We selected organizations that have published their ethical guidelines of AI publicly in Finland. Hence, may be the smaller number of public sector organizations in our study. However, the focus of our study was on transparency and explainability, so we did not make conclusions based on the categories of the organizations.

6 Conclusions

The goal of our study was to investigate what ethical guidelines organizations have defined for the development of transparent and explainable AI systems. Our study shows that explainability is tightly coupled to transparency and trustworthiness of AI systems. This leads to the conclusion that the systematic definition of explainability requirements is a crucial step in the development of transparent and trustworthy AI systems.

In this paper, we propose a model of explainability components that can facilitate to elicit, negotiate, and validate explainability requirements of AI systems. The purpose of our model is to assist practitioners to elaborate four important questions 1) to whom to explain, 2) what to explain, 3) in what kind of situation to explain, and 4) who explains. The paper also proposes a simple template for representing explainability requirements in a structured and consistent way.

One important direction in our future research is to perform case studies to understand how transparency and explainability requirements are defined in AI projects. We also aim to investigate how practitioners implement ethical guidelines in the development of AI systems. In addition, we are planning to conduct action research studies to explore how the model of explainability components and the template for representing explainability requirements can be applied in AI projects. Our long-term plan is to investigate how explainability requirements can be used in the testing of AI systems.

References

1. Abdollahi, B., Nasraoui, O.: Transparency in fair machine learning: the case of explainable recommender systems. In: Zhou, J., Chen, F. (eds.) Human and Machine Learning. HIS, pp. 21–35. Springer, Cham (2018). https://doi.org/10.1007/978-3-319-90403-0_2
2. Ahmad, K., Bano, M., Abdelrazek, M., Arora, C., Grundy, J.: What's up with requirements engineering for artificial intelligent systems? In: International Requirements Engineering Conference, pp. 1–12 (2021)
3. Balasubramaniam, N., Kauppinen, M., Kujala, S., Hiekkanen, K.: Ethical guidelines for solving ethical issues and developing AI systems. In: Morisio, M., Torchiano, M., Jedlitschka, A. (eds.) PROFES 2020. LNCS, vol. 12562, pp. 331–346. Springer, Cham (2020). https://doi.org/10.1007/978-3-030-64148-1_21
4. Charmaz, K.: Constructing Grounded Theory, 2nd edn. SAGE Publications Inc., Thousand Oaks (2014)
5. Chazette, L.: Mitigating challenges in the elicitation and analysis of transparency requirements. In: International Requirements Engineering Conference, pp. 470–475 (2019)
6. Chazette, L., Brunotte, W., Speith, T.: Exploring explainability: a definition, a model, and a knowledge catalogue. In: International Requirements Engineering Conference, pp. 197–208 (2021)
7. Chazette, L., Karras, O., Schneider, K.: Do end-users want explanations? Analyzing the role of explainability as an emerging aspect of non-functional requirements. In: International Requirements Engineering Conference, pp. 223–233 (2019)
8. Chazette, L., Schneider, K.: Explainability as a non-functional requirement: challenges and recommendations. Requirements Eng. 25(4), 493–514 (2020). https://doi.org/10.1007/s00766-020-00333-1
9. Cohn, M.: Agile Estimating and Planning. Prentice Hall, Upper Saddle River (2006)
10. Corbin, J., Strauss, A.: Basics of Qualitative Research, 4th edn. SAGE, Thousand Oaks (2015)
11. Cysneiros, L.M.: Using i* to elicit and model transparency in the presence of other non-functional requirements: a position paper. In: iStar: Citeseer, pp. 19–24 (2013)
12. Cysneiros, L., do Prado, J.: Non-functional requirements orienting the development of socially responsible software. In: Nurcan, S., Reinhartz, I., Soffer, P., Zdravkovic, J. (eds.) BPMDS/EMMSAD - 2020. LNBIP, vol. 387, pp. 335–342. Springer, Cham (2020). https://doi.org/10.1007/978-3-030-49418-6_23
13. Cysneiros, L.M., Raffi, M., Sampaio do Prado Leite, J.C.: Software transparency as a key requirement for self-driving cars. In: International Requirements Engineering Conference, pp. 382–387 (2018)
14. do Prado Leite, J.C.S., Cappelli, C.: Software transparency. Business Inf. Syst. Eng. 2(3), 127–139 (2010)
15. Drobotowicz, K., Kauppinen, M., Kujala, S.: Trustworthy AI services in the public sector: what are citizens saying about it? In: Requirements Engineering: Foundation for Software Quality, pp. 99–115 (2021)

16. European Commission: Ethics Guidelines for Trustworthy AI. https://ec.europa.eu/futurium/en/ai-alliance-consultation/guidelines. Accessed 24 Oct 2021

17. Guizzardi, R., Amaral, G., Guizzardi, G., Mylopoulos, J.: Ethical requirements for AI systems. In: Goutte, C., Zhu, X. (eds.) Canadian AI 2020. LNCS (LNAI), vol. 12109, pp. 251–256. Springer, Cham (2020). https://doi.org/10.1007/978-3-030-47358-7_24

18. Habibullah, K.M., Horkoff, J.: Non-functional requirements for machine learning: understanding current use and challenges in industry. In: International Requirements Engineering Conference, pp. 13–23 (2021)

19. Horkoff, J.: Non-functional requirements for machine learning: challenges and new directions. In: International Requirements Engineering Conference, pp. 386–391 (2019)

20. IEEE: Ethically Aligned Design, 1st edn. https://ethicsinaction.ieee.org/. Accessed 24 Oct 2021

21. Kwan, D., Cysneiros, L.M., do Prado Leite, J.C.S.: Towards Achieving Trust Through Transparency and Ethics (Pre-Print) (2021). http://arxiv.org/abs/2107.02959. Accessed 30 Aug 2021

22. Köhl, M.A., Baum, K., Langer, M., Oster, D., Speith, T., Bohlender, D.: Explainability as a non-functional requirement. In: International Requirements Engineering Conference, pp. 363–368 (2019)

23. Lepri, B., Oliver, N., Letouzé, E., Pentland, A., Vinck, P.: Fair, transparent, and accountable algorithmic decision-making processes. Philos. Technol. 31(4), 611–627 (2018)

24. Paech, B., Schneider, K.: How do users talk about software? Searching for common ground. In: Workshop on Ethics in Requirements Engineering Research and Practice, pp. 11–14 (2020)

25. SIIA (Software and Information Industry Association): Ethical Principles for Artificial Intelligence and Data Analytics, pp. 1–25 (2017)

26. Zieni, B., Heckel, R.: TEM: a transparency engineering methodology enabling users' trust judgement. In: International Requirements Engineering Conference, pp. 94–105 (2021)

Requirements Engineering for Artificial Intelligence: What Is a Requirements Specification for an Artificial Intelligence?

Daniel M. Berry[✉][iD]

Cheriton School of Computer Science, University of Waterloo, Waterloo, ON N2L 3G1, Canada
dberry@uwaterloo.ca
https://cs.uwaterloo.ca/~dberry/

Abstract. Context: This article concerns requirements for an artificial intelligence (AI) that does a non-algorithmic task that requires real intelligence. **Problem**: The literature and practice of AI development does not clarify what is a requirements specification (RS) of an AI that allows determining whether an implementation of the AI is correct. **Principal ideas**: This article shows how (1) measures used to evaluate an AI, (2) criteria for acceptable values of these measures, and (3) information about the AI's context that inform the criteria and tradeoffs in these measures, collectively constitute an RS of the AI. **Contribution**: This article shows two related examples of how such an RS can be used and lists some open questions that will be the subject of future work.

Keywords: Recall and precision · Empirical acceptability criteria · Tradeoff

1 Introduction: Background and Some Related Work

The desire is to develop an artificial intelligence (AI)[1] that does a non-algorithmic *task* that requires real intelligence (RI), i.e., from a human, e.g., to recognize a stop sign in an image. In general, a task is to find *correct answers* in a space of *answers*, some of which are *correct* and the rest of which are *incorrect*. This AI might be

- a *classical* AI, which is an algorithmic attempt to simulate a human's thinking as E[2] does the task, perhaps with the help of logic, or
- a *learned machine* (LM)[3], which is the result of an instance of machine learning (ML) or deep learning, whether the LM is taught, self-taught, or both with relevant real-world (RW) data.

---

[1] Glossary of Non-Standard Acronyms:

HAP humanly achievable precision	RI real intelligence
HAR humanly achievable recall	RW real world
LM learned machine	ZJVF Zave–Jackson Validation Formula.

[2] "E", "em", and "er" are gender non-specific third-person singular pronouns in subjective, objective, and possessive forms, respectively.

[3] a.k.a."ML component (MLC)" [16].

© Springer Nature Switzerland AG 2022
V. Gervasi and A. Vogelsang (Eds.): REFSQ 2022, LNCS 13216, pp. 19–25, 2022.
https://doi.org/10.1007/978-3-030-98464-9_2

This article uses the term "an AI" to mean any of these possibilities.

It has been my observation that no AI worker expects to be able to describe an AI's behavior completely, and everyone works around this limitation to describe an AI's behavior in imprecise terms, such as "usually", "probably", "approximately", etc., giving only empirically determined probabilities. An AI is evaluated with *vague*[4] measures, such as recall and precision. While there might be a simple specification of a task, e.g., "Return only images that contain stop signs.", there is no actionable specification that identifies all and only images containing stop signs. Thus, there is no possibility of a formal mathematical specification. And yet, it is desired to be able to say with some certainty whether an implementation of an AI for a task does indeed do the task, at least well enough [1, 2, 8–10, 12, 15–17, 19–21].

Some have asked a key question that seems not to be satisfactorily answered in the literature [1, 11, 21].

How does one write a requirements specification (RS), S, for an AI, A, for a task, T, in a way that S can be used to decide whether A correctly implements T, by asking whether A satisfies S?

If A is an LM, which is a data-centric system, S includes the RW data with which A learned to do what it does [1, 2, 5, 9, 10].

2 Basic Approach

Fundamentally, an AI for a task must *mimic* humans who are using their RI to perform the task [9, 19, acknowledged Alessio Ferrari]. Lacking any complete specification of the task, we accept that what humans do in practice, while trying to avoid bias [13], is correct. The mimicry will rarely, if ever, be perfect. Thus, an RS for an AI doing the task must describe this mimicry in a way that allows *measuring how well* the AI mimics humans [21]. These measures are vague and whether their values are satisfactory will not have binary, "yes" or "no", answers. Thus, the decision about how well the AI mimics humans will be a matter of judgment. One such set of measures is *recall and precision*, measures of the frequency of correctness w.r.t. a human-determined gold set. See Sect. 7 about other measures.

The measures are not binary, and human performance is part of the decision. Thus, the truth of the claims that the evaluation criteria are met and, thus, an RS is satisfied, is not logical, but is empirical, just as with the Zave–Jackson Validation Formula (ZJVF), which is about systems that interact with the RW [7, 22].

As running examples, this article uses two different AIs, $A1$ and $A2$, for the task of finding stop signs in images, in two different contexts that impose different needs on the measures. Each AI is to classify each input image as to whether or not the image has at least one stop sign, and is to output only those images that do. The difference between $A1$ and $A2$ is in the way the outputs are used. $A1$ finds the images that contain

---

[4] I.e., there is little certainty on what values of the vague measure are good and are bad. Even when there is certainty that some value is good and another value is bad, there is no certainty about what value in between is the boundary between the good and the bad.

stop signs in order to produce a set of images, with which to train $A2$ to identify stop signs in real time for an autonomous vehicle (AV). This article describes these two different AIs with the same base functionality to demonstrate the necessity of including in an RS for the AI, the context of the AI's use. The use of the same algorithm and the same RW training data for these AIs would yield the same recall and precision values, not distinguishing the AIs. Only the context distinguishes them and allows determining whether the recall and precision values are acceptable for the AI's use.

This article tries to show that *any* set of measures that is used to evaluate an AI in an attempt to convince the AI's stakeholders that the AI is what they want can be the basis of an RS of the AI *if* added to this basis is all the information from the AI's context that the stakeholders need about the meanings of the values of the measures, to be able to decide whether the AI is satisfactory for their needs.

In the rest of this paper, Sect. 3 reminds the reader about recall, precision, and summarization. Section 4 describes the two AIs, $A1$ and $A2$, and how they may be evaluated, allowing Sect. 5 to abstract to a general framework for an RS for an AI. Section 6 summarizes related work, and Sect. 7 points to future work.

3 Recall, Precision, Summarization

In the interest of conserving space in this article, this article merely reminds the reader of the meanings of *recall*, *precision*, and *summarization* [3][5]. For an AI, A

- recall (R): percentage of the correct answers that are returned by A,
- precision (P): percentage of the answers returned by A that are correct, and
- summarization (S): percentage of the input to A that are removed in the output that A returns, i.e., $(100\% - (\frac{size(output)}{size(input)}))$ (not the usual AI summarization).

Informally, the output of an AI is correct if it has *all* and *only* correct answers. R and P are the two sides of "*all* and *only*": R measures how close to *all* correct answers are in the output. P measures how close to *only* correct answers are in the output. S measures how much of the task that the AI is supposed to do is done and is not left to be done by humans.

To clarify the measures, the importance of context, and the importance of summarization, consider an application of one of the running examples, $A1$, to a set of 1000 images, of which 200 contain stop signs. Suppose that $A1$ returns 400 images of which 190 truly have stop signs. Then, $R = \frac{190}{200} = 95\%$, $P = \frac{190}{400} = 47.5\%$, and $S = 100\% - \frac{400}{1000} = 60\%$. These particular measure values are not bad, particularly if the average human has poorer than 95% recall in the same task. Because the output of $A1$ is being used to train $A2$, it is essential to get as close as possible to having *all* and *only* images that contain stop signs. Because $P = 47.5\%$ means that more than half of $A1$'s output is false positives, $A1$'s output must be manually searched, i.e., *vetted*, to find them and remove them. The 60% summarization says that the manual vetting search of the only 400 images returned by $A1$ will be considerably faster than a manual search of the original 1000 images. Thus, the poor precision of 47.5% does not matter

---

[5] It was a total surprise that the cited work was so applicable to RSs for AIs.

that much, because the tedium of a manual search has been cut by 60%. As observed by a reviewer, any way of ensuring that vetting is fast is OK, e.g., that a human's correctness decision for an item in the AI's output is considerably faster than for an item in the AI's input [3].

4   Evaluation of $A1$ and $A2$ with the Measures

If we decide to use recall and precision as the basis for the evaluation and, thus, specification of an AI, then the process of determining if an implementation meets the specification involves (1) evaluating and comparing the recall and precision of the AI and of humans doing the same task and (2) using the context of the task, which is thus part of the specification, as the basis for deciding what the comparison means.

For $A1$ and $A2$, each AI is evaluated by its R and P, with respect to a manually developed gold set of classified images. Each human expert in the domain of the AI that participates in developing the gold set computes er own R and P, and the averages of their R and P values are

- the *humanly achievable recall* (HAR) and
- the *humanly achievable precision* (HAP)

of the stop-sign recognition task. Each of these HAR and HAP is probably about 99%, a claim that must be verified empirically.

One possibility is to require an AI for a task to at least mimic people doing the same task. Otherwise, especially for a life-critical task, we're better off leaving the task to humans [4]. So, one possibility for an AI for a task is

- for the AI's R to achieve or beat the task's HAR and
- for the AI's P to achieve or beat the task's HAP.

In the case of $A2$, achieving or beating HAR and HAP is acceptable; accidents are inevitable, particularly if humans are doing the task. If $A2$'s R and P achieve or beat the task's HAR and HAP, then $A2$ will have no more accidents than does a human doing the task. While no accident is good, society can accept an AI's doing this task in this circumstance.

For each of $A1$ and $A2$, achieving or beating the task's HAR is essential. However, for $A1$, a low P means that there are lots of false positives among the output of $A1$. Fortunately, for $A1$'s specific context, these false positives are not really dangerous, because there is plenty of time for vetting to find the false positives and remove them from the output. However, lots of false positives among the output of $A1$ can discourage the human vetters. If S is high, then the vetters can be reminded that manually vetting $A1$'s output is a lot faster than manually searching $A1$'s entire input. Unless S is actually zero, $A1$ *does* reduce the manual searching that needs to be done. In a vetting context, the R and P of the AI is determined only *after* the vetting, because vetting does generally improve P. In the end, for $A1$, if the R after vetting beats the task's HAR, and the time to vet $A1$'s output is less than the time to do the classification task manually, then $A1$ is considered to meet its requirements. After all, since the task of $A1$ is essential, the alternative to running $A1$ is to do the task completely manually at the cost of a lot *more* tedious, *boring* grunt work!

$A2$ runs in an AV, making vetting impossible. Therefore, low P means lots of unnecessary stops by the AV, that could very well lead to dangerous rear-end collisions! Therefore, for $A2$, low P is definitely not tolerable, and reusing $A1$ as $A2$ is not acceptable. Another $A2$ must be found that makes both R and P high enough to achieve or beat the task's HAR and HAP [6].

This example has suggested one particular set of measures,—R, P, and S—and one particular set of criteria—R's and P's achieving HAR and HAP, possibly with the help of vetting assisted by a high S. However, *any* set of measures and *any* criteria that make sense to an AI's stakeholders can be used as the RS for the AI.

5   What an RS for an AI Is

It is now clear that an RS for an AI needs more than just whatever measures $M_1, \ldots,$ and M_n are used in evaluating the AI. The RS needs also criteria for acceptable values of these measures, e.g.,

- minimum, or maximum, threshold values of $M_1, \ldots,$ and M_n, which may be the humanly achievable values of $M_1, \ldots,$ and M_n for the AI's task, with which to compare the AI's $M_1, \ldots,$ and M_n values, respectively;
- the relative importance of the individual measures $M_1, \ldots,$ and M_n to help evaluate any needed tradeoff between $M_1, \ldots,$ and M_n [6];
- in a case in which vetting is possible or required, (1) the S of the AI and (2) the times for a human to decide the correctness of an item in the AI's input and in the AI's output; and
- any data, e.g., training data, that are needed for the AI to function correctly.

Calculating the relative importance of, and thus the tradeoffs between, the measures $M_1, \ldots,$ and M_n in the context of the AI requires a *full* understanding of the context in which the AI is being used, including the cost of achieving a high value in each of the individual measures $M_1, \ldots,$ and M_n, in the context [6]. Non-functional requirements will help define the context and decide the tradeoffs [8,21]. All of this information is what *requirements engineering for an AI* must elicit or invent.

Finally, the decision of whether the AI satisfies its RS and meets its requirements will involve engineering judgement and evaluation of tradeoffs in the AI's context, and will *not* be a simple "yes" versus "no" decision, because of all of the vague elements in the RS. For examples:

1. What should be done if the value of any measure *just misses* its threshold while all the others beat their thresholds?
2. How *critical* must the task be in order that an acceptable alternative to an AI that does not satisfy its RS is doing the task manually?
3. How fast must vetting be for vetters to *tolerate* having to vet?

Questions like these can interact in an engineering way. For example, what should be done in the situation in which the task is *only fairly critical*, the AI *just misses achieving* the task's thresholds, and vetting is *somewhat slow*?

6 Related Work

Most of the related work is cited at any point in this article where an observation or contribution made by the work is mentioned.

Salay and Czarnecki observe that the ISO 26262 standard does not prescribe a single complete specification for partially or fully autonomous vehicles, describing only a collection of specifications for development processes and individual properties of an AV [17]. They address the difficulties, including some mentioned in Sects. 1 and 2 of this article, with these specifications by providing improvements to each of the specifications of the standard. The RS framework suggested by this article will need to incorporate their improvements. See Sect. 7.

Kästner observes that the engineering of the RW training data to yield the desired behavior corresponds to RE rather than implementation of the resulting LM [10]. Checking with the customer that the training data yields the correct behavior is validation. Thus, these training data end up being part of the specification of the LM.

There are methods to test whether an AI does what it is supposed to do [2,18,23]. Implicitly, whatever the test data test are the requirements of the AI.

There is a lot of somewhat related work in the proceedings of the AIRE Workshops (https://ieeexplore.ieee.org/xpl/conhome/1803944/all-proceedings) and of the RE4AI Workshops (http://ceur-ws.org/Vol-2584/, http://ceur-ws.org/Vol-2857/). Papers from these workshops that address the topic of this article are cited in this article.

7 Future Work

Section 5 shows only a first attempt at abstracting from what was learned from the running example to a general framework for RSs for AIs. The details of this framework changed a lot prior to submission of this article and as a result of the reviewers' comments. It is, thus, clear that the main future research will be to examine more AIs to understand their measures, criteria, and contexts in the hopes of arriving at a statement of the framework that works for all AIs. Nevertheless, the basic idea remains: The RS for an AI consists of a description of all measures and criteria plus all information about the AI's context of use that are necessary for the AI's stakeholders to decide if the AI meets their needs.

Some specific topics include:

- Are there measures, other than recall and precision, on which an RS for an AI can be based? Examples include (1) other measures calculable from a confusion matrix [14] and (2) interrater agreement between the AI and some humans using their RI.
- What is the role in an RS of the representativeness of the data with which an LM is trained in the RS of the LM [1,2,5,10]?

Acknowledgments. I benefited from voice and text discussions with Krzysztof Czarnecki, Nancy Day, John DiMatteo, Alessio Ferrari, Vijay Ganesh, Andrea Herrmann, Hans-Martin Heyn, Jeff Joyce, Davor Svetinovic, John Thistle, Richard Trefler, and Andreas Vogelsang and his students and post-docs. I thank the anonymous reviewers for their suggestions, only of few of which could be enacted due to the page limit.

References

1. Ahmad, K., et al.: What's up with requirements engineering for artificial intelligence systems? In: IEEE 29th RE, pp. 1–12 (2021)
2. Ashmore, R., et al.: Assuring the machine learning lifecycle: desiderata, methods, and challenges. ACM Comp. Surv. **54**(5), 111 (2021)
3. Berry, D.M.: Empirical evaluation of tools for hairy requirements engineering tasks. Empir. Softw. Eng. **26**(6), 1–77 (2021). https://doi.org/10.1007/s10664-021-09986-0
4. Berry, D.M., et al.: The case for dumb requirements engineering tools. In: REFSQ, pp. 211–217 (2012)
5. Chuprina, T., et al.: Towards artefact-based requirements engineering for data-centric systems. In: REFSQ-JP 2021: RE4AI (2021)
6. DiMatteo, J., et al.: Requirements for monitoring inattention of the responsible human in an autonomous vehicle: the recall and precision tradeoff. In: REFSQ-JP 2020: RE4AI (2020)
7. Hadar, I., Zamansky, A., Berry, D.M.: The inconsistency between theory and practice in managing inconsistency in requirements engineering. Empir. Softw. Eng. **24**(6), 3972–4005 (2019). https://doi.org/10.1007/s10664-019-09718-5
8. Horkoff, J.: Non-functional requirements for machine learning: challenges and new directions. In: IEEE 27th RE, pp. 386–391 (2019)
9. Hu, B.C., et al.: Towards requirements specification for machine-learned perception based on human performance. In: IEEE 7th AIRE, pp. 48–51 (2020)
10. Kästner, C.: Machine learning is requirements engineering (2020). https://medium.com/analytics-vidhya/machine-learning-is-requirements-engineering-8957aee55ef4
11. Kostova, B., et al.: On the interplay between requirements, engineering, and artificial intelligence. In: REFSQ-JP 2020: RE4AI (2020)
12. Kress-Gazit, H., et al.: Formalizing and guaranteeing human-robot interaction. CACM **64**(9), 78–84 (2021)
13. Mehrabi, N., et al.: A survey on bias and fairness in machine learning. ACM Comp. Surv. **54**(6), 1–35 (2021)
14. Mishra, A.: Metrics to evaluate your machine learning algorithm (2018). https://towardsdatascience.com/metrics-to-evaluate-your-machine-learning-algorithm-f10ba6e38234
15. Parnas, D.L.: The real risks of artificial intelligence. CACM **60**(10), 27–31 (2017)
16. Rahimi, M., et al.: Toward requirements specification for machine-learned components. In: IEEE 27th RE Workshops (REW), pp. 241–244 (2019)
17. Salay, R., Czarnecki, K.: Using machine learning safely in automotive software: an assessment and adaption of software process requirements in ISO 26262 (2018). https://arxiv.org/abs/1808.01614
18. Schmelzer, R.: How do you test AI systems? (2020). https://www.forbes.com/sites/cognitiveworld/2020/01/03/how-do-you-test-ai-systems/
19. Seshia, S.A., et al.: Towards verified artificial intelligence (2020). https://arxiv.org/abs/1606.08514v4
20. Valiant, L.: Probably Approximately Correct: Nature's Algorithms for Learning and Prospering in a Complex World. Basic Books, New York (2013)
21. Vogelsang, A., Borg, M.: Requirements engineering for machine learning: perspectives from data scientists. In: IEEE 27th RE Workshops (REW), pp. 245–251 (2019)
22. Zave, P., Jackson, M.: Four dark corners of requirements engineering. TOSEM **6**(1), 1–30 (1997)
23. Zhang, J., Li, J.: Testing and verification of neural-network-based safety-critical control software: a systematic literature review. IST **123**, 106296 (2020)

Quo Vadis, Explainability? – A Research Roadmap for Explainability Engineering

Wasja Brunotte[1,2]([✉]), Larissa Chazette[1], Verena Klös[3], and Timo Speith[4]

[1] Software Engineering Group, Leibniz University Hannover, Hannover, Germany
{wasja.brunotte,larissa.chazette}@inf.uni-hannover.de
[2] Cluster of Excellence PhoenixD, Leibniz University Hannover, Hannover, Germany
[3] Chair for Software and Embedded Systems Engineering, TU Berlin, Berlin, Germany
verena.kloes@tu-berlin.de
[4] Institute of Philosophy and Department of Computer Science, Saarland University, Saarbrücken, Germany
timo.speith@uni-saarland.de

Abstract. [**Context and motivation**] In our modern society, software systems are highly integrated into our daily life. Quality aspects such as ethics, fairness, and transparency have been discussed as essential for trustworthy software systems and explainability has been identified as a means to achieve all of these three in systems. [**Question/problem**] Like other quality aspects, explainability must be discovered and treated during the design of those systems. Although explainability has become a hot topic in several communities from different areas of knowledge, there is only little research on systematic explainability engineering. Yet, methods and techniques from requirements and software engineering would add a lot of value to the explainability research. [**Principal ideas/results**] As a first step to explore this research landscape, we held an interdisciplinary workshop to collect ideas from different communities and to discuss open research questions. In a subsequent working group, we further analyzed and structured the results of this workshop to identify the most important research questions. As a result, we now present a research roadmap for explainable systems. [**Contribution**] With our research roadmap we aim to advance the software and requirements engineering methods and techniques for explainable systems and to attract research on the most urgent open questions.

Keywords: Explainability · Explainability engineering · Explainable artificial intelligence · Interpretability · Research roadmap · Software engineering · Requirements engineering · Software transparency

1 Introduction

Modern software systems are becoming increasingly complex, and research concerning them is achieving unprecedented degrees of system autonomy. As the

---

All authors have contributed equally to this paper and share the first authorship.

© Springer Nature Switzerland AG 2022
V. Gervasi and A. Vogelsang (Eds.): REFSQ 2022, LNCS 13216, pp. 26–32, 2022.
https://doi.org/10.1007/978-3-030-98464-9_3

number, complexity, and impact of such systems grow, speaking about the features required for high software quality standards becomes more and more vital.

Quality aspects such as ethics, fairness, and transparency have been discussed as essential for building trustworthy systems. Explainability has been identified as a means to achieve all of these three aspects and as a way to calibrate users' sentiments of trust in systems [6]. Essentially, explainability is a non-functional requirement that focuses on disclosing information to a particular audience [8]. An explainable system is capable of providing explanations to an addressee (e.g., an end-user) about a specific aspect of the system (e.g., its reasoning process), helping the addressee understand this aspect [5].

Like other quality aspects, explainability must be discovered and addressed during system design. As requirements engineers, we "translate" these aspects into requirements as part of a project. As simple as it sounds, we know that reality proves to be otherwise. Quality requirements are often a challenge for practice, and explainability is not different [7].

Communities from different areas of knowledge (e.g., machine learning, philosophy, psychology, human-computer interaction, and cyber-physical systems) have been researching explainability actively. However, the software engineering (SE) and requirements engineering (RE) communities have not yet developed specific methods and techniques to elicit, analyze, and document requirements for explainability, nor to address it in practice [2].

We conducted an interdisciplinary workshop to foster research in this direction and to collect ideas from different communities, discussing open research questions (RQs). We analyzed the results of this discussion and created a research roadmap for explainability engineering. Our goals are to advance SE/RE methods and techniques for creating explainable systems, and to attract research on the most pressing open questions. Our vision is to establish explainability as a core property of future systems, which we believe is an essential requirement given the increasing autonomy and impact of software systems.

During the workshop, we were able to identify several areas that need further research. In this short paper, we will describe some of these areas, thus creating a roadmap that should be followed in the quest for explainable systems.

2 State of the Art

Köhl et al. [8] examined explainability from the perspective of RE. Their core contributions were to identify explainability as a non-functional requirement and to propose a first operationalization of explainability in the RE context. Chazette and Schneider [7] surveyed end-users to understand their requirements concerning explainability. They identified challenges for explainability during RE, and proposed recommendations to avoid a negative influence of explanations on the usability of a system.

Based on these works, input from experts, and a literature survey, Chazette et al. [6] proposed a more advanced operationalization of explainability. The focus of their work, however, was to look at the impact of explainability on other quality aspects in a system. In addition, they framed their results in a model and a knowledge catalogue. Focusing on the interplay between explainability and privacy, Brunotte et al. [5] presented a research agenda to explore how explanations might support users in understanding aspects of their online privacy.

Arrieta et al. [1] discuss concepts and taxonomies of, as well as opportunities and challenges surrounding, explainable artificial intelligence (XAI). The authors argue that there is a need for guidelines for implementing XAI systems and agree that the interaction of associated requirements and constraints with other NFRs should be carefully analyzed. In this line of thought, Sadeghi et al. [11] present a taxonomy of different demands for explanations along with scenarios that describe specific situations in which a software system should provide an explanation. Their taxonomy can guide the requirements elicitation for explanation capabilities of interactive intelligent systems.

Blumreiter et al. [2] present the first reference framework for building self-explainable systems that can provide explanations about the system's past, present, and future behavior. Their framework leverages requirements- and explainability models at run-time. While they present first examples for explanation models, they raise many research questions, such as how to detect explanation needs and how to generate explanations automatically. Ziesche et al. [13] follow their framework and present some preliminary solutions for detecting explanation needs. Schwammberger [12] presents an approach to generate explanation models from formal models and proposes to use run-time RE for online updates of the explanation models.

3   Explainability: Research Directions

To overcome the lack of methods and techniques for eliciting, analyzing, and documenting explanation needs, as well as for engineering explainable systems, we held an interdisciplinary workshop at the renowned *2021 IEEE 29th International Requirements Engineering Conference* [3]. Together with researchers from different disciplines, we discussed ideas and open research questions.

3.1   Details on the Workshop and Methodology

The workshop was a mixture of keynote lectures, paper presentations, and collaborative activities. With a steady attendance of about 20 participants and lively discussions, the workshop was very successful. Notably, all participants agreed that explainability engineering is an urgent topic for future systems.

On the first day of the workshop, we discussed impulses from current research in an author panel after the first few paper presentations. Subsequently, we deepened and extended the ideas from this discussion in a brainstorming session with all workshop participants using a virtual board. The goal was to identify problems and challenges to advance research in the area of explainability.

On the second day, we had the remaining paper presentations. All participants were asked to contribute to the virtual board whenever they had new insights. In the end, we discussed the identified research questions in small working groups. The results were several artifacts (e.g., a mind map, but also loose notes) outlining research directions for future work on explainability.

After the workshop, the authors of this paper came together in several sessions to further organize the created artifacts. We clustered the research ideas in a mind map and extracted actionable questions. We further divided the extracted questions into two broad categories: questions concerning *fundamental* topics and those explicitly related to *explainability engineering*. This division is based on the idea that some research questions are rather general (fundamental RQs), while others primarily concern the actual engineering of explainable systems (explainability engineering). The final mind map, constituting the basis for our roadmap, can be found in our additional material [4].

3.2   Fundamental Research Questions

We have identified three categories of fundamental research questions: *Defining and Measuring Explainability*, *Stakeholders and Contexts*, and *Goals and Desiderata*. We discuss these categories and some of the questions related to them in the next paragraphs.

Defining and Measuring Explainability. One of the biggest problems related to explainability is the lack of an actionable definition. While there is a lot of research on explainability in different research domains, there is no common definition of *what it means to be explainable* and *how exactly explainability differs from related concepts such as transparency, explicability, and traceability.*

While Chazette et al. [6] and Köhl et al. [8] have taken the first steps in this direction, we still need a more thorough overview of *what types of explanations exist*, and we need to explore *which ones are best suited for particular goals.* According to Chazette et al. [6] and Köhl et al. [8], explainability depends on various factors, such as the explanation's recipients, the behavior and context of the system to explain, the entity explaining, and the explanation goal. These insights indicate that a definition of explainability needs several parameters.

Finally, we need to establish standardized methods for measuring explainability. Finding standards for explainability enables common quality models for certification or auditing, as proposed by Langer et al. [9]. To achieve a common understanding across different disciplines, we suggest continuing the discussion in interdisciplinary workshops, working groups, or even projects.

As suggested above, a parameterized definition or a meta-model of explainability could help define aspects of explainability that can be measured and evaluated. Similar to the ISO models for safety, we envision a standard for explainability that specifies ways of ensuring that a system is explainable.

Stakeholders and Contexts. Two major factors that influence the explanations that a system must provide are the stakeholder and the context. For this reason, it is crucial to know *which stakeholders and contexts have to be considered when designing the explainability faculties of a system.*

For both factors, some underlying questions are the same: *which stakeholders and contexts should be considered for explainability* and *how to adjust explanations to fit a particular stakeholder and/or context*. However, these factors also interact: when there is time pressure, the explanation should be most likely less detailed than when there is no time pressure. Consequently, the context determines the granularity of the explanation needed by a particular stakeholder. These interactions need to be better explored in the future.

Goals and Desiderata. People want explanations with a particular goal or, more general, desideratum in mind. A developer, for instance, may want to receive explanations to debug a system. Since goals and desiderata directly determine the type and content of an explanation, we need to study *how to adjust explanations to fit certain goals*. There are already studies on such goals (see, for instance, [6] and [10]), but they need to be explored further.

As different goals of stakeholders can conflict, an important question is *how to balance them*. Companies, for example, may wish to protect their trade secrets about how particular systems operate while being legally obligated to disclose parts of their workings. In this and many other cases, the challenge is finding out how to design explanations that meet both goals and *how to prioritize explanation goals*. Solutions to these questions might be context-dependent and, thus, require dynamic decisions.

3.3   Explainability Engineering

The most prominent topics of discussion during our workshop were SE issues. More specifically, they were concrete aspects that influence the software process or the product itself. We grouped "explainability engineering" to highlight that they require SE and RE knowledge.

Similar to usability engineering, which is a discipline that focuses on improving the usability of interactive systems, explainability engineering focuses on improving the explainability of a system. It uses theories from computer science, psychology, and philosophy to identify comprehension problems and explanation needs that arise when interacting with a system. Subsequently, it helps mitigate these problems at various stages of development. Overall, it is concerned with the requirements related to explanations, design strategies, and testing.

Technical Aspects. Under *technical aspects*, we grouped research questions that relate to concrete aspects of creating explanations, for instance, concerning the requirements for *explanation models*, most urgently *which information should be presented* and *which information sources to take*; but also *which kind of semantics we need* and *how to arrive at common semantics*. Another critical issue is *how to design and implement* explanations, whether they are on-demand or adaptable to specific contexts and individual characteristics of stakeholders.

Technical challenges. were also discussed, such as *how to present tailor-fitted explanations at run-time*. Here, we propose cooperating with and learning from the models-at-run-time and the self-adaptive systems communities.

Design Process in RE/SE. The design process is also a pivotal aspect that needs to be better researched. One of the biggest questions is *whether the existing RE and SE activities and methods are sufficient in the case of explainability.* In particular, it is essential to clarify whether we need new methods and activities to elicit and model explainability requirements or whether we merely need to enrich existing ones. To design explainable systems, we also need to investigate *how to operationalize explainability requirements.*

As a first step, we propose to integrate explainability requirements into existing RE/SE methods and activities (e.g., requirement models, user stories, design processes) and to evaluate them on different case studies. The user-centered methodologies of the human-computer interaction community should also be explored, particularly when it comes to interface-related aspects of explainability.

Quality Aspects and Testing. A crucial aspect of SE is quality assurance. When designing explainable systems, we need to explore testing and verification methods for explanations. *How do we know that the explanation provided is satisfactory and meets the specified requirements? Can we prove that the explanation is helpful and understandable?* As is already known, poor explanations can have a negative impact on the system instead of contributing to the satisfaction of specific quality requirements such as user satisfaction and usability [7].

For these critical research questions, we first need to define quality metrics for explanations and then develop methods to evaluate them. Furthermore, we need to investigate how explanations influence other quality aspects of software systems, such as safety, security, or user satisfaction.

Costs and Resources. Clearly, the issue of cost (e.g., economic and effort) needs to be investigated and mitigated, as it is one of the most considerable constraints in the software industry. Here, we need to find answers to the question of *how difficult it is to deal with explainability requirements in terms of activities and costs* through various studies. Finally, the creation of artifacts was also identified as a possible line of research. Such artifacts can reach from taxonomies and catalogs to a database of examples of explanation cases (similar to [11]).

4   Conclusion

Qualities such as ethics, fairness, and transparency play a key role in modern software systems, translating into an increasing need for the explainability of systems. Currently, there is little research that addresses explainability engineering systematically. To foster research in this direction, we present a research roadmap for explainability engineering that highlights where research should be heading in terms of fundamental research questions as well as more specific questions concerning this field. With this roadmap paper, we aim to advance SE/RE methods and techniques for creating explainable systems and to stimulate research on the most pressing open questions.

Acknowledgments. This work was supported by the research initiative Mobilise between the Technical University of Braunschweig and Leibniz University Hannover, funded by the Ministry for Science and Culture of Lower Saxony and by the Deutsche Forschungsgemeinschaft (DFG, German Research Foundation) under Germany's Excellence Strategy within the Cluster of Excellence PhoenixD (EXC 2122, Project ID 390833453). Work on this paper was also funded by the Volkswagen Foundation grant AZ 98514 "Explainable Intelligent Systems" (EIS) and by the DFG grant 389792660 as part of TRR 248.

References

1. Arrieta, A.B., et al.: Explainable artificial intelligence (XAI): concepts, taxonomies, opportunities and challenges toward responsible AI. Inf. Fusion **58**, 82–115 (2020)
2. Blumreiter, M., et al.: Towards self-explainable cyber-physical systems. In: ACM/IEEE 22nd International Conference on Model Driven Engineering Languages and Systems Companion (MODELS-C), pp. 543–548. IEEE (2019)
3. Brunotte, W., Chazette, L., Klös, V., Knauss, E., Speith, T., Vogelsang, A.: Welcome to the first international workshop on requirements engineering for explainable systems (RE4ES). In: IEEE 29th International Requirements Engineering Conference Workshops (REW), pp. 157–158. IEEE (2021)
4. Brunotte, W., Chazette, L., Klös, V., Speith, T.: Supplementary Material for Vision Paper "Quo Vadis, Explainability? - A Research Roadmap for Explainability Engineering" (2022). https://doi.org/10.5281/zenodo.5902181
5. Brunotte, W., Chazette, L., Korte, K.: Can explanations support privacy awareness? a research roadmap. In: IEEE 29th International Requirements Engineering Conference Workshops (REW), pp. 176–180. IEEE (2021)
6. Chazette, L., Brunotte, W., Speith, T.: Exploring explainability: a definition, a model, and a knowledge catalogue. In: IEEE 29th International Requirements Engineering Conference (RE), pp. 197–208. IEEE (2021)
7. Chazette, L., Schneider, K.: Explainability as a non-functional requirement: challenges and recommendations. Requirements Eng. **25**(4), 493–514 (2020). https://doi.org/10.1007/s00766-020-00333-1
8. Köhl, M.A., Baum, K., Langer, M., Oster, D., Speith, T., Bohlender, D.: Explainability as a non-functional requirement. In: IEEE 27th International Requirements Engineering Conference (RE), pp. 363–368. IEEE (2019)
9. Langer, M., Baum, K., Hartmann, K., Hessel, S., Speith, T., Wahl, J.: Explainability auditing for intelligent systems: a rationale for multi-disciplinary perspectives. In: IEEE 29th International Requirements Engineering Conference Workshops (REW), pp. 164–168. IEEE (2021)
10. Langer, M., et al.: What do we want from explainable artificial intelligence (XAI)? - a stakeholder perspective on XAI and a conceptual model guiding interdisciplinary XAI research. Artif. Intell. **296**, 103473 (2021)
11. Sadeghi, M., Klös, V., Vogelsang, A.: Cases for explainable software systems: characteristics and examples. In: IEEE 29th International Requirements Engineering Conference Workshops (REW), pp. 181–87. IEEE (2021)
12. Schwammberger, M.: A quest of self-explainability: when causal diagrams meet autonomous urban traffic manoeuvres. In: IEEE 29th International Requirements Engineering Conference Workshops (REW), pp. 195–199. IEEE (2021)
13. Ziesche, F., Klös, V., Glesner, S.: Anomaly detection and classification to enable self-explainability of autonomous systems. In: 2021 Design, Automation & Test in Europe Conference & Exhibition (DATE), pp. 1304–1309. IEEE (2021)

Machine Learning

How Effective Is Automated Trace Link Recovery in Model-Driven Development?

Randell Rasiman[ID], Fabiano Dalpiaz[✉][ID], and Sergio España[ID]

Utrecht University, Utrecht, The Netherlands
{f.dalpiaz,s.espana}@uu.nl

Abstract. **[Context and Motivation]** Requirements Traceability (RT) aims to follow and describe the lifecycle of a requirement. RT is employed either because it is mandated, or because the product team perceives benefits. **[Problem]** RT practices such as the establishment and maintenance of trace links are generally carried out manually, thereby being prone to mistakes, vulnerable to changes, time-consuming, and difficult to maintain. Automated tracing tools have been proposed; yet, their adoption is low, often because of the limited evidence of their effectiveness. We focus on vertical traceability that links artifacts having different levels of abstraction. **[Results]** We design an automated tool for recovering traces between JIRA issues (user stories and bugs) and revisions in a model-driven development (MDD) context. Based on existing literature that uses process and text-based data, we created 123 features to train a machine learning classifier. This classifier was validated via three MDD industry datasets. For a trace recommendation scenario, we obtained an average F_2-score of 69% with the best tested configuration. For an automated trace maintenance scenario, we obtained an $F_{0.5}$-score of 76%. **[Contribution]** Our findings provide insights on the effectiveness of state-of-the-art trace link recovery techniques in an MDD context by using real-world data from a large company in the field of low-code development.

Keywords: Requirement traceability · Trace link recovery · Model-driven development · Low-code development · Machine learning

1 Introduction

Requirements Trace Link Recovery (RTR) is the process of establishing trace links between a requirement and another trace artefact [13]. Many techniques for (requirements) trace link recovery propose semi-automatic processes that rely on information retrieval (IR) [2]. The premise of IR-based approaches is that when two artefacts have high a degree of textual similarity, they should most likely be traced [18]. Commonly used IR algorithms include Vector Space Models, Latent Semantic Indexing, Jenson-Shannon Models, and Latent Dirichlet Allocation [2,5].

More recently, developments from Machine Learning (ML) have been employed in automatic Trace Link Recovery (TLR) [2]. ML approaches treat TLR as a classification problem: the Cartesian product of the two trace artefact sets defines the space of candidate trace links [11,16], a subset of which are valid links (manually defined by

© Springer Nature Switzerland AG 2022
V. Gervasi and A. Vogelsang (Eds.): REFSQ 2022, LNCS 13216, pp. 35–51, 2022.
https://doi.org/10.1007/978-3-030-98464-9_4

the domain experts). A ML classifier is tasked to build a model for predicting whether unseen trace links are valid or invalid. This is achieved by representing the trace links as a vector, derived from features. Most ML TLR approaches use similarity scores of IR-based methods as features [11,16,23] and outperform IR-based TLR approaches [16].

However, in most of the studies, the classifiers are trained either using open-source datasets from universities, or proprietary data regarding safety-critical systems, and this entails an external validity concern [5]. Although using the same datasets is useful for benchmarking and for comparing methods, it poses the risk that the new traceability tools are being over-optimised for these specific datasets. To advance the current state-of-the-art traceability tools, the research community has called for gaining feedback from additional industrial datasets in a broad range of application domains [2,5].

In this paper, we aim to acquire new insights on automated RTR in a model-driven development (MDD) context, a domain which has shown potential for RT integration [27]. Following the Design Science research methodology [26], we conduct a case study at Mendix, a large-scale MDD-platform producer, and we develop a software tool for automated RTR that focuses on vertical traceability [21], which allows for the automated recovery of trace links between artifacts at different abstraction levels. The main contributions of this research are:

1. We provide new insights on the application of RTR in MDD, narrowing the gap between academic research and industrial demands, and moving steps toward the vision of ubiquitous requirements traceability [14].
2. To the best of our knowledge, this is the first study that experiments with the use of Gradient Boosted Trees for RTR.
3. We evaluate the relative importance of four families of features for establishing trace links between requirements (represented as JIRA issues) and model changes (commit files generated by the Mendix Studio low-code development platform).

We follow the recommendations of context-driven research [6]: specifying working assumptions based on a real-world context in order to attain practicality and scalability. We do so by collaborating with Mendix, which allowed us to use their data and to obtain rich insights on their development processes and the possible role of traceability.

This paper is structured as follows: Sect. 2 presents the background on requirements traceability. Section 3 describes how MDD and requirements are supported with the Mendix Studio platform within the Mendix company. Section 4 presents the construction of our automated RTR classifier. Section 5 shows the results, while Sect. 6 discusses the threats to validity. Finally, Sect. 7 concludes and outlines future work.

2   Related Work on Automated RTR

RT practices are mandated by well-known standards such as CMM, ISO 9000, and IEEE 830-1998 [4,9]. Thus, organisations who aim to comply with such standards embrace RT practices. These are expected to deliver benefits for project management and visibility, project maintenance, and verification & validation. Despite the clear benefits, the practice itself is not evident. RT activities are found to be "time-consuming, tedious and fallible" [25]. Even when conducted, manual tracing is favoured, leading to traces which are error-prone, vulnerable to changes, and hard to maintain.

Information Retrieval. For this reason, a considerable amount of RT research focuses on automating the task. Many of the proposed IR-based methods employ Vector Space Models (VSM), which use the cosine distance to measure the semantic similarity between documents. An alternative is the Jenson-Shannon Models (JSM), which consider documents as a probabilistic distribution [1,8], and the Jenson-Shannon Divergence as a measure of the semantic difference. There are two fundamental problems in IR-methods. *Synonymy* refers to using different terms for the same concept (e.g., 'drawing' and 'illustration'), and this decreases the recall. *Polysemy* refers to using terms that have multiple meanings (e.g. 'fall'), and this decreases precision [10]. Latent Semantic Indexing (LSI) aims to solve this problem by replacing the *latent semantics* (what terms actually mean) to an implicit higher-order structure, called latent semantics. This latent structure can then be used as feature set, which better reflects major associative data patterns and ignores less important influences. An example of this approach is the work by Port *et al.* [19]. Although other approaches have further improved performance, the performance gain has flattened, and more recent works make use of machine learning.

Machine Learning. Most state-of-the-art techniques for RTR employ ML nowadays, taking the field to new levels. ML approaches treat the TLR process as a classification problem: the Cartesian product of the two trace artefact sets is calculated, and the resulting elements represent candidate trace links [11,16]. A ML classifier learns from sample data, which is manually traced, and the classifier is then used to predict whether unseen couples of artefacts should be traced to one another. Most ML TLR approaches use the similarity scores from IR-based methods as features [11,16,23], although other features have been proposed. Besides feature representation, researchers have also analysed which ML classification algorithms would perform best. Falessi *et al.* [12] have compared multiple algorithms: decision trees, random forest, naïve Bayes, logistic regression, and bagging, with random forests yielding the best results.

Deep Learning. Recent advances in neural networks can also be employed in automated TLR [15]. Although this an interesting direction with the potential of achieving excellent results, neural networks are only suitable when large datasets are available. This is not the case in many industrial situations, like the one described in this paper.

3   Case Study at Mendix

We conducted a case study at Mendix, the producer of the Mendix Studio Low-Code Platform (MLCP). The MLCP employs MDD principles and allows creating software by defining graphical models for the domain, business logic, and user interface [24]. We study MLCP developers employed by Mendix, who are building applications with the MLCP for Mendix itself. These developers follow the SCRUM development process. Product Owners are responsible for managing and refining requirements, which are documented as JIRA issues and are added to the product backlog. The issues for the Sprint Backlog are chosen by the MLCP development team. Each selected item is assigned to one MCLP developer during a sprint, who is responsible for implementation.

The implementation is broken down into several activities. First, the MCLP developer examines the JIRA issue to become familiar with it. Second, the MCLP developer opens the latest MLCP model, navigates to the relevant modules, and makes the required changes. These changes are stored in a revision and are committed to the repository once they to fulfil the JIRA issue's acceptance criteria. Each revision is supplemented with a log message, in which the MCLP developer outlines the changes he or she made, as well as the JIRA issue ID for traceability purposes.

3.1 Studied Artefacts

We focus on tracing *JIRA* issues to committed revisions, because manual trace information was available from some development teams who followed traceability practices. Figure 1 shows the relationships among the trace artefacts.

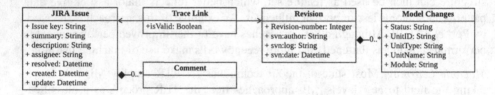

Fig. 1. Model showing the relationships between JIRA issues and revisions

JIRA Issues. Several teams at Mendix use the widespread project management tool Atlassian JIRA. In JIRA, project members define work items called issues, which Mendix uses to document requirements. The following attributes are shared by all JIRA issues: I1) a unique *issue key* serving as identifier, I2) a *summary*, used by Mendix to document a user story written in the Connextra template, I3) a *description*, which further explains the requirements alongside the acceptance criteria, I4) an *assignee*: the person who is responsible for implementing the issue. Finally, each issue has three date/time indicating when the issue was I5) created, I6) last updated, and I7) resolved.

Revisions. The MLCP, like any modern development environment, employs version control. An adapted version of Apache Subversion is integrated into the MLCP, which the developer can access through a GUI. Each revision contains: R1) *revision-number*, a unique integer, R2) *author*, the email of the person who committed the *revision*, R3) *log*, an optional field to write text, and R4) *date*, the date/time when the revision was committed. Finally, each revision contains the changes made to the units, which are stored as an element of an array that contains R5) *unitID*, R6) the *status* (either added, deleted, or modified), R7) *unitName*: the name of that unit, R8) *unitType*: the category of the unit (e.g., microflow or form), R9) *module*, the module where the unit is located.

3.2 Studied Datasets

We acquired data from three internal MLCP projects, produced by two development teams. We refer to them as i) *Service*, ii) *Data*, and iii) *Store*. For each project, we used a data export of one JIRA project and one MLCP repository. We analysed the availability of manual traces (see Table 1). We distinguished between revisions that trace to a single issue, to two or more issues, and to no issues. A large percentage of revisions is untraced. This could be because the revision is too generic (e.g., creation of a branch), or because the developer forgot about tracing. Also, the revisions were not always traced to issue keys of the JIRA projects we acquired. This happens because multiple teams, each with their own JIRA project, may operate on the same repository.

Table 1. Summary of the acquired project data

Dataset	Service	Data	Store
Total JIRA issues	173	58	634
Total revisions	2,930	818	713
Revisions traced to 1 issue	1,462 (49.90%)	556 (67.97%)	202 (28.33%)
Revisions traced to 2+ issues	33 (1.13%)	26 (3.18%)	3 (0.42%)
Revisions traced to no issues	1,435 (48.98%)	236 (28.85%)	508 (71.25%)

3.3 Objective and Evaluation Scenarios

Our objective is to automate the MLCP developers' tracing process, which is currently manual. We adapt the two scenarios put forward by Rath *et al.* [23]: *Trace Recommendation* and *Trace Maintenance*. Our automated artefact is evaluated for both scenarios using a common traceability metric, the F-measure, which quantifies the harmonic mean between precision and recall. However, in line with Berry's recommendations [3], we employ adjusted versions of the F-measure, as described below.

Trace Recommendation. MLCP developers use a GUI to commit changes to the remote repository. When doing this, the developer outlines the changes made and writes an issue key out of those in JIRA. Integrating a trace recommendation system can improve this scenario (see Fig. 2): the issues that the developer may choose among can be filtered based on the likelihood for that issue to be linked to the current revision. Only those issues above a certain threshold are shown.

The only manual task left for the developer is to vet the trace links. It is cognitively affordable and relatively fast since developers generally know which specific JIRA issue they have implemented. This scenario requires a high level of recall, for valid traces must be present in the list for a developer to vet it. Precision is less important because developers can ignore invalid traces. Therefore, in this scenario, we evaluate the system using the F_2-measure, an F-measure variant favouring recall above precision.

Trace Maintenance. Not all the revisions are traced to a JIRA issue. As visible in the last row of Table 1, between 28% and 71% of the revisions were not traced to issues. Thus, maintenance is needed to recover traces for the untraced revisions, which leads to the goal of the second scenario: an automated trace maintenance system. Such a system would periodically recover traces that were forgotten by the developer, ultimately leading to a higher level of RT. No human intervention is foreseen to correct invalid traces, so precision needs to be favoured above recall. Thus, we evaluate the system using the $F_{0.5}$-measure.

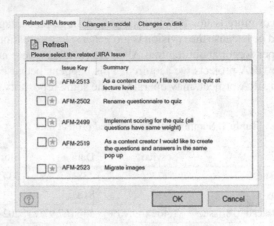

Fig. 2. Mock-up of a trace recommendation system

4 Requirement Trace Link Classifier

To accommodate both scenarios, we present an ML classifier to classify the validity of
traces, based on the TRAIL framework [16]. Our classifier, which we call *LCDTrace*,
is publicly available as open source[1], and a permanent copy of the version used in this
paper is part of our online appendix [22].

After describing the dataset the data available at Mendix for training, and how we
pre-processed it, we describe the feature engineering process, data rebalancing, and the
employed classification algorithms.

4.1 Data Description and Trace Construction

To train the ML classifier, we used the data from the Service, Data and Store datasets.

Revisions. The data was provided in text-format. We used Regular Expressions to transform the data and to extract the issue key(s) from the log message and store it in a
distinct issue key column. After extraction, the issue key was removed from the log
message, and the log message was pre-processed using common pre-processing steps:
1) all words were lowercased, 2) all the interpunction was removed, 3) all numeric characters were removed, 4) all sentences were tokenised with NLTK, 5) the corpus from
NLTK was used to eliminate all stop words, and 6) all remaining terms were stemmed
using the Porter Stemming Algorithm [20]. These activities resulted in a pre-processed
dataset that consists of (labels were defined in Sect. 3.1): R1 (Revision Number), R2
(Author), R3 (Log), R4 (Date), R7 (Unit Names), R8 (merge of log and unit names),
and associated JIRA key (a reference to I1).

JIRA Issues. The JIRA datasets were provided as delimited text files. Pre-processing
was carried out in the same manner as for the revisions. This led to a dataset that consists
of I1 (Issue key), I2 (Summary), I3 (Description), I4 (Assignee), I5 (Created date),

---

[1] https://github.com/RELabUU/LCDTrace.

I6 (Last updated date), I7 (Resolved date), plus one additional feature: I9 (JIRA All-Natural Text): the union of I2 and I3.

Trace Link Construction. Because a classifier can only be trained using labelled data, we discarded data that were not traced to issues. For the remaining data, we calculated the Cartesian product between the JIRA project dataset and the repository dataset. Each element is a candidate trace link whose validity was determined by comparing the issue key to the revision's related issue key. If the issue key was present, the trace link was classified as valid; else, the trace link was classified as invalid. Also, we applied causality filtering to the trace links [23]: when a trace link had revision antecedent to the creation of an issue, it was deemed invalid due to causality. The result is in Table 2.

Table 2. Valid and invalid traces before and after applying causal filtering to the project data

Dataset	Causality filtering	Total traces	Invalid traces	Valid traces
Service	Before	258,635	258,215 (99.84%)	420 (0.16%)
	After	89,233	88,813 (99.53%)	420 (0.47%)
Data	Before	33,756	33,305 (98.66%)	451 (1.34%)
	After	27,815	27,364 (98.38%)	451 (1.62%)
Store	Before	129,970	129,884 (99.93%)	86 (0.07%)
	After	33,627	33,541 (99.74%)	86 (0.26%)

4.2 Feature Engineering

The previously produced candidate trace links were then used for training the classifier. For this, we had to represent the candidate trace links as a set of features. Based on literature in the field, we engineered a total of 123 features grouped into four categories: process-related, document statistics, information retrieval and query quality.

Process-Related. These four features build on Rath *et al.* [23]. F1, the first feature, captures stakeholder information by indicating if the assignee of a JIRA issue is the same person as the author of a revision. The remaining three features capture temporal information. F2 is the difference between the date of revision (R4) and the date the issue was created (I5), F3 is the difference between R4 and the date the issue was last updated (I6), and F4 is the difference between R4 and the date the JIRA issue was resolved (I7).

Document Statistics. These features rely on the work of Mills *et al.* [16]: they gauge document relevance and the information contained within the documents. Within this category, seven metrics (hence, 7 features) are included:

- *Total number of terms*, calculated for the JIRA issue (F5) and the revision (F6).
- *Total number of unique terms* for the JIRA issue (F7) and the revision (F8).
- *Overlap of terms between the JIRA issue and the revision.* To calculate this metric, the overlap of terms is divided by the set of terms that are compared to. This is done in three ways, each leading to a feature: F9 divides the overlap of terms by the terms in the JIRA issue, F10 divides is by the terms in the revision, and F11 divides it by the union of the terms in the JIRA issue and in the revision.

Information Retrieval. This feature set captures the semantic similarity between two trace artefacts. We first apply VSM with TF-IDF weighting to transform the trace arte-facts to a vector representation. Because we use TF-IDF weighting, the chosen corpus used for weighting impacts the resulting vector. For instance, the term 'want' occurs commonly in the JIRA summary, for Mendix developers put their user story in there. However, it might be a rare term when considering all the terms in a JIRA issue. Since we could not determine which corpus best represents the trace artefact, we opted to explore multiple representations: we have constructed three issues vector representation (I2: Summary, I3: Description, I9: Summary & Description) and three representations for the revisions (R3: log message, R7: unit names, and R8: log & unit names). This results in 9 distinct pairs for each trace link candidate, as shown in Table 3. The cosine similarity of each pair was computed and utilised as a feature. Mills and Haiduc [17] showed that the chosen trace direction (i.e., which artefact in the trace link is used as a query) affect traceability performance. Thus, we calculated the cosine distance in either direction, resulting in a total of 18 IR-features (F12–F29) in Table 3. We used Scikit-learn for TF-IDF weighting and SciPy for calculating the cosine distance.

Table 3. TF-IDF combinations used for VSM

ID	Revision artefact	Issue artefact	Features
1	Log message	Summary	F12–F13
2	Log message	Description	F14–F15
3	Log message	JIRA all-natural text	F16–F17
4	Unit names	Summary	F18–F19
5	Unit names	Description	F20–F21
6	Unit names	JIRA all-natural text	F22–F23
7	Revision all-natural text	Summary	F24–F25
8	Revision all-natural text	Description	F26–F27
9	Revision all-natural text	JIRA all-natural text	F28–F29

Query Quality. The quality of a query determines how well a query is expected to retrieve relevant documents from a document collection. A high-quality query returns the relevant document(s) towards the top of the results lists, whereas a low-quality query returns them near the bottom of the list or not at all. It is important to differentiate between high- and low-quality queries, when using IR-techniques for TLR. Do two artefacts have a low cosine similarity because they are actually invalid, or is it because the similarity was computed using a low-quality query?

Mills and Haiduc [17] devised metrics for measuring query quality (QQ). These QQ metrics are organised into pre-retrieval and post-retrieval metrics. Pre-retrieval metrics merely consider the properties of the query, whereas post-retrieval metrics also consider the information captured by the list returned by the executed query. We focused on implementing pre-retrieval QQ metrics in this study, evaluating three different aspects:

– *Specificity* refers the query's ability to express the relevant documents and to distin-guish them from irrelevant documents. Highly-specific queries contain terms which are rare in the document collection, while lowly-specific queries contain common terms. Highly specific queries are desired, for documents can be differentiated based on the terms.

- *Similarity* refers to the degree to which the query is similar to the document collection. Queries that are comparable to the collection suggest the existence of many relevant documents, increasing the possibility that a relevant document is returned.
- *Term relatedness* refers to how often terms in the query co-occur in the document collection. If query terms co-occur in the document collection as well, the query is considered of high quality.

The computation of these metrics was executed for the six corpora mentioned in the information retrieval paragraph (log message, unit names, revision all-natural text, summary, description, and JIRA all-natural text), because the outcome of the metrics depends on the corpus of which the query is a part. This resulted in a total of 102 QQ features: F30–F131, listed in Table 4.

Table 4. Query quality features from the work by Mills and Haiduc [17]

Family	Measure	Metric	Features	
			Query: Revision	Query: JIRA
Specificity	TF-IDF	{Avg, Max, Std-Dev}	F30–F38	F39–F47
	TF-ICTF	{Avg, Max, Std-Dev}	F48–F56	F57–F65
	Entropy	{Avg, Med, Max, Std-Dev}	F66–F77	F78–F89
	Query Scope		F90–F92	F93–F95
	Kullback-Leibler divergence		F96–F98	F99–F101
Similarity	SCQ	{Avg, Max, Sum}	F102–F110	F111–F119
Relatedness	PMI	{Avg, Max}	F120–F125	F126–F131

4.3 Data Rebalancing

In traceability settings, the training data is generally highly imbalanced because only a few valid links exist [15,23], making classifier training problematic [23]. Table 2 shows this occurs in our datasets too, with a percentage of valid links between 0.26% and 1.62%. The positive samples that the classifier would view are quite low, compared to the negative ones. Thus, we applied four rebalancing strategies [16] to the training data:

1. *None.* There is no rebalancing method applied to the data.
2. *Oversampling.* The minority class is oversampled until it reaches the size of the majority class, by applying SMOTE.
3. *Undersampling.* The majority class is randomly undersampled until it has the same size as the minority class, by applying the random undersampling technique.
4. *5050.* Oversampling via SMOTE is applied to the minority class with a sampling strategy of 0.5. Then undersampling is applied to the majority class until the sizes of both classes are equal.

4.4 Classification Algorithms

We considered two state-of-the-art supervised ML algorithms for classifying trace links as valid or invalid: Random Forests and Gradient Boosted Decision Trees. While the former are shown to be the best RTR classifier in earlier research [16,23], Gradient Boosted Decision Trees outperformed Random Forests in other domains [7,29]. To implement the Random Forest algorithm, we used the framework of Scikit-learn. To implement the Gradient Boosted Decision Trees we used two different frameworks: XGBoost, and LightGBM. These frameworks differ in two major respects. The first distinction is in the method of splitting. XGBoost splits the tree level-wise rather than leaf-wise, whereas LightGBM splits the tree leaf-wise. The second difference is how best split value is determined. XGBoost uses a histogram-based algorithm, which splits a feature and its data points into discrete bins, which are used to find the best split value. LightGBM uses a subset of the training data rather than the entire training dataset. Its sampling technique uses gradients, resulting in significantly faster training times.

5 Results

We performed an evaluation on the different combinations of the rebalancing strategies of Sect. 4.3 and of the classification algorithms of Sect. 4.4. This evaluation was conducted for each dataset independently by dividing each dataset into a training (80%) and testing (20%) sets using stratified sampling, so that the two sets have a comparable proportion of positives and negatives. Due to insufficient memory, we use only 4 out of the 12 relatedness-based QQ features listed in Table 4, leading to a total of 123 features.

To mitigate randomisation effects, we repeated the evaluation (training-testing set splitting, classifier training on the 80%, testing on the 20%) for 25 times, then we averaged the outputs, leading to the results we show in Sect. 5.1. In addition to the quantitative results, we discuss the relative importance of the features in Sect. 5.2.

5.1 Quantitative Results

Table 5 shows the precision, the recall, and the $F_{0.5}$- and F_2-measure for the results, which were obtained using non-normalised data. The table compares the three algorithms (Random Forests, XGBoost, LightGBM) that are visualised as macro-columns; the results for each project are presented in a different set of rows. Per project, the results are shown by showing, one per line, the four rebalancing strategies (none, oversampling, undersampling, 5050). The results for the normalised data were found to be slightly worse, and are therefore only included in the online appendix.

For the trace recommendation scenario, XGBoost ($\overline{x} = 56.25$) has the highest mean F_2 across all rebalancing strategies. LightGBM follows ($\overline{x} = 55.16$), and Random Forests are the least effective ($\overline{x} = 42.24$). This is interesting, for Random Forests have consistently been found to be the best performing algorithm in prior RTR research [16,23]. This finding indicates that, similar to other tasks [7,29], Gradient Boosted Decision Trees can outperform Random Forests in RTR-tasks too. A similar result holds for the trace maintenance scenario ($F_{0.5}$), where XGBoost ($\overline{x} = 55.45$) performs best, and LightGBM achieves results that are as low as those of random forests.

Table 5. Mean precision, recall, and $F_{0.5}$- (trace maintenance scenario) and F_2-measure (trace recommendation) across all 3 datasets. The green-coloured cells indicate the best results per each dataset. For accuracy and readability, the table shows F-scores in percentage.

Proj.	Rebal.	Random Forests				XGBoost				LightGBM			
Service	None	94.96	19.71	53.13	23.37	81.77	48.86	71.89	53.07	64.56	48.62	60.45	51.07
	Over	5.90	95.52	7.26	23.61	6.98	96.33	8.56	27.01	6.59	97.62	8.10	25.92
	Under	69.12	44.67	62.17	48.01	70.23	60.24	67.89	61.94	60.02	65.71	61.02	64.42
	5050	59.59	54.33	58.41	55.27	59.62	69.86	61.37	67.47	53.49	72.10	56.34	67.31
Data	None	90.34	29.78	63.91	34.35	84.87	62.65	79.21	66.09	82.50	61.75	77.24	64.98
	Over	16.42	92.04	19.65	47.84	20.28	94.44	24.05	54.50	20.01	94.11	23.74	53.99
	Under	75.52	48.33	67.78	52.03	77.08	69.27	75.34	70.68	70.67	69.96	70.47	70.05
	5050	62.33	54.51	60.52	55.86	65.96	74.98	67.54	72.94	63.22	76.26	65.42	73.19
Store	None	93.13	42.12	73.66	46.99	86.56	59.06	78.77	62.85	46.78	47.53	45.51	45.27
	Over	4.31	90.35	5.32	17.96	2.51	90.35	3.12	11.23	2.98	92.47	3.70	13.17
	Under	72.61	44.47	63.21	47.70	70.51	62.59	68.02	63.42	69.43	65.18	68.18	65.67
	5050	65.31	52.00	61.58	53.84	58.84	65.88	59.63	63.73	55.34	71.06	57.68	66.89
Macro-Avg	None	92.81	30.54	63.57	34.90	84.40	56.86	76.62	60.67	64.61	52.63	61.07	53.77
	Over	8.88	92.64	10.74	29.80	9.92	93.71	11.91	30.91	9.86	94.73	11.85	31.03
	Under	72.42	45.82	64.39	49.25	72.61	64.03	70.42	65.35	66.71	66.95	66.56	66.71
	5050	62.41	53.61	60.17	54.99	61.47	70.24	62.85	68.05	57.35	73.14	59.81	69.13
	Mean	*59.13*	*55.65*	*49.72*	*42.24*	*57.10*	*71.21*	*55.45*	*56.25*	*49.63*	*71.86*	*49.82*	*55.16*

Also, our findings show that the rebalancing strategy has a greater effect than the classification algorithm. With no rebalancing, we achieve the highest precision in 11/12 combinations (algorithm × dataset), with the only exception of LightGBM on the Store dataset. So, for the trace maintenance scenario, no oversampling is the best option.

SMOTE oversampling reduces precision and increases recall: in extreme cases where recall is considerably more important than precision (missing a valid trace is critical and the cost of vetting many invalid candidates is low), it may be a viable option. However, for our two scenarios with $F_{0.5}$ and F_2, SMOTE is the worst alternative.

When we use undersampling for rebalancing, we get a better trade-off than when we use oversampling: the recall increases with respect to no re-balancing, at the expense of precision. However, the decrease in precision is less substantial than for oversampling.

The 5050 rebalancing strategy improves this balance by trading recall for precision. As a result, the classifiers using this rebalancing strategy preserve high recall while offering a more practical precision. The F_2-measure quantifies this: 5050 rebalancing is the best alternative for the trace recommendation scenario.

When taking both the rebalancing and classification algorithm into account, we achieve highest F2-score by combining LightGBM with 5050 rebalancing ($\overline{x} = 69.13$), making it the best configuration for trace recommendation. The XGBoost/5050 combination is, however, very close, and slightly outperforms LightGBM/5050 for the Service dataset. For the Trace Recommendation scenario, we get the best by combining XGBoost with no data rebalancing, which achieves a mean F0.5-measure of 76.62.

5.2   Features Importance

We report on the feature importance to contribute to the model's explainability. We consider the average gain of each feature category, as defined in Sect. 4.2, with QQ broken down into its subcategories due to the many features. The cumulative (total), max, and average gain is shown in Table 6, while Fig. 3 presents them visually.

Table 6. The total, max, and average gain (in percentage over the total gain given by all features) per feature category for the trace recommendation and trace maintenance scenarios.

		Trace recommendation			Trace maintenance		
		Total	Max	Avg	Total	Max	Avg
Process-related	Service	30.79	26.14	7.70	11.43	4.66	2.86
	Data	52.61	32.14	13.15	10.93	3.86	2.73
	Store	7.61	4.48	1.19	5.14	1.705	1.29
Information retrieval	Service	52.82	49.33	2.94	17.83	3.04	0.99
	Data	20.29	15.45	1.12	19.99	2.97	1.11
	Store	46.81	42.71	2.60	14.20	2.46	0.79
Document statistics	Service	3.20	1.76	0.46	7.60	2.17	1.09
	Data	4.08	1.34	0.58	5.06	1.66	0.72
	Store	3.67	1.75	0.52	15.66	8.04	2.23
Query quality (Specificity)	Service	10.59	2.20	0.15	51.01	1.71	0.71
	Data	18.89	4.89	0.26	51.51	5.08	0.72
	Store	39.17	19.85	0.54	51.97	2.96	0.72
Query quality (Similarity)	Service	2.35	0.45	0.13	9.93	1.59	0.55
	Data	3.03	0.59	0.17	10.14	2.35	0.56
	Store	2.54	0.59	0.14	11.65	1.94	0.65
Query quality (Term Relatedness)	Service	0.25	0.14	0.06	2.20	0.74	0.55
	Data	1.09	0.75	0.27	2.37	1.01	0.59
	Store	0.20	0.16	0.05	1.38	0.70	0.34

In the Trace Recommendation scenario, we see that process-related feature categories are important in the Service and Data projects, with gains of 30.79 and 52.61, respectively. Further investigation reveals that the top two process-related features for Service and Data are F4: the difference between the date the issue was resolved and the revision date (18.99 for Data, 26.14 for Service) and F1: whether the issue assignee is the same person who committed the revision (32.14 for Data, 3.8 for Service).

Process-related features contribute much less for the Store dataset, in both scenarios. One explanation is that Service and Data are produced by a different development team than Store. Both teams may have a different level of discipline when it comes to managing JIRA-problems (i.e., promptly updating the status of JIRA issues), resulting in a different level of importance for this feature category.

The Information Retrieval feature category is shown to be important for the Trace recommendation scenario, with total Gains of 52.82, 20.29, and 46.81. Similar to the Process-related feature category, the majority of this increase comes from a single feature, which is the cosine similarity between all-text from a revision and a JIRA-issue summary, utilising summary as a query (F25) for all three datasets. This means that a TF-IDF representation of merely the JIRA issues via the summary is better for the model than a combination of summary and description.

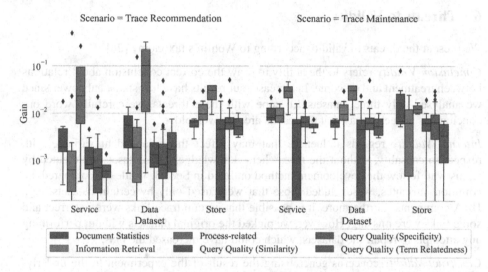

Fig. 3. Average gain per feature family for the trace recommendation scenario (left) and for the trace maintenance scenario (right). The y-axis uses an exponential scale to improve readability.

Furthermore, we find that this feature category is less important in the trace maintenance scenario, with each unique feature contributing more evenly.

Table 6 also reveals that the Document Statistics feature category have a low total gain. Figure 3, however, shows that the average gain per feature in this category is rather significant. Because of this finding, the cost-benefit ratio of implementing this feature category is favourable due to its relative simplicity of implementation.

Finally, for the QQ feature family, only the Specificity sub-category is frequently present in the model, with a total gain of 10.59, 18.89, and 19.89 in the Trace Recommendation scenario and 51.01, 51.51, and 51.97 in the Trace Maintenance scenario for Service, Data, and Store, respectively. It should be emphasised, however, that this sub-category accounts for 58% (72 out of 123) of the total number of features. In the Trace Recommendation scenario, we can observe that the maximum value of QQ (Specificity) for Store is 19.85. Further analysis reveals that this feature is the medium entropy of the JIRA descriptions as query, which was likewise the top performing for Data and the second best for Service in its category. The original intent of the QQ metrics may explain why Specificity has a greater information gain than the Similarity and Term Relatedness QQ metrics. In IR, queries are deemed high-quality when the relevant information is obtained, independent of the document in which it is stored. Both the Similarity and Term relatedness metrics assume that a document collection with many relevant documents is valuable because it raises the likelihood of retrieving a relevant document. However, for TLR, where there is only one genuine artifact to be identified, this is irrelevant. Because of this disparity, the Similarity and Term relatedness metrics are less suited for the TLR task. Specificity can still help since it seeks to differentiate the relevant document from the irrelevant documents, which is also visible in Table 6.

6   Threats to Validity

We present the threats to validity according to Wohlin's taxonomy [28].

Conclusion Validity refers to the ability to draw the correct conclusion about relations between treatment and outcome. In our case, our results have low statistical power since we analysed only three datasets. To cope with these threats, we carefully word our conclusions in such a way that the results are not oversold.

Internal Validity regards influences that may affect the independent variable with respect to causality, without the researchers' knowledge. The datasets are created by teams who follow the development method outlined in Sect. 3. While we compared the common attributes, we excluded those that were used only by certain datasets, e.g., JIRA comments. Furthermore, it is possible that certain trace links were incorrect and some links were missing. However, we picked the original datasets without performing any attempts to repair the datasets, which could have increased the bias.

Construct Validity concerns generalising the result of the experiment to the underlying concept or theory. The main threat concerns the research design: we approximate performance in the two scenarios via the $F_{0.5}$ and F_2 metrics. Although our method is aligned with the state-of-the-art in traceability research, in-vivo studies should be conducted for a more truthful assessment of the effectiveness, e.g., by deploying a system based on our employed algorithms and measuring the performance in use.

External Validity regards the extent to which we can generalise the results of our experiment to industrial practice. Our claims are limited to the low-code development domain, and, in particular, to the case of our industrial collaborator: Mendix. Although we collected projects from two separate teams, using more data would be beneficial. Finally, to minimise overfitting and enhance generalisability, we followed the standard practice of having a distinct training and test set.

Despite our best efforts to mitigate the threats, not everything can be accounted for. All the results were obtained from a single organisation, which could lead to a potential bias. Consequently, we had to be cautious in how we expressed our conclusions. Our results show promising avenues, but we are not yet in a position to generalise.

7   Conclusion and Future Work

In this study, we have provided initial evidence regarding requirements trace classification within an MDD-context. Upon analysing the MDD development process of our research collaborator (Mendix), we identified two scenarios which could benefit from a requirement trace link classifier: trace recommendation and trace maintenance. These scenarios require different performance metrics: F_2 for the former, $F_{0.5}$ for the latter.

After examining the three datasets under four rebalancing strategies, we obtained an average F_2-score (for trace recommendation) across the datasets of 69% with the LightGBM classifier with a mix of under- and oversampling (5050 strategy). For trace maintenance, we obtained an average $F_{0.5}$-score of 76% when employing XGBoost as the ML classifier and with no rebalancing of the training data.

The results are positive when considering that the percentage of traces in our datasets is low, ranging between 0.26% and 1.62% (see Table 1). This imbalance poses serious challenges when training a classifier and it represents a key obstacle to its performance.

We have also analysed which feature families from the literature, which we embedded in our tool, lead to the highest information gain. We found that process-related features seem to lead to the highest information gain, and that most query-quality features have a very marginal information gain and can therefore be discarded.

More research is needed about the specific features to include in production environments. Indeed, a high number of features may lead to overfitting. Also, we need to compare our ML-based approach to its deep learning counterparts. Studying additional dataset is one of our priorities, especially through the collaboration with Mendix. Moreover, analysing the performance of the tool in use is a priority: while we have based our analysis and discussion in F-measures, only a user study can reveal the actual quality of the recommended and recovered traces, that is, whether the developers who have to vet and use the traces find them useful, and whether they actually approve of integrating our approach into their development environment. Finally, studying horizontal traceability, i.e., the existence of links between artifacts at the same abstraction level (e.g., between requirements) is an interesting future direction.

This paper, which takes existing features for ML-based traceability and applies them to the low-code or model-driven domain, calls for additional studies on the effectiveness of the existing techniques in novel, emerging domains. We expect that such research will incrementally contribute to the maturity of the field of requirements traceability.

Acknowledgment. The authors would like to thank Mendix, and especially to Toine Hurkmans, for the provision of the datasets used in this paper and for giving us access to their development practices through numerous interviews and meetings.

References

1. Abadi, A., Nisenson, M., Simionovici, Y.: A traceability technique for specifications. In: Proceedings of ICPC, pp. 103–112 (2008)
2. Aung, T.W.W., Huo, H., Sui, Y.: A literature review of automatic traceability links recovery for software change impact analysis. In: Proceedings of ICPC, pp. 14–24 (2020)
3. Berry, D.M.: Empirical evaluation of tools for hairy requirements engineering tasks. Empir. Softw. Eng. **26**(6), 1–77 (2021). https://doi.org/10.1007/s10664-021-09986-0
4. Blaauboer, F., Sikkel, K., Aydin, M.N.: Deciding to adopt requirements traceability in practice. In: Krogstie, J., Opdahl, A., Sindre, G. (eds.) CAiSE 2007. LNCS, vol. 4495, pp. 294–308. Springer, Heidelberg (2007). https://doi.org/10.1007/978-3-540-72988-4_21

5. Borg, M., Runeson, P., Ardö, A.: Recovering from a decade: a systematic mapping of information retrieval approaches to software traceability. Empir. Softw. Eng. **19**(6), 1565–1616 (2013). https://doi.org/10.1007/s10664-013-9255-y
6. Briand, L., Bianculli, D., Nejati, S., Pastore, F., Sabetzadeh, M.: The case for context-driven software engineering research: generalizability is overrated. IEEE Softw. **34**(5), 72–75 (2017)
7. Callens, A., Morichon, D., Abadie, S., Delpey, M., Liquet, B.: Using Random forest and Gradient boosting trees to improve wave forecast at a specific location. Appl. Ocean Res. **104**, 102339 (2020)
8. Capobianco, G., De Lucia, A., Oliveto, R., Panichella, A., Panichella, S.: On the role of the nouns in IR-based traceability recovery. In: Proceedings of the ICPC, pp. 148–157, May 2009
9. Cleland-Huang, J., Berenbach, B., Clark, S., Settimi, R., Romanova, E.: Best practices for automated traceability. Computer **40**(6), 27–35 (2007)
10. Deerwester, S., Dumais, S.T., Furnas, G.W., Landauer, T.K., Harshman, R.: Indexing by latent semantic analysis. J. Am. Soc. Inf. Sci. **41**(6), 391–407 (1990)
11. Falessi, D., Di Penta, M., Canfora, G., Cantone, G.: Estimating the number of remaining links in traceability recovery. Empir. Softw. Eng. **22**(3), 996–1027 (2016). https://doi.org/10.1007/s10664-016-9460-6
12. Falessi, D., Roll, J., Guo, J.L.C., Cleland-Huang, J.: Leveraging historical associations between requirements and source code to identify impacted classes. IEEE Trans. Software Eng. **46**(4), 420–441 (2018)
13. Ghannem, A., Hamdi, M.S., Kessentini, M., Ammar, H.H.: Search-based requirements traceability recovery: a multi-objective approach. In: Proceedings of the CEC, pp. 1183–1190 (2017)
14. Gotel, O., et al.: The grand challenge of traceability (v1.0). In: Cleland-Huang, J., Gotel, O., Zisman, A. (eds.) Software and Systems Traceability, pp. 343–409. Springer, London (2012). https://doi.org/10.1007/978-1-4471-2239-5_16
15. Guo, J., Cheng, J., Cleland-Huang, J.: Semantically enhanced software traceability using deep learning techniques. In: Proceedings of ICSE, pp. 3–14. IEEE (2017)
16. Mills, C., Escobar-Avila, J., Haiduc, S.: Automatic traceability maintenance via machine learning classification. In: Proceedings of ICSME, pp. 369–380, July 2018
17. Mills, C., Haiduc, S.: The impact of retrieval direction on IR-based traceability link recovery. In: Proceedings of ICSE NIER, pp. 51–54 (2017)
18. Oliveto, R., Gethers, M., Poshyvanyk, D., De Lucia, A.: On the equivalence of information retrieval methods for automated traceability link recovery. In: Proceedings of ICPC, pp. 68–71 (2010)
19. Port, D., Nikora, A., Hayes, J.H., Huang, L.: Text mining support for software requirements: traceability assurance. In: Proceedings of HICSS, pp. 1–11. E (2011)
20. Porter, M.F.: An algorithm for suffix stripping. Program (1980)
21. Ramesh, B., Edwards, M.: Issues in the development of a requirements traceability model. In: Proceedings of ISRE, pp. 256–259 (1993)
22. Rasiman, R., Dalpiaz, F., España, S.: Online appendix: how effective is automated trace link recovery in model-driven development? January 2022. https://doi.org/10.23644/uu.19087685.v1
23. Rath, M., Rendall, J., Guo, J.L.C., Cleland-Huang, J., Maeder, P.: Traceability in the wild: automatically augmenting incomplete trace links. In: Proceedings of ICSE, vol. 834–845 (2018)

24. Umuhoza, E., Brambilla, M.: Model driven development approaches for mobile applications: a survey. In: Younas, M., Awan, I., Kryvinska, N., Strauss, C., Thanh, D. (eds.) MobiWIS 2016. LNCS, vol. 9847, pp. 93–107. Springer, Cham (2016). https://doi.org/10.1007/978-3-319-44215-0_8
25. Wang, B., Peng, R., Li, Y., Lai, H., Wang, Z.: Requirements traceability technologies and technology transfer decision support: a systematic review. J. Syst. Softw. **146**, 59–79 (2018)
26. Wieringa, R.J.: Design Science Methodology for Information Systems and Software Engineering. Springer, Heidelberg (2014). https://doi.org/10.1007/978-3-662-43839-8
27. Winkler, S., von Pilgrim, J.: A survey of traceability in requirements engineering and model-driven development. Softw. Syst. Model. **9**(4), 529–565 (2010)
28. Wohlin, C., Runeson, P., Höst, M., Ohlsson, M.C., Regnell, B., Wesslén, A.: Experimentation in software engineering, vol. 9783642290 (2012)
29. Yoon, J.: Forecasting of real GDP growth using machine learning models: gradient boosting and random forest approach. Comput. Econ. **57**(1), 247–265 (2020). https://doi.org/10.1007/s10614-020-10054-w

A Zero-Shot Learning Approach to Classifying Requirements: A Preliminary Study

Waad Alhoshan[1]([✉]) [iD], Liping Zhao[2]([✉]) [iD], Alessio Ferrari[3] [iD],
and Keletso J. Letsholo[4] [iD]

[1] Al-Imam Mohammad Ibn Saud Islamic University, Riyadh, Saudi Arabia
wmaboud@imamu.edu.sa
[2] University of Manchester, Manchester, UK
liping.zhao@manchester.ac.uk
[3] CNR-ISTI, Pisa, Italy
alessio.ferrari@isti.cnr.it
[4] Higher Colleges of Technology, Abu Dhabi, UAE
kletsholo@hct.ac.ae

Abstract. *Context and motivation:* Advances in Machine Learning (ML) and Deep Learning (DL) technologies have transformed the field of Natural Language Processing (NLP), making NLP more practical and accessible. Motivated by these exciting developments, Requirements Engineering (RE) researchers have been experimenting ML/DL based approaches for a range of RE tasks, such as requirements classification, requirements tracing, ambiguity detection, and modelling. *Question/problem:* Most of today's ML/DL approaches are based on supervised learning techniques, meaning that they need to be trained using annotated datasets to learn how to assign a class label to examples from an application domain. This requirement poses an enormous challenge to RE researchers, as the lack of requirements datasets in general and annotated datasets in particular, makes it difficult for them to fully exploit the benefit of the advanced ML/DL technologies. *Principal ideas/results:* To address this challenge, this paper proposes a novel approach that employs the Zero-Shot Learning (ZSL) technique to perform requirements classification. We build several classification models using ZSL. We focus on the classification task because many RE tasks can be solved as classification problems by a large number of available ML/DL methods. In this preliminary study, we demonstrate our approach by classifying non-functional requirements (NFRs) into two categories: Usability and Security. ZSL supports learning without domain-specific training data, thus solving the lack of annotated datasets typical of RE. The study shows that our approach achieves an average of 82% recall and F-score. *Contribution:* This study demonstrates the potential of ZSL for requirements classification. The promising results of this study pave the way for further investigations and large-scale studies. An important implication is that it is possible to have very little or no training data to perform requirements classification. The proposed approach thus contributes to the solution of the long-standing problem of data shortage in RE.

Keywords: Requirements Engineering · Zero-Shot Learning · Machine Learning · Deep Learning · Transfer Learning · Language models · Natural Language Processing

© Springer Nature Switzerland AG 2022
V. Gervasi and A. Vogelsang (Eds.): REFSQ 2022, LNCS 13216, pp. 52–59, 2022.
https://doi.org/10.1007/978-3-030-98464-9_5

1   Introduction

Data shortage, particularly lack of annotated task-specific data, has been a major challenge for requirements engineering (RE) researchers interested in applying natural language processing (NLP) and machine learning (ML) techniques to requirements documents [6,24]. Even for the lively field of app review analysis, Dabrowki *et al.* [3] has shown that most studies have not released their annotated dataset. Also when datasets are available, the annotation process is time consuming and error prone [4], thus calling for solutions that can work well with limited data. Transfer learning makes it possible to address this issue, by training language models on largely available NL datasets, and then fine tuning on a smaller set of domain specific ones [20]. Zero-Shot Learning (ZSL) further improves the idea by treating sentence classification as a problem of predicting whether a NL sentence is related to a NL tag or not, by reasoning solely on the embedding of the sentence and of the tag, and not resorting on pre-annotated classes for training. In this paper, we perform a preliminary study on using zero-shot learning for the problem of non-functional requirements (NFRs) classification. Our results show comparable performances to other supervised approaches that use a considerable amount of annotated datasets for training or fine-tuning existing models. The affordability of the approach makes it possible to be further investigated and extended. In the paper, we also discuss our future steps in the application of this solution to other classification-related tasks in RE.

2   Background: From Transfer Learning to Zero-Shot Learning

Transfer learning refers to the ability of a ML model to recognize and apply knowledge learned in previous tasks to novel, but related tasks [11]. For example, we can train a model with a sentiment analysis task and then transfer the model to perform a related task such as spam detection [20]. The power of transfer learning lies in enabling a high-performance ML model trained with easily obtained data from one domain to be 'transferred' to a different, but related target domain [11,20]. In so doing, transfer learning aims to improve the performance of a ML model in the target domain, whilst avoiding many expensive data-labeling efforts and alleviating the training data shortage problem [11,17,20].

Transfer learning has become a commonplace in advanced *language models (LMs)*, which are machine learning frameworks for NLP tasks. These models can be *pre-trained* on a data-rich task before being *fine-tuned* on different downstream tasks [14]. In particular, the LMs such as BERT [5] and GPT [13] allow a model to be pre-trained using *unsupervised learning* on *unlabeled data* and then fine-tuned using *supervised learning* on *labelled data* from the downstream tasks. These approaches have achieved state-of-the-art results in many of the most common NLP benchmark tasks [5,14].

What makes BERT and GPT so powerful is their underlying *transformer* architecture [18], which transforms a given sequence of elements, such as the sequence of words in a sentence, into another sequence, with the help of an Encoder and a Decoder. The output sequence can be in another language, symbols, a copy of the input, etc. Both Encoder and Decoder are composed of modules, which are made of multi-head *self-attention* functions and feed forward layers. The self-attention mechanism looks at an input sequence and decides at each step which parts of the sequence are important or unimportant; which parts should be remembered or forgotten. As sentences in natural language are sequence-dependent—that is, the order of the words is crucial for understanding a sentence—, transformers are particularly useful for NLP tasks, such as language understanding and machine translation. In addition, transformers are capable of performing transformation sequentially as well as in parallel, by stacking multiple self-attention mechanisms on top of each other or by using them side by side. However, while transformer-based LMs can avoid expensive data-labeling efforts, they are very expensive to pre-train, as they require a large amount of training data, as well as expensive computational resources. For example, to pre-train a $BERT_{base}$ model[1], it requires 128,000 words $\times$ 1,000,000 steps on 4 Cloud TPUs with 16 TPU chips for four days [5]. Although fine-tuning of these models is relatively less expensive, it still requires thousands or tens of thousands of labelled task-specific examples [2,5].

Zero-Shot Learning (ZSL) has been originally used in image processing to predict unseen images [16], and has recently been adapted to text classification to predict unseen classes [12]. Unlike other text classifiers that learn to classify a given sentence as one of the possible classes, the ZSL models (also called *learners*) learn to predict *whether the sentence is related to a tag or not*. Thus, ZSL treats a classification task (binary, or multi-class) as a problem of finding relatedness between sentences and classes [12].

To train a ZSL classifier, we need to add all the tags (labels) to each sentence in the training set for the model to learn the likelihood of each tag for each sentence. The learning involves measuring the semantic relatedness of a given input sequence (e.g., a sentence) to each class or tag and assigning a probabilistic score to the input in relation to the tag to establish if the input belongs to the corresponding class. After the assignment of all the tags to the input, the classifier proposes a threshold value to suggest if the input should be classified into one or more classes represented by the tags. Effectively, ZSL performs a multi-label classification for each input.

The real potential of ZSL is its partnership with large pre-trained LMs. By piggybacking on such models, the ZSL models can perform competitively on downstream NLP tasks *without fine-tuning (zero-shot) or with only a handful of labelled task-specific examples (few-shot)*, thus removing the burden of expensive data-labeling efforts, the goal set out by transfer learning. There are two general methods which are available for training a ZSL model: the *embedding-based* method and the *entailment-based* method. The *embedding-based* method integrates the text embedding layer with the tag embedding layer, and then measures the probability of their relatedness using some similarity function [12]. The embeddings are commonly extracted from pre-trained LMs and the embedding layers could be at the word or sentence level, a word-based embedding layer aims to learn the probability of words in entire datasets, while a sentence-based embedding layer aims to contextualize the words at sentence-level, thus exploiting the

---

[1] BERT has two basic models: $BERT_{base}$ and $BERT_{large}$. $BERT_{base}$ has 12 encoder layers whereas $BERT_{large}$ has 24. Which BERT model to use depends on the application and $BERT_{base}$ is usually sufficient for experiments, as it takes less time and resource to fine-tune comparing to $BERT_{large}$.

whole sentence structure and content in the learning process. On the other hand, the *entailment-based* method treats an input text sequence as a premise and the candidate tags as a hypothesis, and then infers if the input text is an entailment of any of the given tags or not [23]. In this preliminary study, we choose the embedding-based method due to the widely availability of embedding technologies.

3   Preliminary Study

Dataset In this study we use the popular PROMISE dataset[2] to demonstrate the potential of ZSL for requirements classification. The dataset contains 625 FRs and NFRs with associated labels, and has frequently been used as a benchmark for requirements classification [4,7,8]. In our feasibility study, we select only the subset of the dataset that contains the usability and security requirements. The two classes of requirements are evenly distributed, with 67 usability and 66 security requirements, labelled as US and SE respectively. The classification task in our study is to apply different ZSL models to predict *whether a requirement in this dataset is related to a usability tag or not, or whether a requirement in this dataset is related to a security tag or not.*

Setting-up the ZSL Classifiers. We use the embedding-based method to study the ZSL models and select the following nine pre-trained Transformer models from Hugging Face models hub [21]:

- **BERT family** [5]: $BERT_{base-uncased}$, $BERT_{base-cased}$, $BERT_{large-uncased}$, $BERT_{large-cased}$;
- **RoBERTa family** [9]: $RoBERT_{base}$, $XLM-RoBERT_{base}$;
- **XLNet family** [22]: $XLNet_{base-cased}$;
- **Sentence-based LMs**: Sentence-BERT [15] and MiniLM-L12-v2 [19] which is fine-tuned by one billion sentence pairs dataset from different online technical feeds such as Reddit comments.

Based on these nine LMs, we implement nine embedding-based ZSL classifiers by fitting each model to the default ZSL pipeline from the Transformers library [21]. Afterwards we apply each ZSL classifier as follows: 1) We feed each requirement sentence and its labels to the classifier. 2) The LM within the classifier carries out tokenization and then creates a sentence embedding and a label embedding layer. 3) The classifier processes the embedding results by computing the relatedness between the sequences embedding and the label embeddings using cosine similarity. 4) Finally, the overall similarity scores are fed into a classification function, and the probabilities of all labels are computed to select the maximum score as the most related label to a given requirement.

Evaluation and Results Analysis. We implement the ZSL classifiers on Google Colab with a standard CPU at 2.30 GHz with 12 GB of RAM. The entire experiment took less than 5 min (4.39 mis) to run, with 0.77 GB of RAM usage. The results are then exported into structured (.csv) files for further investigation[3]. We computed the ZSL classifiers performance in comparison to the original annotated PROMISE dataset. For performance evaluation, we use precision (P), recall (R), F1, weighted F-score (w.F), and accuracy (A). Results are shown in Table 1.

---

[2] https://doi.org/10.5281/zenodo.268542.
[3] The results are available at: https://github.com/waadalhoshan/ZSL4REQ.

Table 1. The experiment results. The **bold** font indicates the best results obtained from the ZSL-based experiments, and the underlined scores refer to the best results reported in the related work [8] and [7].

Classification approach	Usability (US)			Security (SE)			A	w.F
	P	R	F1	P	R	F1		
[8] Supervised$_{mulit}$ (w/o feature sel.)	0.65	0.82	0.70	0.81	0.77	0.74	0.76	0.73
[8] Supervised$_{mulit}$ (500 best features)	0.70	0.66	0.64	0.64	0.53	0.56	0.61	0.6
[7] NoRBERT$_{basemulti}$ (ep. = 50)	0.78	0.85	0.81	0.78	<u>0.92</u>	0.85	0.85	0.83
[7] NoRBERT$_{largemulti}$ (ep. = 50)	<u>0.83</u>	<u>0.88</u>	<u>0.86</u>	<u>0.90</u>	<u>0.92</u>	<u>0.91</u>	<u>0.87</u>	<u>0.86</u>
ZSL BERT$_{base-uncased}$	**0.83**	0.52	0.64	0.65	0.90	0.75	0.71	0.70
ZSL BERT$_{base-cased}$	**0.83**	0.58	0.68	0.68	0.88	0.77	0.73	0.73
ZSL BERT$_{large-uncased}$	**0.83**	0.15	0.26	0.54	0.97	0.69	0.56	0.48
ZSL BERT$_{large-cased}$	0.52	0.18	0.27	0.51	0.84	0.63	0.51	0.45
ZSL RoBERTa$_{base}$	0.00	0.00	0.00	0.50	**1.00**	0.67	0.50	0.34
ZSL XLM-RoBERTa$_{base}$	0.49	**1.00**	0.66	0.00	0.00	0.00	0.50	0.33
ZSL XLNet$_{base-cased}$	0.47	0.68	0.56	0.45	0.25	0.32	0.47	0.44
ZSL sentence BERT	0.71	0.80	0.76	0.78	0.69	0.73	0.74	0.75
ZSL MiniLM-L12-v2	0.73	**1.00**	**0.85**	**1.00**	0.64	**0.78**	**0.82**	**0.82**

Considering that our ZSL classification models have not been trained on any sample requirements from the dataset, in contrast to fully supervised or fine-tuned classification approaches, the reported results from some of the used LMs are considered to be *encouraging* for further investigation. In particular, we notice that recall (R) is equal to 100% for some of the LM, as recommended by Berry [1]. We compared the performance of ZSL classifiers with existing work ([8] and [7]) which used the same NFR dataset. The results provided by fine-tuned BERT$_{large}$ model namely NoRBERT [7] has still the highest performance rates in terms of precision rates and F1 scores. However, one of the ZSL classifiers, which applied Sentence-based (MiniLM-L12-v2 LM [19], has a comparable performance of a weighted F-score of 82% comparing to 86% provided by NoRBERT$_{large}$ model. In addition, two of the ZSL classifier models which are based on sentence embeddings (Sentence BERT and MiniLM-L12-v2) have outperformed the fully-supervised learning approaches by Kurtanovic and Maalej [8] with more than 75% of weighted F-scores. Example requirements with their similarity scores according to the given labels set and based on Sentence-based embedding are shown in Table 2. However, we noticed that word-based LMs can be biased towards a specific label. For example, both RoBERTa models (i.e., RoBERTa$_{base}$ and XLM-RoBERTa) are word-based and have the tendency to label all the requirements as Security only or Usability only, as shown in the recall and F1-score results in Table 1. This is predictable with any pre-trained LMs as those models are trained on general-domain datasets, making them less accurate when working with domain-specific data. Therefore, what we regard as a Security requirements (as requirement engineers) could be classified by those general models into more general categories not related to the security aspects of a software.

Overall, the sentence-based LM with ZSL classifier have provided almost best results in our initial experiments comparing to other word-based LM (e.g., BERT, RoBERTa, and XLNet). This observation suggests that sentence-based LMs are to be preferred over word-based LMs as methods for generating requirement and label embedding. As a next step of this research, we will fine-tune an existing sentence-based LM (e.g., Sentence BERT) for specific RE tasks. In the following section, we will briefly outline our future research plan.

Table 2. Requirement examples with their associated similarity scores using the ZSL classifier which is based on the sentence-based embedding. The strike (*) refers to a mislabeling.

Requirement text	Label	Sentence-BERT	Sentence-transformers
The website will provide a help section with answers and solutions to common problems	US	Usability: 0.26	Usability: 0.14
Data integrity scripts will be run on a weekly basis to verify the integrity of the database	SE	Security: 0.18	Security: 0.20
The product should be able to be used b 90% of novice users on the internet	US	*Security: 0.17	Usability: 0.25
The product shall conform to the Americans with disabilities Act	US	Usability: 0.37	*Security: 0.19

4   Conclusion and Future Plan

The promising performance of ZSL observed in our study indicates its potential for requirements classification. We plan to expand this study to conduct further experiments. First, we will extend the current approach to the entire PROMISE dataset, to consider more fine-grained semantic categories, similar to the work of Hey *et al.* [7]. To this end, we plan to experiment different deep learning architectures for implementing the ZSL requirements classifier, as described by Pushp and Srivastava [12], and then apply different fine-tuning techniques to the LMs with promising performances, such as the Sentence-BERT model [15]. For example, by training the high-level layer of the pre-trained LM and freeze the low-level layers, and then fine-tuning by freezing the entire LM and train additional layers on the top. In addition, we will expand the fine-tuning and training of the LMs to different requirement datasets and different classification taxonomies. Second, we will extend the ZSL approach to few-shot learning (FSL) by using one shot (one labelled task-specific requirement) and a few shot (a handful of labelled requirements) to fine-tune the LMs to see if the performance of ZSL can be improved. According to the study carried out by OpenAI [2], even using just one labelled example can substantially improve the classifier performance.

Finally, we will apply ZSL/FSL to other classification related tasks in RE such as those identified in our recent mapping study [24], including *Detection* (detecting linguistic issues in requirements documents) and *Extraction* (identifying key domain abstractions and concepts). We will also repeat our study on the app review classification problem, addressed, e.g., by [10], to see if the models we developed for requirements classification can be transferred to the app review classification task.

References

1. Berry, D.M.: Empirical evaluation of tools for hairy requirements engineering tasks. Empir. Softw. Eng. **26**(6), 1–77 (2021). https://doi.org/10.1007/s10664-021-09986-0
2. Brown, T.B., et al.: Language models are few-shot learners. arXiv preprint arXiv:2005.14165 (2020)
3. Dabrowski, J., Letier, E., Perini, A., Susi, A.: App review analysis for software engineering: a systematic literature review. University College London, Technical report (2020)
4. Dalpiaz, F., Dell'Anna, D., Aydemir, F.B., Çevikol, S.: Requirements classification with interpretable machine learning and dependency parsing. In: RE 2019, pp. 142–152. IEEE (2019)
5. Devlin, J., Chang, M.W., Lee, K., Toutanova, K.: BERT: pre-training of deep bidirectional transformers for language understanding. arXiv preprint arXiv:1810.04805 (2018)
6. Ferrari, A., Dell'Orletta, F., Esuli, A., Gervasi, V., Gnesi, S.: Natural language requirements processing: a 4d vision. IEEE Softw. **34**(6), 28–35 (2017)
7. Hey, T., Keim, J., Koziolek, A., Tichy, W.F.: NoRBERT: transfer learning for requirements classification. In: RE 2020, pp. 169–179. IEEE (2020)
8. Kurtanović, Z., Maalej, W.: Automatically classifying functional and non-functional requirements using supervised machine learning. In: RE 2017, pp. 490–495. IEEE (2017)
9. Liu, Y., et al.: A robustly optimized BERT pretraining approach. arXiv preprint arXiv:1907.11692 (2019)
10. Maalej, W., Kurtanović, Z., Nabil, H., Stanik, C.: On the automatic classification of app reviews. Requirements Eng. **21**(3), 311–331 (2016). https://doi.org/10.1007/s00766-016-0251-9
11. Pan, S.J., Yang, Q.: A survey on transfer learning. IEEE Trans. Knowl. Data Eng. **22**(10), 1345–1359 (2009)
12. Pushp, P.K., Srivastava, M.M.: Train once, test anywhere: zero-shot learning for text classification. arXiv preprint arXiv:1712.05972 (2017)
13. Radford, A., Narasimhan, K., Salimans, T., Sutskever, I.: Improving language understanding by generative pre-training. Technical report, OpenAI (2018)
14. Raffel, C., et al.: Exploring the limits of transfer learning with a unified text-to-text transformer. arXiv preprint arXiv:1910.10683 (2019)
15. Reimers, N., Gurevych, I.: Sentence-BERT: sentence embeddings using Siamese BERT-networks. arXiv preprint arXiv:1908.10084 (2019)
16. Romera-Paredes, B., Torr, P.: An embarrassingly simple approach to zero-shot learning. In: ICML 2015, pp. 2152–2161 (2015)
17. Ruder, S., Peters, M.E., Swayamdipta, S., Wolf, T.: Transfer learning in natural language processing. In: NACL 2019, pp. 15–18 (2019)
18. Vaswani, A., et al.: Attention is all you need. In: NeurIPS 2017, pp. 5998–6008 (2017)
19. Wang, W., Wei, F., Dong, L., Bao, H., Yang, N., Zhou, M.: MiniLM: deep self-attention distillation for task-agnostic compression of pre-trained transformers. arXiv preprint arXiv:2002.10957 (2020)
20. Weiss, K., Khoshgoftaar, T.M., Wang, D.D.: A survey of transfer learning. J. Big Data **3**(1), 1–40 (2016). https://doi.org/10.1186/s40537-016-0043-6

21. Wolf, T., Debut, L., Sanh, V., et al.: Transformers: state-of-the-art natural language processing. In: EMNLP 2020, pp. 38–45 (2020)
22. Yang, Z., Dai, Z., Yang, Y., Carbonell, J., Salakhutdinov, R.R., Le, Q.V.: XLNet: generalized autoregressive pretraining for language understanding. In: NeurIPS 2019, vol. 32 (2019)
23. Yin, W., Hay, J., Roth, D.: Benchmarking zero-shot text classification: datasets, evaluation and entailment approach. CoRR abs/1909.00161 (2019)
24. Zhao, L., et al.: Natural language processing for requirements engineering: a systematic mapping study. ACM Comput. Surv. **54**(3), 55:1–55:41 (2021)

Natural Language Processing

Abbreviation-Expansion Pair Detection for Glossary Term Extraction

Hussein Hasso[1]($\boxtimes$), Katharina Großer[2], Iliass Aymaz[1], Hanna Geppert[1], and Jan Jürjens[2,3]

[1] Fraunhofer FKIE, 53343 Wachtberg (Bonn), Germany
{hussein.hasso,iliass.aymaz,hanna.geppert}@fkie.fraunhofer.de
[2] University of Koblenz-Landau, 56070 Koblenz, Germany
{grosser,juerjens}@uni-koblenz.de
[3] Fraunhofer ISST, 44227 Dortmund, Germany

Abstract. *Context and motivation:* Providing precise definitions of all project specific terms is a crucial task in requirements engineering. In order to support the glossary building process, many previous tools rely on the assumption that the requirements set has a certain level of quality. *Question/problem:* Yet, the parallel detection and correction of quality weaknesses in the context of glossary terms is beneficial to requirements definition. In this paper, we focus on detection of uncontrolled usage of abbreviations by identification of abbreviation-expansion pair (AEP) candidates. *Principal ideas/results:* We compare our feature-based approach (ILLOD) to other similarity measures to detect AEPs. It shows that feature-based methods are more accurate than syntactic and semantic similarity measures. The goal is to extend the glossary term extraction (GTE) and synonym clustering with AEP-specific methods. First experiments with a PROMISE data-set extended with uncontrolled abbreviations show that ILLOD is able to extract abbreviations as well as match their expansions viably in a real-world setting and is well suited to augment previous term clusters with clusters that combine AEP candidates. *Contribution:* In this paper, we present ILLOD, a novel feature-based approach to AEP detection and propose a workflow for its integration to clustering of glossary term candidates.

Keywords: Requirements engineering · Glossary term extraction · Abbreviation-expansion pair detection · Synonym detection

1 Introduction

One of the goals in requirements engineering is to improve an opaque system comprehension into a complete system specification [28]. Activities related to glossary building support that goal, since glossaries serve to improve the accuracy and understandability of requirements written in natural language [3].

Second author supported by European Space Agency's (ESA) NPI program under NPI No. 4000118174/16/NL/MH/GM.

© Springer Nature Switzerland AG 2022
V. Gervasi and A. Vogelsang (Eds.): REFSQ 2022, LNCS 13216, pp. 63–78, 2022.
https://doi.org/10.1007/978-3-030-98464-9_6

According to the *International Requirements Engineering Board* (IREB) [12], a glossary is a collection of definitions of terms that are relevant in a specific domain. In addition, a glossary frequently contains cross-references, synonyms, homonyms, and abbreviations [12]. Glossaries serve to enrich the requirement texts with additional important information, which ensures that technical terms are used and understood correctly, and supports communication among project participants [19]. The consequent use of a complete and accurate glossary leads to a more consistent language, resulting in coherent structures for the requirements, which in turn enhances automatic analysability [8,26]. Finally, a glossary can be reused for future projects within the same application domain to facilitate requirements elicitation and analysis [18].

In order to obtain the mentioned benefits, a glossary should be developed during the requirements elicitation phase, which is also compliant to best practices [19,27]. For various reasons, many projects tend to build their glossary after the requirements elicitation phase [1,2,11]. However, this complicates the task, since requirements written without the use of a glossary are more likely to contain imprecise or ambiguous wordings. When multiple terms are used to refer to the same meaning (synonyms), denote specializations (hyponyms), or terms have multiple meanings (homonyms), this presents a major challenge for the identification of glossary terms. Therefore, beforehand, the analyst has to ensure that the terminology is used consistently, e.g. through syntactic or semantic adjustments. This task affects various inter-requirement relations in parallel.

With this paper, we present an approach that encourages the analyst to start with the glossary building, even when the requirements quality still shows weaknesses, and contributes to resolve two tasks in parallel: (1) quality improvement through reduction of lexical variation and (2) glossary term identification. In particular, we integrate the detection of abbreviations and their expansions.

2 Problem Definition

We briefly focus on the main problems to be solved by an automated tool for the identification of glossary terms (GTE) [3,8,11].

First, since 99% of glossary entries are *noun phrases* (NPs) [14,17]:

(A) A GTE tool needs to have an *accurate noun phrase detection*.

Second, as glossaries deal with domain specific terms and omit duplicates:

(B) A GTE tool needs to *filter* detected NPs to *glossary term candidates*.

Considering (A), *Natural Language Processing* (NLP) pipelines for noun phrase detection, e.g., through *chunking approaches*, are shown to be effective [1,2]. As such, in this paper we focus on devising an effective technique for (B). Here, *statistical filters* composed of *specificity* and *relevance* measures, as presented by Gemkow et al. [11], could be used, in which beforehand identification of homonyms, synonyms, and different spelling variants among detected noun phrases is expected to have a positive effect on accuracy. Since we explicitly consider requirement sets with such quality weaknesses, we first focus on:

(B1) A GTE tool needs to *identify and/or merge homonyms, synonyms, hyponyms and different spelling variants* among detected noun phrases.

To detect such relations among domain terms is also beneficial for the building of initial domain models. In order to check whether a given pair of terms is synonymous, homonymous, or hypernymous, the underlying concepts themselves must be disambiguated [14], which requires good knowledge about the relevant domain. Therefore, candidate term pairs still have to be confirmed or rejected by the analyst. To keep the manual effort low, *term clusters* are a suitable method of representation [2]. A cluster of size n can combine $(n(n-1))/2$ term pairs. For example, the *REGICE* tool [2] follows a synonym clustering approach. Yet, only *context-based* (semantic) and *text-based* (syntactic) similarity [34] are considered and *abbreviations* must have been cleaned up and defined beforehand. Homonyms and hyponyms are not explicitly addressed. Yet, they can be spotted as bycatch. However, for homonyms this is only the case for non-disjoint clusters.

For higher recall in synonym detection, additionally *pattern-based* similarity [34] for *controlled abbreviations* can be applied. It refers to clauses where abbreviations are defined by their corresponding expansions using parentheses or keywords such as *"also known as"*, *"abbreviated"* and *"a.k.a."*, e.g.,

- Common Business Oriented Language **abbreviated** COBOL
- AES (Advanced Encryption Standard)
- Compression/Decompression, **also known as** Codec

More interesting, however, is an algorithm that also supports to resolve *uncontrolled abbreviations*, which are not defined in place when they are used. Uncontrolled abbreviations in requirements are rather common, especially when requirements elicitation is carried out by different persons (in different organizations) and when guidelines for the use of abbreviations are missing or not followed. Abbreviations can be homonymous by having multiple possible expansions within the same requirements set, as they are predominantly used in a project- or domain-specific context, and new projects regularly come up with new word creations. Thus, simple look-up techniques on predefined lists are not sufficient. This leads us to the next problem statement:

(B1.1) A GTE tool needs to exploratorily resolve hitherto unknown abbreviations in comparison to other terms present in the given text.

Since the abbreviation list is part of the glossary, both should be built in parallel. The goal is to enable a specific synonym detection optimized for matching of abbreviations with their expansions, which can be integrated to the clustering in glossary term extraction (GTE) tools. For that, we first compare the accuracy of syntactic and semantic similarity measures with feature-based classification approaches applied to abbreviation-expansion pairs (AEPs). Further, we introduce *ILLOD*, a binary classifier extending the algorithm of Schwartz and Hearst [31]. It checks **I**nitial **L**etters, term **L**engths, **O**rder, and **D**istribution of characters. Finally, we propose how tools like ILLOD can be integrated into the clustering of glossary term candidates.

3   Related Work

For glossary term extraction (GTE), Gemkow et al. [11] showed how to reduce the number of glossary term candidates by using relevance and specificity *filters*. Improving the precision of glossary term extraction like this is important especially for large data-sets. Yet, they do not regulate the possible presence of synonyms and homonyms when determining term frequencies.

Arora et al. [2] argue that *clustering* of glossary term candidates has the advantage to better mitigate false positives from noun phrase detection (A) and to support candidate filtering (B). In addition, their approach provides guidelines on how to tune clustering for a given requirements set, to detect synonyms with high accuracy. They conclude that disjoint clusters should be produced in order to keep the workload for term identification low. In Sect. 6 of this paper, we look at this from a new perspective.

There are various approaches for the extraction and recognition of *abbreviation-expansion pairs* (AEPs). In addition to *statistical* [24,36] and *rule-based* methods [29,32], there are also *machine learning* methods [35]. Many publications deal with biomedical texts and a few, like Park et al. [25], with the field of computer science. Most work assumes that AEPs are predefined in the text via certain patterns and focus their analyses on the surrounding context of the detected abbreviations, which is also the case for Schwartz and Hearst [31]. In our work, we extend the algorithm *findBestLongForm* presented by Schwartz and Hearst [31] to make it applicable for cross-comparisons where an abbreviation and its expansion may occur in different sentences/requirements and are distributed over the given text. We also show that this extension—ILLOD—can be used beneficially in extraction and identification of requirements glossary terms.

4   Abbreviation Detection

The first step to AEP-matching is the identification of abbreviations. Since "[t]he styling of abbreviations is inconsistent and arbitrary and includes many possible variations" [21], abbreviation extraction is usually achieved by finding *single words* that are *relatively short* and have *several capital letters* [20,31,33]. This way, not only acronyms are addressed, but also other forms of abbreviations.

For this task, we implement a simple detection algorithm. It returns *"true"* for a given word w, if the capital letter portion and the word length exceed respectively fall below specified parameter values, otherwise it returns *"false"*. We test this method on a cleaned list of 1786 abbreviation-expansion pairs known from the field of information technology [7][1] with abbreviations of different styles. We reference this list with L, all abbreviations $a \in L$ with A, and all expansions $e \in L$ with E. To identify suitable parameters for word length and the proportion of capital letters, we perform *F1-optimisation* through an exhaustive search on all possible combinations of the two parameters. The search is conducted in the range from 0.01 to 1.0 (in 1/100 steps) for the capital letter portion parameter

---

[1] For reproduction purposes, this list is also included in the supplemental material [13].

and from 1 to 20 for the word length parameter. The algorithm is once tested on all $a \in A$ and once on all $e \in E$ to obtain false negative and false positive assignments respectively.

After optimization, with **word-length** $<= 13$ and **proportion of capital letters** $>= 0.29$ we achieve Precision $= 0.922$, Recall $= 0.923$, and F1 $= 0.922$. On full written text, to keep such high accuracy, we apply an additional stop word filter sorting out words whose lower case matches a stop word and which only have one uppercase letter, as first letter, e.g. "The", "Any", or "If".

5   Detection of AEP Candidates

For AEP detection, different types of similarity measures are eligible. In a nutshell, words are *semantically* similar if they have the same meaning and *syntactically* similar if they have a similar character sequence [10]. Semantic measures rely on data from large corpora or *semantic nets*—models of terms and their relations, whereas "syntactic measures operate on given words and their characters without any assumption of the language or the meaning of the content" [10]. Finally, *feature-based* similarity rates features that are common to a given pair of words, e.g. the order of certain letters. Below, we compare three different types of classifiers for AEP detection based on these three types of similarity measures.

5.1   AEP Detection with Semantic Similarity Measures

Most methods to semantic similarity need to know queried terms in advance. This applies to knowledge-based methods that rely on lexical databases such as *WordNet* [23] and corpus-based methods such as *Word2vec* [22]. As a result, these methods are not suitable to solve (B1.1). Thus, we chose FastText (FT) [4] as a generic approach and state-of-the-practice technique to assess the suitability of semantic similarity methods for AEP detection. To assign an abbreviation a to a *potential* expansion t in the upcoming evaluation, our simple semantic classifier returns whether

$$cosine\_similarity(embed_{FT}(a), embed_{FT}(t)) \geq threshold,$$

where the *cosine_similarity* for two vectors x and y is defined as $\frac{x^T y}{\|x\|\|y\|}$, and $embed_{FT}$ stands for embedding with FastText.

5.2   AEP Detection with Syntactic Similarity Measures

The second type of classifier uses syntactic similarity measures between a and t. For this, several measures, as summarized by Gali et al. [10], can be used, like *Levenshtein-Distance* (LD)[2], *Jaro-Winkler-Similarity* (JWS), an extension

---

[2] We do not choose the extended *Damerau-Levenshtein-Distance* as it considers transpositions and LD is therefore more sensitive to changes in the sequence of letters.

of *Jaro-Similarity*, and the *Dice-Coefficient* (DC). However, the use of syntactic similarity measures to detect AEPs is limited. Typically, abbreviations contain only a small proportion of the letters of their respective extensions. E.g., the pair ("ISO", "International Organization for Standardization") has only a share of 3/14 common characters compared in lower case. This is also reflected in Table 1, where the similarities between randomly selected pairs from L are rather low.

Table 1. Syntactic and semantic similarities between randomly chosen AEPs $(a, e) \in L$ *Distance measures d normalized to similarity in $[0, 1]$ by $1 - (d(a, e)/max(|a|, |e|))$ [10]

Abbreviation-expansion pair (a, e)	LD*	JWS	DC	FT
(LED monitor, Light-emitting diode)	0.15	0.435	0.818	0.30
(Int, integer)	0.286	0.651	0.667	0.20
(PS/2, Personal System/2)	0.235	0.436	0.444	0.19
(IANA, Internet Assigned Numbers Authority)	0.114	0.612	0.316	0.093
(SMM, System Management Mode)	0.136	0.586	0.307	0.142
(U/L, upload)	0.0	0.0	0.444	0.025
(IAP, Internet access provider)	0.042	0.458	0.375	0.06
(CLNS, connectionless network service)	0.0	0.0	0.471	0.076
(MMC, MultiMediaCard)	0.214	0.603	0.333	0.533
(I/O, input/output)	0.083	0.472	0.6	0.147

Table 2. Average syntactic similarities for all $(a, e) \in L$ and $(a, \hat{a})$ with $\hat{a} = potAbb(e)$ *Distance measures d normalized to similarity in $[0, 1]$ by $1 - (d(a, x)/max(|a|, |x|))$ [10]

Compared pairs	LD*	JWS	DC	With pre-processing
(a, e)	0.092	0.309	0.419	No
	0.183	0.637	0.422	Yes
$(a, \hat{a})$	0.361	0.422	0.861	No
	0.797	0.896	0.865	Yes

To overcome this difficulties, the matching between an abbreviation a and some possible expansion t can be estimated by creating a *potential* abbreviation $\hat{a} = potAbb(t)$ out of the initial letters of the single tokens of t. Similarity is then measured between a and $\hat{a}$. This contraction allows to compare a and t on a homogeneous representation level. Table 2 summarizes the average values of the syntactic comparisons between (a, e) as well as $(a, \hat{a})$ for all pairs $(a, e) \in L$, where $\hat{a} = potAbb(e)$ following the just mentioned contraction approach.

Further, we apply *pre-processing* by converting the string into lower case letters, removing punctuation marks and the stop words "for", "and", "of", "in", "via" and "be". Table 2 shows, that pre-processing and contraction have a positive effect for all three examined measures. For (a, e), the average (normalized) Levenshtein-Distance improves by 0.705, average Jaro-Winkler-Similarity by 0.587, and the average Dice Coefficient by 0.446. Thus, with $a^c = preprocess(a)$ and $t^c = preprocess(t)$, the second type of classifiers returns whether

$$syntacticSimilarityMeasure(a^c, potAbb(t^c)) \geq threshold.$$

Although abbreviations usually have short length—in our dataset the average after pre-processing is 3.55—it can be assumed that $\hat{a}$ and a still differ in many cases despite pre-processing. For the Levenshtein-Distance, there is a relative difference of 20.3% in average between $\hat{a}$ and a even after pre-processing, which shows that, as assumed [21], the formation and use of abbreviations in computer science is not subject to fixed guidelines/regulations in practice. Even though the average Jaro-Winkler-Similarity and the average Dice-Coefficient-Similarity are close to their ideal value of 1.0, they are potentially prone to many false positive assignments. We address this assumption in Sect. 5.4.

5.3   AEP Detection with Feature-Based Similarity Measures

The third type of classifier is represented by *ILLOD*, an extension of the algorithm *findBestLongForm* [31] that we implemented in *Python*. Whether (a, t) is a candidate AEP is decided by ILLOD solely on the basis of features of a and the words in t. Thus, it is a feature-based approach, although each feature is identified using conditional rules. Algorithm 1 specifies ILLOD in pseudo-code:

Algorithm 1: ILLOD

---

1 $a^c = preprocess(a)$; $t^c = preprocess(t)$;
2 **if** $check\_initial\_letters(a, t)$ **then**
3 | return True ;
4 **else if** $check\_initial\_letters(a^c, t^c)$ **then**
5 | return True ;
6 **else if** $check\_order(a^c, t^c)$ **and** $compare\_lengths(a^c, t^c)$ **and** $check\_distribution(a^c, t^c)$ **then**
7 | return True ;
8 **else**
9 | return False ;

The method $check\_initial\_letters(a, t)$ examines for all letters in a whether they correspond to the initial letters of the words in t. Thus, the calls in lines 2 and 4 check intuitively if the expansion fits the abbreviation, but have difficulties with pairs like ("QnA", "Questions a̲nd A̲nswers"). To solve this, in line 6 additional features are evaluated:

$check\_order(a, t)$ examines if the order of the letters in a can also be found in t and if the initial letters of a and t correspond. Based on Schwartz and

Hearst [31], we compare the letters in backward reading direction to favour an even distribution of the letters over the words of the expansion.

compare_lengths(a, t) checks whether the length (count of letters) of a is $\geq$ the number of words in t. This sorts out pairs like ("A", "Advanced Configuration and Power Interface"), based on the assumption that a should reference as many words in t as possible.

check_distribution(a, t) tests if the letters from a, if present in t, are uniformly distributed over the words in t, to sort out pairs like ("SMS", "Systems Network Architecture") or ("PaaS", "Palo Alto Research Center").

5.4 Evaluation of the Approaches on a Synthesized Data-Set

To estimate the accuracy of AEP detection approaches, a data-set D is needed that contains incorrect and correct AEPs. For this purpose, we compiled D as $D = L \cup S$, where L corresponds to the list from Sect. 4 and S consists of the pairs (a, e) in which a random element e from E was assigned to a given abbreviation a, not matching the real abbreviation of e. To be more formal, the set S can be described as $S = \{(a, e) \mid a \in A, e \in E, (a, e) \notin L\}$.

While $|L| = 1786$, S grows to $|S| = 2\,710\,125$. S could be reduced by filtering to pairs with identical initial letter. However, since L contains AEPs in which the initial letters differ, this option is discarded. Since we aim to test on a *balanced* data-set, where the proportion of abbreviations among all terms approximately corresponds to that in requirement texts, we test the presented approaches on different $D_\alpha = L \cup S_\alpha$, where $S_\alpha \subset S$ is randomly chosen from S each time, under the condition that $|S_\alpha| = \alpha * |L|$. To obtain an estimate for α, we extract 3195 NPs from 1102 requirements from ten projects of the *PURE* data-set [9]. To increase the recall, all words (not only words in NPs) are checked by our extraction rules from Sect. 4. In total, we extract 138 abbreviations and therefore estimate $\alpha = 3195/138 = 23.152$. Since requirement sets vary in use of abbreviations, several values for α (8, 16, 24, 48, 72) are considered. To avoid disadvantages for classifiers based on syntactic and semantic similarity, threshold values are F1-optimized for all α, given as *thold* in Table 3.

Table 3. F1 performance of AEP detection for different α. *Sem* (FT) corresponds to the semantic classifier in Sect. 5.1, *Syn* corresponds to the different variants of the syntactic classifier in Sect. 5.2 and *Feat* (ILLOD) corresponds to the feature-based classifier in Sect. 5.3. Best thresholds are given in the *thold* columns. *Normalised LD: $LD^*(a, t) = 1 - (LD(a^c, potAbb(t^c))/max(|a^c|, |potAbb(t^c)|))$ [10]

Classifier		$\alpha = 8$		$\alpha = 16$		$\alpha = 24$		$\alpha = 48$		$\alpha = 72$	
		F1	*thold*	F1	*thold*	F1	*thold*	F1	*thold*	F1	*thold*
Sem	FT	0.287	*0.13*	0.191	*0.13*	0.146	*0.16*	0.088	*0.16*	0.064	*0.18*
Syn	LD*	0.861	*0.55*	0.841	*0.54*	0.825	*0.52*	0.780	*0.70*	0.776	*0.68*
	JWS	0.874	*0.73*	0.849	*0.79*	0.831	*0.79*	0.800	*0.79*	0.778	*0.84*
	DC	0.841	*0.75*	0.811	*0.79*	0.789	*0.77*	0.746	*0.82*	0.723	*0.85*
Feat	ILLOD	**0.948**	–	**0.942**	–	**0.937**	–	**0.917**	–	**0.900**	–

The results in F1-scores summarized in Table 3 show that the FastText-based classifier performs poorly. This might be because a word embedding obtained from FastText can only inaccurately represent a certain word sense if the corresponding abbreviation has multiple expansions with heterogeneous meanings. Classifiers based on syntactic similarity measures have F1-scores between 72 and 87%—on average 80%, but are outperformed by ILLOD, which has between 90 and 94%. In the majority of cases, ILLOD achieves higher precision and recall at the same time. With increasingly larger α ($= 48, 72$), a weakening of the precision for ILLOD becomes apparent. Here, it is surpassed by the LD classifier. However, ILLOD is able to retain the best F1-score across all α thanks to its consistently high recall in particular. While Table 3 only states F1-scores, these more detailed results can be obtained within supplemental material [13].

5.5   Evaluation of the Approaches on a Requirements Data-Set

We evaluate the practicability of ILLOD for the intended use case with requirements from 15 projects comprised in a *PROMISE* [30] data-set [5,37]. In order to simulate their uncontrolled usage, 30 undefined abbreviations are inserted as replacements for written-out terms into various requirements. Only terms that appear in at least two requirements are abbreviated in at most one of those. No further guidelines for abbreviation are followed and different styles, not only acronyms, are used. This is performed by an independent person, not involved in this work and without the knowledge of the authors.

We read in the modified data-set as CSV-file. In independent runs, first abbreviations, as described in Sect. 4, and then *ordinary terms without undefined abbreviations* (OT), obtained through noun-chunk extraction [2], are gathered. In the next step, ILLOD is used to determine AEP-candidates by pairwise comparison of the abbreviations with the ordinary terms. The pairs created this way are then merged to *AEP groups*—clusters of exactly one abbreviation and all its potential expansions. For the modified PROMISE data-set, ILLOD creates 115 term tuples, combined to 51 AEP groups. Subsequently, this list of all determined AEP candidates is compared with the actual replacements. As a result, the extraction approach detects 29 of 30 inserted abbreviations and ILLOD is able to indicate the correct expansions for 25 of them.

We performed the same experiment with the semantic and syntactic classifiers. The results show that the other classifiers generate more than twice as many term tuples (AEP candidates) compared to ILLOD in order to indicate the correct expansion for fewer abbreviations—at maximum 22. Detailed results can be found again in the supplemental material [13].

6   Integration into Clustering Workflow

On the lines of Wang et al. [34], the preceding results confirm that different types of synonyms require different adapted approaches to calculating similarity, in particular for AEP-detection. Before we describe how AEP-specific methods like ILLOD can be integrated into clustering of GTE tools, it is necessary to discuss how to ensure that the clusters created are meaningful and useful.

Arora et al. [2] create an ideal cluster solution from a given domain model against which the clusters obtained by different clustering algorithms have to be measured/compared/evaluated. We adopt this guiding principle in order to find a good strategy for the integration of ILLOD. We do not intend to evaluate different clustering algorithms, but rather to show how two already optimized clustering results—one for ordinary terms according to Arora et al. [2] and one for AEP groups—can be merged. To do so, some theoretical considerations on how ideal clusters can be constructed for this are required.

6.1 Ideal Clustering Solution

Arora et al. [2] create ideal clusters around a single concept c from the domain model, where the clusters also contain variants of terms that are conceptually equivalent to c and terms that are related to c according to the domain model.

Terms within individual AEP groups have a different relation to each other—indicating that two terms can be used as an expansion/definition for the same, as yet undefined, abbreviation. Thus, AEP groups differ in type from the ideal clusters of Arora et al. [2]. As AEP groups are designed to indicate probable ambiguities, they should not be separated in an ideal cluster solution.

As the ordinary terms within the individual AEP groups do not have to be conceptually related to each other according to the domain model, we must assume that they are distributed over the different clusters of the ideal clusters.

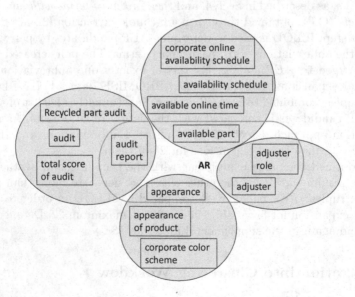

Fig. 1. Glossary term clusters of ordinary terms (grey) and overlay cluster for abbreviation *"AR"* and its possible expansions (blue) for a *"vehicle parts finder system"*. (Color figure online)

This leads to the conclusion that AEP groups in an ideal cluster solution must be considered as so-called overlay clusters, which implies that the AEP groups are included as additional clusters. Figure 1 shows an example for this, based on the requirements from a *"Vehicle Parts Finder System"* part of the PROMISE data-set [5] as project #5.

6.2 GTE Processing Steps

Considerations from the previous section lead us to propose the approach for the integration of ILLOD into a given GTE tool, as outlined in Fig. 2.

First, abbreviations are extracted from the given text, as described in Sect. 4 and then reduced to only consider yet undefined ones. Further, general glossary term candidates are extracted, e.g., through noun-chunking, and then cleaned from the abbreviations to a set of ordinary terms. ILLOD is then used to cluster abbreviations with their potential expansions into AEP groups, while a general synonym clustering approach, such as presented by Arora et al. [2], is used to cluster the ordinary terms.

As AEP groups are added into the final cluster solution in the last step, this will produce overlapping clusters. To evaluate the solutions generated by this approach, in addition to an ideal cluster solution, a metric is required to determine the score of agreement between an overlapping clustering solution and an overlapping ground truth—the ideal cluster solution. The *OMEGA-Index* Ω, a metric based on pair counts, introduced by Collins et al. [6], can achieve this.

Another argument for generating disjoint clusters of ordinary terms in the second-last step, besides the ones given by Arora et al. [2], is indicated by Ω. It shows the difficulty of making overlapping cluster solutions more similar to the ground truth clustering. For calculation, Ω uses the *contingency table C*. The entries $c_{i,j} \in C$ indicate the number of all pairs that appear in exactly i clusters in the solution and in exactly j clusters in the ground truth. A necessary condition to increase Ω between a generated cluster solution and a given ground truth is to modify the cluster solution so, that their agreement (sum of all diagonal values in C) is increased and their disagreement (sum of all values outside the diagonal) is decreased. Finally, an enlargement of the matrix would cause only a linear increase in the number of agreement fields, while the number of disagreement fields increases quadratically. Therefore, we propose the combination of disjoint clustering with separately calculated AEP group overlay clusters as introduced in Sect. 6.1.

7 Discussion

In the following, we discuss limitations and potential threats to validity [15] of our ILLOD approach to AEP detection, its evaluation, as well as considerations on its strengths and its integration to glossary term candidate clustering.

Repeatability. We provide our source code and data-sets, as well as additional evaluation data [13] for replication.

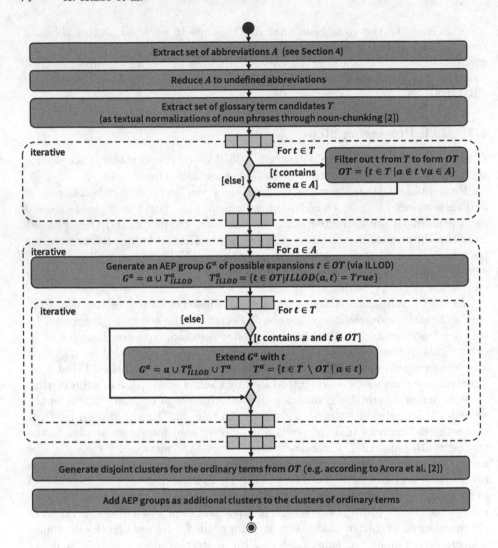

Fig. 2. Proposed workflow for the integration of ILLOD into a given GTE tool

Construct Validity. Regarding (B1.1) threats are neglectable, as we directly work on extracted terms obtained via well known and reliable NLP techniques, and parameters for the identification of abbreviations are retrieved from real world examples and can be adjusted to fit domain specific peculiarities. Towards the more general (B1), homonyms and hyponyms are not detected explicitly. Yet, the analyst might be enabled to spot some during manual inspection of the clusters, although in general this problem needs to be addressed in a separate solution. However, focus of this work is on abbreviations, as defined in (B1.1).

Internal Validity. To minimize the risk of threats, we tested the similarity measures and classifiers with the same cleaned list of defined abbreviations and under several portions α of abbreviations within the text. Semantic and syntactic similarity measures, are tested with different thresholds.

External Validity. Parameters and features for abbreviation detection might be context and language specific. E.g., two examples from the German armed forces to abbreviate a unit of organization and an employment title exceed the limits of our detection: First, ("SABCAbwGSchAufg", "Schule ABC-Abwehr und Gesetzliche Schutzaufgaben") is with 15 letters longer than our limit of 13. Second, ("Schirrmstr", "Schirrmeister") has with 0.1 a too low portion of capital letters—this is presumably typical for simply truncated words. It shows that parameters need to be adjusted or some specific rules have to be added for domains with notably different guidelines. The list we used [7] is open community built without guidelines and thus heterogeneous abbreviation styles not limited to acronyms. Yet, it is domain specific. Further, we only used English terms. Parameters and accuracy might vary for other languages, e.g. in German rules for noun-splitting differ. However, parameters can be easily adapted through optimization on other data-sets. Similar, features evaluated by ILLOD can be easily adapted to domain specific patterns. Yet, the tests on the PROMISE data-set with requirements from 15 projects from different domains, indicate some general applicability. We plan to verify our approach on further data-sets in future research.

Conclusion Validity. To mitigate threats, the modifications to the PROMISE data-set as well as the evaluation of detection results is conducted by an external independent person without exposure of details to the authors.

The considerations on cluster integration are based on related work [2] and initial experiments on optimization of different clustering algorithms with the OMEGA-Index. However, we plan to substantiate this in future experiments. Based on our findings, the proposed workflow has the following advantages:

(1) By using AEP groups, we avoid to decide which pair of terms belong together automatically, which is a challenging problem according to Jiang et al. [16].
(2) AEP groups have ergonomic as well as procedural advantages:
   (a) The analyst is motivated to build the list of abbreviations in parallel.
   (b) The analyst has direct insight into how an abbreviation could be expanded alternatively, as alternative expansions are likely to be encountered in the same cluster, and thus the analyst gets another opportunity to reduce ambiguities.
(3) Since the AEP groups are added to the generated cluster of ordinary terms in a post-processing step from a clustering point of view, the AEP groups ensure that unknown abbreviations and proposed expansions are placed in the same cluster, regardless of the clustering algorithm.
(4) Adding additional AEP groups lead to a final result with overlapping clusters, but mitigates the disadvantages of such, as these additional clusters are of different type than those of the ordinary terms.
(5) Using a feature-based approach to AEP detection, as ILLOD, provides high flexibility to adjust to domain specific rules, as new rules can easily be added.

We further conducted preliminary experiments with *hybrid* approaches to AEP detection, combining different types of classifiers. For example, to check the *initial letter equivalence* rule contained in ILLOD in a pre-processing step for all syntactic measures. This leads to increased accuracy for this type of classifier, as can be learned from the detailed evaluation data [13]. However, due to the nature of feature-based approaches of combining and potentially weighting different rules/features, it appears to be more plausible, to potentially integrate syntactic measures as additional rules here, rather than to outsource other features to excessive pre-processing.

8 Conclusions

Early glossary building and synonym detection is relevant to reduce ambiguity in requirements sets, e.g. through definition of preferred terms [14]. We demonstrate that different types of synonyms [14] need different treatments in detection. In particular, classical syntactic and semantic similarity measures perform poorly on abbreviations, as we show with our experiments in Sect. 5. With our ILLOD tool, we present a new feature-based approach to AEP detection, which outperforms those classic approaches. It is also more flexible, as rule sets can be easily adapted to context specific characteristics, e.g., guidelines or other languages. Initial experiments indicate that investigation of hybrid approaches might be promising, though. We further propose how to integrate groups of abbreviations and their potential expansions to clusters of ordinary glossary term candidates as additional separate type of clusters.

This enables analysts to build the abbreviation list in parallel to the glossary and start this process early already on preliminary requirements. Further, we assume our approach not only to be relevant for early harmonization of requirements document terminology, but also if glossary and abbreviation list have to be built over several documents spanning multiple project phases and/or involved organizations and domains. In addition, different clusters for different synonym types can support the building of synonym groups for glossaries or thesauri with cross references [14] and context specific grouping as well as domain models.

References

1. Arora, C., Sabetzadeh, M., Briand, L., Zimmer, F.: Automated checking of conformance to requirements templates using natural language processing. IEEE Trans. Softw. Eng. **41**(10), 944–968 (2015). https://doi.org/10.1109/TSE.2015.2428709
2. Arora, C., Sabetzadeh, M., Briand, L., Zimmer, F.: Automated extraction and clustering of requirements glossary terms. IEEE Trans. Softw. Eng. **43**(10), 918–945 (2017). https://doi.org/10.1109/TSE.2016.2635134
3. Bhatia, K., Mishra, S., Sharma, A.: Clustering glossary terms extracted from large-sized software requirements using FastText. In: 13th Innovations in Software Engineering Conference, Formerly Known as India Software Engineering Conference (ISEC 2020), pp. 1–11 (2020). https://doi.org/10.1145/3385032.3385039

4. Bojanowski, P., Grave, E., Joulin, A., Mikolov, T.: Enriching word vectors with subword information. Trans. Assoc. Comput. Linguist. **5**, 135–146 (2017). https://doi.org/10.1162/tacl_a_00051
5. Cleland-Huang, J., Settimi, R., Zou, X., Solc, P.: Automated classification of non-functional requirements. Requirements Eng. **12**(2), 103–120 (2007). https://doi.org/10.1007/s00766-007-0045-1. http://ctp.di.fct.unl.pt/RE2017//downloads/datasets/nfr.arff
6. Collins, L.M., Dent, C.W.: Omega: a general formulation of the rand index of cluster recovery suitable for non-disjoint solutions. Multivar. Behav. Res. **23**(2), 231–242 (1988). https://doi.org/10.1207/s15327906mbr2302_6
7. Computer Hope: computer acronyms and abbreviations. https://www.computerhope.com/jargon/acronyms.htm. Accessed 16 Oct 2021
8. Dwarakanath, A., Ramnani, R.R., Sengupta, S.: Automatic extraction of glossary terms from natural language requirements. In: 21st IEEE International Requirements Engineering Conference (RE 2013), pp. 314–319. IEEE (2013). https://doi.org/10.1109/RE.2013.6636736
9. Ferrari, A., Spagnolo, G.O., Gnesi, S.: PURE: a dataset of public requirements documents. In: 25th IEEE International Requirements Engineering Conference (RE 2017), pp. 502–505 (2017). https://doi.org/10.1109/RE.2017.29
10. Gali, N., Mariescu-Istodor, R., Hostettler, D., Fränti, P.: Framework for syntactic string similarity measures. Expert Syst. Appl. **129**, 169–185 (2019). https://doi.org/10.1016/j.eswa.2019.03.048
11. Gemkow, T., Conzelmann, M., Hartig, K., Vogelsang, A.: Automatic glossary term extraction from large-scale requirements specifications. In: 26th IEEE International Requirements Engineering Conference (RE 2018), pp. 412–417. IEEE (2018). https://doi.org/10.1109/RE.2018.00052
12. Glinz, M.: A glossary of requirements engineering terminology. Technical report, International Requirements Engineering Board IREB e.V., May 2014
13. Hasso, H., Großer, K., Aymaz, I., Geppert, H., Jürjens, J.: AEPForGTE/ILLOD: Supplemental Material v(1.5). https://doi.org/10.5281/zenodo.5914038
14. ISO: 25964-1: information and documentation—thesauri and interoperability with other vocabularies—part 1: thesauri for information retrieval. ISO (2011)
15. Jedlitschka, A., Ciolkowski, M., Pfahl, D.: Reporting experiments in software engineering. In: Shull, F., Singer, J., Sjøberg, D.I.K. (eds.) Guide to Advanced Empirical Software Engineering, pp. 201–228. Springer, London (2008). https://doi.org/10.1007/978-1-84800-044-5_8
16. Jiang, Y., Liu, H., Jin, J., Zhang, L.: Automated expansion of abbreviations based on semantic relation and transfer expansion. IEEE Trans. Softw. Eng. (2020). https://doi.org/10.1109/TSE.2020.2995736
17. Justeson, J.S., Katz, S.M.: Technical terminology: some linguistic properties and an algorithm for identification in text. Nat. Lang. Eng. **1**(1), 9–27 (1995). https://doi.org/10.1017/S1351324900000048
18. Kiyavitskaya, N., Zeni, N., Mich, L., Berry, D.M.: Requirements for tools for ambiguity identification and measurement in natural language requirements specifications. Requirements Eng. **13**(3), 207–239 (2008). https://doi.org/10.1007/s00766-008-0063-7
19. van Lamsweerde, A.: Requirements Engineering. Wiley, Hoboken (2009)
20. Larkey, L.S., Ogilvie, P., Price, M.A., Tamilio, B.: Acrophile: an automated acronym extractor and server. In: 5th ACM Conference on Digital Libraries, pp. 205–214 (2000). https://doi.org/10.1145/336597.336664

21. Merriam-Webster: what is an abbreviation? https://www.merriam-webster.com/dictionary/abbreviation. Accessed 17 Oct 2021
22. Mikolov, T., Chen, K., Corrado, G., Dean, J.: Efficient estimation of word representations in vector space. arXiv preprint arXiv:1301.3781 (2013)
23. Miller, G.A.: WordNet: a lexical database for English. Commun. ACM **38**(11), 39–41 (1995). https://doi.org/10.1145/219717.219748
24. Okazaki, N., Ananiadou, S.: A term recognition approach to acronym recognition. In: COLING/ACL 2006 Main Conference Poster Sessions, pp. 643–650. ACM (2006)
25. Park, Y., Byrd, R.J.: Hybrid text mining for finding abbreviations and their definitions. In: Conference on Empirical Methods in Natural Language Processing (2001)
26. Park, Y., Byrd, R.J., Boguraev, B.K.: Automatic glossary extraction: beyond terminology identification. In: 19th International Conference on Computational Linguistics (COLING 2002), vol. 1, pp. 1–7 (2002). https://doi.org/10.3115/1072228.1072370
27. Pohl, K.: Requirements Engineering. Springer, Heidelberg (2010)
28. Pohl, K.: The three dimensions of requirements engineering. In: Rolland, C., Bodart, F., Cauvet, C. (eds.) CAiSE 1993. LNCS, vol. 685, pp. 63–80. Springer, Heidelberg (2013). https://doi.org/10.1007/978-3-642-36926-1_5
29. Pustejovsky, J., Castano, J., Cochran, B., Kotecki, M., Morrell, M.: Automatic extraction of acronym-meaning pairs from MEDLINE databases. In: MEDINFO 2001, pp. 371–375. IOS Press (2001). https://doi.org/10.3233/978-1-60750-928-8-371
30. Sayyad Shirabad, J., Menzies, T.: PROMISE software engineering repository. School of Information Technology and Engineering, University of Ottawa, Canada (2005). http://promise.site.uottawa.ca/SERepository/
31. Schwartz, A.S., Hearst, M.A.: A simple algorithm for identifying abbreviation definitions in biomedical text. In: Biocomputing 2003, pp. 451–462. World Scientific (2002). https://doi.org/10.1142/9789812776303_0042
32. Sohn, S., Comeau, D.C., Kim, W., Wilbur, W.J.: Abbreviation definition identification based on automatic precision estimates. BMC Bioinform. **9**(1), 402–412 (2008). https://doi.org/10.1186/1471-2105-9-402
33. Song, M., Chang, P.: Automatic extraction of abbreviation for emergency management websites. In: 5th International Conference on Information Systems for Crisis Response and Management (ISCRAM), pp. 93–100 (2008)
34. Wang, Y., Manotas Gutièrrez, I.L., Winbladh, K., Fang, H.: Automatic detection of ambiguous terminology for software requirements. In: Métais, E., Meziane, F., Saraee, M., Sugumaran, V., Vadera, S. (eds.) NLDB 2013. LNCS, vol. 7934, pp. 25–37. Springer, Heidelberg (2013). https://doi.org/10.1007/978-3-642-38824-8_3
35. Yeganova, L., Comeau, D.C., Wilbur, W.J.: Identifying abbreviation definitions machine learning with naturally labeled data. In: 9th International Conference on Machine Learning and Applications, pp. 499–505. IEEE (2010). https://doi.org/10.1109/ICMLA.2010.166
36. Zhou, W., Torvik, V.I., Smalheiser, N.R.: ADAM: another database of abbreviations in MEDLINE. Bioinformatics **22**(22), 2813–2818 (2006). https://doi.org/10.1093/bioinformatics/btl480
37. Zou, X., Settimi, R., Cleland-Huang, J.: Improving automated requirements trace retrieval: a study of term-based enhancement methods. Empir. Softw. Eng. **15**(2), 119–146 (2009). https://doi.org/10.1007/s10664-009-9114-z. http://ctp.di.fct.unl.pt/RE2017//downloads/datasets/nfr.arff

Towards Explainable Formal Methods: From LTL to Natural Language with Neural Machine Translation

Himaja Cherukuri[1], Alessio Ferrari[2](✉) [iD], and Paola Spoletini[1] [iD]

[1] Kennesaw State University, Atlanta, GA, USA
pspoleti@kennesaw.edu
[2] CNR-ISTI, Pisa, Italy
alessio.ferrari@isti.cnr.it

Abstract. **[Context and motivation]** Requirements formalisation facilitates reasoning about inconsistencies, detection of ambiguities, and identification critical issues in system models. Temporal logic formulae are the natural choice when it comes to formalise requirements associated to desired system behaviours. **[Question/problem]** Understanding and mastering temporal logic requires a formal background. Means are therefore needed to make temporal logic formulae interpretable by engineers, domain experts and other stakeholders involved in the development process. **[Principal ideas/results]** In this paper, we propose to use a neural machine translation tool, named OPENNMT, to translate Linear Temporal Logic (LTL) formulae into corresponding natural language descriptions. Our results show that the translation system achieves an average BLEU (BiLingual Evaluation Understudy) score of 93.53%, which corresponds to high-quality translations. **[Contribution]** Our neural model can be applied to assess if requirements have been correctly formalised. This can be useful to requirements analysts, who may have limited confidence with LTL, and to other stakeholders involved in the requirements verification process. Overall, our research preview contributes to bridging the gap between formal methods and requirements engineering, and opens to further research in explainable formal methods.

Keywords: Requirements engineering · Formal methods · Machine translation · Neural networks · Temporal logic · LTL · Natural language processing · NLP

1 Introduction

Temporal logic enables the expression of time-related system requirements and has widely been used in requirements and software engineering research [5,21]. Linear temporal logic (LTL) is a well-known type of temporal logic that treats time as a linear sequence of states. In LTL, each state has only one possible future, and an LTL formula describes the behavior of a single computation of a program. With LTL, system engineers can formalize temporal properties that express the absence, universality, existence, precedence, and the response of predicates about observable system variables.

© Springer Nature Switzerland AG 2022
V. Gervasi and A. Vogelsang (Eds.): REFSQ 2022, LNCS 13216, pp. 79–86, 2022.
https://doi.org/10.1007/978-3-030-98464-9_7

LTL has been used in requirements engineering (RE) for several tasks, including the formalization of goals in goal-oriented requirements engineering (GORE) [15], the expression of desired properties for run-time verification [3], and model checking [6]. The correct specification and interpretation of LTL formulae requires a strong mathematical background and can hardly be done by domain experts [5,7]. Therefore, researchers have dedicated efforts to translate natural language (NL) requirements into temporal logic formulae [5,10,11,18] to support domain experts in the formalization of requirements. However, these approaches still require domain experts to have an understanding of the produced formulae, so to make sure that the translation is correctly preserving the meaning of the original requirement. To support them in this task, we propose to provide a way to translate LTL formulae into their NL explanation. To address this goal, we plan to exploit the potential of neural machine translation platforms, and in particular the open-source framework OpenNMT (https://opennmt.net). Indeed, though the goal of translating LTL into corresponding explanations can in principle be addressed by means of a rule-based or heuristic approach, a neural machine translation strategy is more flexible, as it can facilitate language simplification and transformations—i.e., summaries and paraphrases [2,13,20], without requiring the maintenance of a complex rule-based system. In addition, it can better support the readability of the expressions [2], while ensuring the correctness of the translation. As LTL formulae can often be better understood when associated with visual representations [1], we also plan to augment the translation with a graphical representation that could help clarifying possible ambiguities introduced by the NL translation. At the current stage, we have performed a feasibility study, in which we trained an LTSTM encoder-decoder architecture, implemented in the OpenNMT framework, with a set of manually defined examples. In the next steps, we will consolidate the approach, we will develop the visual part of our idea, and we will validate the resulting prototype with potential users.

2   Towards Explainable LTL Requirements

The overall goal of our research is to facilitate the correct understanding of requirements expressed in LTL by subjects who have a limited expertise in formal logic. To this end, we plan to implement a system that translates LTL formulae into corresponding NL explanations, augmented by visual diagrams with annotations. We will also empirically evaluate the approach, first by ensuring that the automatic translation is actually correct, and then by evaluating to what extent the translation facilitates the understanding of LTL requirements. More specifically, our research questions (RQs) are the following:

- **RQ1:** *To what extent can neural machine translation be used to translate LTL formulae into NL explanations?*
- **RQ2:** *How can NL explanations of LTL formulae be augmented with visual representations?*
- **RQ3:** *Does the automatic explanation of LTL formulae help users in understanding them?*

To answer RQ1, we first perform a feasibility study, reported in this paper (cf. Sect. 2.1), and then we consolidate the approach by (a) ensuring that the approach does not introduce errors in the translation, and (b) ensuring that the readability of the formulae is acceptable, according to standard metrics and through human assessment. To answer RQ2, we plan to devise solutions by combining visual representation of formulae and annotation of traces. Finally, RQ3 will be addressed through an empirical evaluation with students. RQ3 will consider NL explanations alone and also augmented with visual representations.

2.1   RQ1: From LTL to NL with Neural Machine Translation

Dataset Definition.   To assess the feasibility of using neural machine translation for providing explanation of LTL formulae, the 3rd author defined 54 unique formulae including Boolean operators $(!, |, \&, =>)$ and temporal operators (X—next, G—always, F—eventually, U—until), with associated NL translations. The 2nd author independently checked the correctness of the translation. For simplicity, the dataset considers only formulae with no nested temporal operators and the expressions are edited according to the typical LTL patterns as defined by Dwyer et al. [8], so as to provide representative LTL requirements that could occur in real-world projects. This initial dataset is composed of domain-agnostic requirements, in which variables were expressed as alphabetic letters, e.g. $G(a => b)$, translated as *In every moment of the system execution, if a holds, b should hold (a does not need to hold for the formula to be true)*. In providing the translations, the 3rd author made an effort to be consistent across formulae, using always the same terminology, and the same structure. However, no translation rule was established beforehand. The repetitiveness of terminology and structure aims to facilitate learning of the neural model, while the absence of specific rules decided beforehand enables flexibility. As the set of examples would be too limited for successfully training a neural network, the dataset was clerically augmented, by repeating the same formulae—and associated translations—with combinations of 26 different alphabetic letters. The resulting dataset is composed of 12,192 LTL formulae and associated translations. At this exploratory stage, our goal is not to translate unseen syntactic pattern, but to check whether the unwritten rules adopted for translation can be successfully learned. Therefore, we feed the network with similar examples that differ solely for the variable names. The idea is to enable the network to distinguish between operators and variables, "learn" the LTL syntax for these simple cases, and translate accordingly.

Training and Evaluation.   To experiment with our dataset, we selected the OpenNMT framework for machine translation [14]. This is a widely used platform, supporting different translation tasks, including summarization, image to text, speech-to-text, sequence-to-sequence (our case), and offering two implementations, OpenNMT-py, based on PyTorch, and OpenNMT-tf, based on TensorFlow. In our case, we selected OpenNMT-py, as it is claimed by the developers to be more user-friendly, and thus we consider it more appropriate for the exploratory nature of our study. The architecture adopted for the task is a 2-layer Long short-term memory (LSTM) neural network with 500 hidden units on both the encoder and decoder. This is a recurrent neural network (RNN) often used for sequence-to-sequence learning. We use the default settings of OpenNMT at this stage, given the exploratory nature of the study.

To avoid oversimplifying the problem, we built the training set by first eliminating the formulae with only one variable from the dataset and then randomly selecting 19% (of the size of the original dataset) formulae for a total of 2,308. The remaining formulae were randomly split into training (8,048 items, 66% of the total) and validation (1,836, 15%). The validation set is used to evaluate the convergence of the training. The model that achieves the lowest perplexity value on this dataset is considered the best and selected for evaluation in the test set. The whole training activity lasted 7.8 h on a common laptop.

We evaluate the results on the test set by means of different metrics to check the quality of the translation. Evaluation is carried out by means of the Tilde MT online tool (https://www.letsmt.eu/Bleu.aspx). The readability of the resulting formulae is assessed with the BLEU score (BiLingual Evaluation Understudy) [19]. The BLEU score takes into account both the difference in lengths of the sentences it compares (automatic translation and expected one), and their compositions. It is computed as the product of the *brevity penalty* and the *N_Gram overlap*. Roughly speaking, the former assigns a penalization to translations that are too short compared to the closest reference length with an exponential decay, while the latter counts how many single worlds, pairs, triplets, and quadruples of words match their counterpart in the expected translations.

The visual representation provided by Tilde MT is used to identify translations with BLEU score lower than 100%—suggesting incorrect translations—and manually assess them. Indeed, here we want to ensure that the translation is actually 100% correct, and while a high BLEU score between expected and translated sentence could indicate high similarity, the actual difference (e.g., in terms of variable names, or in case a negation is missing) could be crucial for the correctness of the translation.

The BLEU score is 93.53%, indicating high-quality translations, thus suggesting that the translation of LTL formulae with neural machine translation is feasible. It is worth noting that issues are known with the usage of automatic scores in machine translation applied to software engineering problems [12], and further studies with human subjects need to be performed to actually assess the quality of the translation.

Looking at single cases with lower BLEU score, we see that while the syntax is somehow correct, there are some difficulties with the U operator. For example, the formula $(c \mathbin{\&} q) U o$ is translated as *There has to be a moment (the current one or in the future) in which $\underline{u}$ holds, and, if it is not the current one, from the current moment to that moment both c and q have to hold*, BLEU = 94%. The translator introduces the spurious u variable, possibly confused by the letter U of the operator. Similar situations however occur also with other letters. Low BLEU scores are obtained also for complex expressions such as $(c \, U \, q) \mathbin{\&} (o \, U \, q)$, in which only the initial part of the formula is translated, while the second part is entirely missing: *There has to be a moment (the current one or in the future) in which q holds, and, if it is not the current one, from the current moment to that moment c has to hold*, BLEU = 35.9%. The first issue could be addressed by using specific keywords or characters for the operators, or experimenting with longer translation units (i.e., words). The second problem could be solved by segmenting the formula beforehand with rule-based approaches before feeding it to the translator.

Consolidation. The preliminary evaluation carried out suggests that the project idea is feasible with currently available technologies. Further work is required, however, to provide empirically sound evidence to answer RQ1. In particular, besides replicating the current experiments with different neural network architectures, the next steps of our research will address the issue of correctness, by studying the possible problems leading to inaccuracy, and providing solutions towards the goal of 100% correctness [4]. Furthermore, we will extend the evaluation to nested operators, so that full coverage of LTL formulae is possible.

Concerning readability of the translations, we plan to work in three directions. The first one consists in assessing the readability of the translations in the context of the experiments with human subjects carried out in relation to RQ3 (cf. Sect. 2.2). The second direction aims to enhance the approach with automatic text simplification techniques [2], which can be particularly useful in case of lengthy and hard-to-process translations. Finally, to be able to consider more complex variables, we will analyze the possibility of having a pre-processing system to simplify the formulae before translating them, and a post-processing to integrate the original variables into the translation.

2.2 RQ2, RQ3: Visual Representations and Empirical Evaluation

The research activities related to RQ2 and RQ3 will be carried out in parallel with the consolidation of the results of RQ1.

In relation to **RQ2**, we will first investigate possible solutions to augment LTL explanations with visual information. This investigation will consider both the graphical representation of the formulae, in line with e.g., Ahmed *et al.* [1], the representation of the associated traces as done by the LTL Visualiser tool (https://quickstrom.github. io/ltl-visualizer/), and the annotation of traces with NL text generated from the formulae. To select the appropriate means for graphical representation of formulae, we will follow a design science approach [22]. Stemming from the literature, we will design an innovative prototypical solution, and we will perform iterations to refine and validate it. Differently from the deep learning-based translation of LTL formulae, the graphical representation is expected to leverage a rule-based algorithm. Therefore, its correctness is to be ensured by construction—provided that systematic tests against the requirements are carried out.

To answer **RQ3**, we will conduct a controlled experiment to measure if the generated explanations improve the understandability of LTL formulae. We will consider NL explanations alone, and also in conjunction with the graphical representations developed according to RQ2. The experiment will be run with senior undergraduate students and graduate students attending an RE course covering temporal logic. Participants of control group and experimental one will be given a set of LTL formulae. For each formula, they will be also given a set of traces, and their task will be to select all the traces that satisfy the given formula—this exercise is regarded as a way to assess their correct understanding of the formula. In addition to the formulae, the experimental group will also be given as input the automatically generated textual explanation, also aided by the graphical representation, for each of the formulae. Checking the performance of the two groups will allow us to measure the quality of the support provided by our solution in this activity. The experiment will be designed to evaluate the different contributions given by the NL explanations, and by the graphical representations. After the activity, participants will be asked to fill out a questionnaire to gather their perceptions about the task and, for the experimental group, the support obtained by the explanation. To support evaluation of readability, we plan to also repeat the experiment with eye-tracking devices. As an additional assessment, we will design an experiment specifically targeted to understand if the explanations can be useful to check the correctness of the formalization of the requirements. In this case, students in the control group will receive a set of requirements, each one associated with a supposedly matching LTL formula, and will need to check whether the formula is correct. The experimental group will have to do the same, but will also receive the automatically generated NL translation of the LTL formulae, augmented with visual information.

3   Conclusion and Future Works

This paper presents a research preview on providing means to make requirements expressed through LTL understandable to subjects with limited expertise in formal logic. The proposed approach exploits state-of-the-art natural language processing (NLP) techniques for machine translation to produce NL explanations of LTL formulae. Our usage of machine translation is innovative with respect to previous literature in NLP applied to RE [23], which focused more on translating NL into logic formulae or models, rather than providing textual explanations. As part of our approach, we also plan to combine NL explanations with visual representations to improve understandability.

The proposed approach has the potential to be a useful tool to support students and practitioners in learning LTL, but can also have applications in practice. For example, it can facilitate mutual understanding in those industry-academia collaborations in which practitioners provide the informal system specification, and formal methods experts provide formal designs, as common, e.g. in the railway domain [9]. Furthermore, the approach can be used to support verification via model checking of incomplete systems, which is needed when a software is developed incrementally or through decomposition. Existing solutions to this problem (e.g., Menghi *et al.* [17]) rely on the generation of LTL constraints to be satisfied by novel components to be developed. In these contexts, NL explanations can be particularly useful to requirements analysts and developers in the design of the novel components.

Future works will address the RQs of this research preview, with the development of appropriate visual representations, and with extensive empirical evaluations. At this stage, to have a preliminary assessment of the feasibility of our idea, we focused only on simple structures and we built the dataset using single letter variables, and providing very "mechanical" translations. In the next steps of our work, we will enrich our dataset to include more flexibility, and improve the naturalness of the translations. To extend the applicability of our idea, we will also explore how to translate LTL statements into structured NL requirements, for example in EARS [16] or FRETISH [11]. Using consistent sentence structures improves readability and understandability. This approach would help towards your goal of making LTL formulae easier to understand.

References

1. Ahmed, Z., et al.: Bringing LTL model checking to biologists. In: Bouajjani, A., Monniaux, D. (eds.) VMCAI 2017. LNCS, vol. 10145, pp. 1–13. Springer, Cham (2017). https://doi.org/10.1007/978-3-319-52234-0_1
2. Al-Thanyyan, S.S., Azmi, A.M.: Automated text simplification: a survey. ACM Comput. Surv. (CSUR) **54**(2), 1–36 (2021)
3. Bauer, A., Leucker, M., Schallhart, C.: Runtime verification for LTL and TLTL. ACM Trans. Softw. Eng. Methodol. (TOSEM) **20**(4), 1–64 (2011)
4. Berry, D.M.: Empirical evaluation of tools for hairy requirements engineering tasks. Empirical Softw. Eng. **26**(6) (2021). Article number: 111. https://doi.org/10.1007/s10664-021-09986-0
5. Brunello, A., Montanari, A., Reynolds, M.: Synthesis of LTL formulas from natural language texts: state of the art and research directions. In: 26th International Symposium on Temporal Representation and Reasoning (TIME 2019) (2019)
6. Clarke, E., Grumberg, O., Kroening, D., Peled, D., Veith, H.: Model Checking. Cyber Physical Systems Series. MIT Press, Cambridge (2018)
7. Czepa, C., Zdun, U.: On the understandability of temporal properties formalized in linear temporal logic, property specification patterns and event processing language. IEEE Trans. Softw. Eng. **46**(1), 100–112 (2018)
8. Dwyer, M.B., Avrunin, G.S., Corbett, J.C.: Patterns in property specifications for finite-state verification. In: ICSE 1999, pp. 411–420 (1999)
9. Ferrari, A., ter Beek, M.H.: Formal methods in railways: a systematic mapping study. ACM Comput. Surv. (2022). https://doi.org/10.1145/3520480
10. Ghosh, S., Elenius, D., Li, W., Lincoln, P., Shankar, N., Steiner, W.: ARSENAL: automatic requirements specification extraction from natural language. In: Rayadurgam, S., Tkachuk, O. (eds.) NFM 2016. LNCS, vol. 9690, pp. 41–46. Springer, Cham (2016). https://doi.org/10.1007/978-3-319-40648-0_4
11. Giannakopoulou, D., Pressburger, T., Mavridou, A., Schumann, J.: Automated formalization of structured natural language requirements. IST **137**, 106590 (2021)
12. Gros, D., Sezhiyan, H., Devanbu, P., Yu, Z.: Code to comment "translation": data, metrics, baselining & evaluation. In: ASE 2020, pp. 746–757. IEEE (2020)
13. Gupta, A., Agarwal, A., Singh, P., Rai, P.: A deep generative framework for paraphrase generation. In: Proceedings of the AAAI Conference on Artificial Intelligence, vol. 32 (2018)
14. Klein, G., Kim, Y., Deng, Y., Senellart, J., Rush, A.: OpenNMT: open-source toolkit for neural machine translation. In: ACL 2017, pp. 67–72 (2017)
15. Letier, E., Kramer, J., Magee, J., Uchitel, S.: Deriving event-based transition systems from goal-oriented requirements models. Autom. Softw. Eng. **15**(2), 175–206 (2008). https://doi.org/10.1007/s10515-008-0027-7
16. Mavin, A., Wilkinson, P., Harwood, A., Novak, M.: Easy approach to requirements syntax (EARS). In: 2009 17th IEEE International Requirements Engineering Conference, pp. 317–322. IEEE (2009)
17. Menghi, C., Spoletini, P., Chechik, M., Ghezzi, C.: Supporting verification-driven incremental distributed design of components. In: Russo, A., Schürr, A. (eds.) FASE 2018. LNCS, vol. 10802, pp. 169–188. Springer, Cham (2018). https://doi.org/10.1007/978-3-319-89363-1_10
18. Nikora, A.P., Balcom, G.: Automated identification of LTL patterns in natural language requirements. In: ISSRE 2009, pp. 185–194. IEEE (2009)
19. Papineni, K., Roukos, S., Ward, T., Zhu, W.J.: BLEU: a method for automatic evaluation of machine translation. In: ACL 2002, pp. 311–318 (2002)

20. Siddharthan, A.: A survey of research on text simplification. ITL-Int. J. Appl. Linguist. **165**(2), 259–298 (2014)
21. Van Lamsweerde, A., Letier, E.: Handling obstacles in goal-oriented requirements engineering. IEEE Trans. Softw. Eng. **26**(10), 978–1005 (2000)
22. Wieringa, R.J.: Design Science Methodology for Information Systems and Software Engineering. Springer, Heidelberg (2014). https://doi.org/10.1007/978-3-662-43839-8
23. Zhao, L., et al.: Natural language processing for requirements engineering: a systematic mapping study. ACM Comput. Surv. (CSUR) **54**(3), 1–41 (2021)

Req2Spec: Transforming Software Requirements into Formal Specifications Using Natural Language Processing

Anmol Nayak[1]([✉]), Hari Prasad Timmapathini[1], Vidhya Murali[1],
Karthikeyan Ponnalagu[1], Vijendran Gopalan Venkoparao[1],
and Amalinda Post[2]

[1] ARiSE Labs at Bosch, Bengaluru, India
{Anmol.Nayak,Hariprasad.Timmapathini,Vidhya.Murali,
Karthikeyan.Ponnalagu,GopalanVijendran.Venkoparao}@in.bosch.com
[2] Robert Bosch GmbH, Stuttgart, Germany
Amalinda.Post@de.bosch.com

Abstract. [**Context and motivation**] Requirement analysis and Test specification generation are critical activities in the Software Development Life Cycle (SDLC), which if not done correctly can lead to defects in the software system. Manually performing these tasks on Natural Language Requirements (NLR) is time consuming and error prone. [**Question/problem**] The problem is to facilitate the automation of these activities by transforming the NLR into Formal Specifications. [**Principal ideas/results**] In this paper we present Req2Spec, a Natural Language Processing (NLP) based pipeline that performs syntactic and semantic analysis on NLR to generate formal specifications that can be readily consumed by HANFOR, an industry scale Requirements analysis and Test specification generation tool. We considered 222 automotive domain software requirements at BOSCH, 71% of which were correctly formalized. [**Contribution**] Req2Spec will be an aid to stakeholders of the SDLC as it seamlessly integrates with HANFOR enabling automation.

Keywords: Requirements formalization · Natural Language Processing · Requirements analysis · Test specification generation · Language model

1 Introduction

Software requirements analysis is one of the initial phases in the SDLC where requirements are analyzed on several aspects before being passed on to the downstream stakeholders for design, implementation and testing of the system. As there are many stakeholders involved in a software project delivery starting from the requirements engineer to the software tester, errors in the handling of requirements can percolate unnoticed. Getting early insights on the requirements is vital and recommended as it can reveal issues like inconsistencies, ambiguities, incompleteness [1]. There have been a few works that perform analysis of NLR [2–5],

V. Gervasi and A. Vogelsang (Eds.): REFSQ 2022, LNCS 13216, pp. 87–95, 2022.
https://doi.org/10.1007/978-3-030-98464-9_8

however they lack support for integration with HANFOR [6] and have not provided an end-to-end pipeline utilizing recent advances in NLP techniques for it to be leveraged across industry scale software projects. Industry scale NLR analysis tools such as IBM RQA [7] and QRA QVscribe [8] predominantly perform syntactic analysis (e.g. identifying vague terms, passive voice etc.) and minimal semantic analysis (e.g. they do not check for properties such as vacuity, consistency etc.). Test specification generation is another important phase in the later stages of the SDLC where significant amount of time and effort is spent. Some of the recent works have proposed automatic generation of test specification from NLR [9–12] using NLP techniques from which we have leveraged some of the components for syntactic and semantic information extraction.

Requirements formalization aims to transform NLR into pre-defined boilerplates having a restricted grammar, enabling large scale automated processing of requirements for downstream tasks such as requirements analysis and test specification generation. There have been previous attempts to formalizing NLR [13–15], however they expect the NLR to follow a restricted template/structure. Further, automated analysis of formal requirements for properties such as consistency and vacuity have been proposed [16–19], however they need the requirements to be already formalized or in the form of mathematical descriptions. While there exist several methods using formalized requirements, the widespread adoption in industry is still lacking as the hurdle to manually formalize requirements seems to be too high. With our Req2Spec method we want to lower this hurdle and we believe that it will enable utilization of formalized requirements even by requirements engineers without a background in formal methods.

We have integrated Req2Spec with HANFOR as it is an industry scale tool based on the specification pattern system by Konrad et al. [20]. It can also automatically translate the formal specifications into logics for downstream processing. HANFOR currently relies on manually formalized requirements prior to performing requirements analysis and test specification generation. Our work attempts to automate this step by using NLP techniques.

2   Background

HANFOR tool [21] consumes formalized NLR defined by an ID, a scope and a pattern. It supports 5 scopes, 4 regular patterns, 7 order patterns and 12 realtime patterns. A scope describes the boundary of the requirement. For e.g. a requirement with a *Globally* scope will hold true throughout the system, while a requirement with a *After EXPR* scope will hold true only after the expression (*EXPR*) is satisfied. A pattern describes the category of the requirement based on the pre-conditions, post-conditions, sequence of pre-conditions and post-conditions, and time duration elements. For example, a requirement with a time duration element only in the post-condition could have the pattern *If EXPR holds, then EXPR holds for at least DURATION*. The scopes and patterns are parameterized by expressions over system observables and durations. Our proposed pipeline is shown in Fig. 1. It is demonstrated with 2 scopes (*Globally* and *After EXPR*),

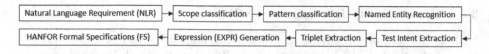

Fig. 1. Req2Spec pipeline.

1 regular pattern (*It is always the case that if EXPR holds, then EXPR holds as well*) and 1 realtime pattern (*If EXPR holds, then EXPR holds after at most DURATION*).

3   Req2Spec Pipeline

3.1   Dataset

NLR dataset consisted of 222 automotive domain requirements corresponding to the aforementioned chosen scopes and patterns as they cover the most common types of requirements found at BOSCH. For training and validation of the various NLP models, automotive software description documents dealing with functionalities such as cruise control, exhaust system, braking etc., along with the ground truths of the NLR dataset were annotated by experts.

3.2   Scope and Pattern Classification

Each NLR has to be associated with a scope and pattern to comply with HANFOR. We trained classification models for scope and pattern identification respectively using the SciBERT-Base-Scivocab-Uncased encoder [22] (a state-of-the-art model used in scientific domains) with a sequence classification head. The encoder and head were kept unfrozen and trained with the Adam [23] optimizer (lr $= 1e-5$, $\beta_1 = 0.9$, $\beta_2 = 0.999$, $\epsilon = 1e-7$). The following requirements are illustrative examples adhering to the chosen 2 scopes and 2 patterns:

1. Scope: *Globally*, Pattern: *It is always the case that if EXPR holds, then EXPR holds as well*:- If ignition is on, then fuel indicator is active.
2. Scope: *Globally*, Pattern: *If EXPR holds, then EXPR holds after at most DURATION*:- If ignition is on, then the wiper movement mode is enabled within 0.2 s.
3. Scope: *After EXPR*, Pattern: *It is always the case that if EXPR holds, then EXPR holds as well*:- Only after the vehicle speed is larger than 60 kmph, If the cruise control button is pressed, then the cruise control mode is activated.
4. Scope: *After EXPR*, Pattern: *If EXPR holds, then EXPR holds after at most DURATION*:- Only after the vehicle is in reverse gear, If the accelerator is pressed, then the rear view camera is activated within 2 s.

3.3   Named Entity Recognition (NER)

NER is the task of identifying and classifying named entities of a domain. We trained the NER model by using the SciBERT-Base-Scivocab-Uncased encoder along with a token classification head in the following setting (as described by a recent work which addresses many of the challenges of NER in the automotive domain [24]): Masked Language Modelling was performed on the pretrained SciBERT encoder with automotive domain text using the Adam optimizer ($lr = 5e-5$, $\beta_1 = 0.9$, $\beta_2 = 0.999$, $\epsilon = 1e-8$). This encoder and the head were then kept unfrozen for NER training with the Adam optimizer ($lr = 1e-5$, $\beta_1 = 0.9$, $\beta_2 = 0.999$, $\epsilon = 1e-7$). The annotation for NER was consisting of 9 automotive specific classes: Other (words outside named entities e.g. the, in), Signal (variables holding quantities e.g. torque), Value (quantities assigned to signals e.g. true, false), Action (task performed e.g. activation, maneuvering), Function (domain specific feature e.g. cruise control), Calibration (user defined setting e.g. number of gears), Component (physical part e.g. ignition button), State (system state e.g. cruising state of cruise control) and Math (mathematical or logical operation e.g. addition).

3.4   Test Intent Extraction

Software requirements describe the expected functionality in terms of test intent components, namely Pre-conditions and Post-conditions. Pre-conditions are the conditions which are expected to be satisfied before the Post-conditions can be achieved. For example in the requirement: *If ignition is on, then fuel indicator is active*, the Pre-condition is *ignition is on* and the Post-condition is *fuel indicator is active*. The test intent components are the primary source of information used to fill the *EXPR* slots of the scope and pattern. We utilized the Constituency Parse Tree (CPT) based syntactic test intent extraction algorithm [11] as it is able to separate dependent clauses (Pre-conditions) and independent clauses (Post-conditions) using grammar sub-tree structures.

3.5   Triplet Extraction

The test intent components have to be converted into expressions before being filled into the *EXPR* slots of the scope and patterns. For this we first convert each test intent component into a Subject-Verb-Object (SVO) triplet. Since traditional triplet extraction algorithms such as OpenIE [25] and ClausIE [26] have been designed from open source text (similar to Wikipedia articles), the quality of the extracted triples is hampered when applied to software engineering domain corpus which contains lexica and sentence structure that is niche. Hence, we have designed the following CPT based triplet extraction algorithm in our pipeline:

1. CPT is constructed using the Stanford CoreNLP [27] library for the condition and recursively traversed.

2. Subject is the sub-string until a Verb Phrase (VP) is encountered. Verb is the sub-string from the beginning of the VP until a Noun Phrase (NP) or Adjective (JJ) is encountered. Object is the sub-string from NP/JJ to the end of the condition. If a Infinitival to (TO)/VP is encountered in the Object, then the words occurring until (including) the TO/VP are concatenated to the Verb string of the triplet and the remaining sub-string is the Object.
3. This step is triggered if Step 2 resulted in a triplet with no Verb and Object strings: Subject is the sub-string until a TO/Preposition (IN) is encountered. Verb is the sub-string corresponding to TO/IN. Object is the sub-string after the TO/IN sub-string. If a TO is encountered in the Object, then the words until (including) the TO are concatenated to the Verb string of the triplet and the remaining sub-string is kept as the Object.
4. This step is triggered if Step 3 resulted in a triplet with no Object string: Subject is the sub-string until a VP/TO is encountered. Verb is the sub-string from the beginning of the VP/TO until any VB (all verb forms)/RB (Adverb)/IN is encountered. Object is the sub-string beginning from VB/RB/IN until the end of the condition.

3.6 Expression (EXPR) Generation

The natural language SVO triplets have to be rewritten into an equation format where natural language aliases are resolved. The Subject and Object are mapped to system observables (can be thought of as variables used in software code development) and the Verb is mapped to an operator. For example, *ignition (S) - is (V) - on (O)* will be mapped to $ig\_st = on$. A system observables (variables) dictionary is used for mapping the Subject and Object, whose keys are natural language descriptions of the variables and the values are the variables. Similarly, the Verb is mapped to operators using an operator dictionary, whose keys are natural language descriptions of the operators and the values are the operators. This mapping happens in 4 steps:

1. The triplet is tagged with the NER model.
2. A vector representation is created for the Subject, Verb and Object of the triplet using a pre-trained Sentence-BERT (SBERT) [28] model.
3. Subject is mapped to the variable whose vector representation of its natural language description was closest based on cosine similarity. Similarly, the Verb is mapped to the closest matching operator in the operator dictionary.
4. Object mapping follows the above process only if it does not contain a Value named entity, otherwise the Value named entity is retained as the Object.

3.7 HANFOR Formal Specifications (FS)

As the final step the *EXPR* and *DURATION* slots of the scope and pattern corresponding to the requirement have to be filled. Once filled, the scope and pattern are tied together resulting in the formal specification. Table 1 shows the intermediate outputs generated during the formalization of an illustrative sample NLR. The scope *EXPR* slot filling happens as follows:

- If the scope is *Globally*, then there is no *EXPR* slot to fill.
- If the scope is *After EXPR*, then each pre-condition whose Subject contains temporal prepositions indicating time following such as *after, beyond, subsequent to, following* etc., its expression will be filled in this *EXPR* slot.
- In case there exist multiple such pre-conditions, their expressions are then tied together with AND and OR operators appropriately.

The pattern *DURATION* slot filling happens as follows:

- If the pattern is *It is always the case that if EXPR holds, then EXPR holds as well*, then there is not *DURATION* to fill.
- If the pattern is *If EXPR holds, then EXPR holds after at most DURATION*, then the Regular Expression $\backslash d+[.]?\backslash d+?$?(?:seconds|minutes|hours|time units') is checked against each post-condition to extract any time duration element. As this pattern applies a single *DURATION* element across all the post-conditions, the sub-string returned from the Regular Expression will be stripped from the post-conditions and filled in the *DURATION* slot.

The pattern *EXPR* slot filling happens as follows:

- In case there are multiple pre-conditions and post-conditions, their expressions are then tied together with AND and OR operators appropriately.
- For both the selected patterns, the pre-condition expressions are filled in the *EXPR* slot attached to the *If* clause, and the post-conditions expressions are filled in the *EXPR* slot attached to the *then* clause.

Table 1. End-to-end flow of a sample requirement through the Req2Spec pipeline.

Component	Output
NLR	If ignition is on, then fuel indicator is active
Scope	Globally
Pattern	It is always the case that if EXPR holds, then EXPR holds as well
NER	Signal: ignition; Component: fuel indicator; Value: on, active
Test intent extraction	Pre-cond: ignition is on, Post-cond: fuel indicator is active
Triplet extraction	Pre-cond: ignition-is-on, Post-cond: fuel indicator-is-active
Expression generation	Pre-cond: ig_st = on, Post-cond: fuel_ind = active
Formal specification	Globally, It is always the case that if ig_st = on holds, then fuel_ind = active holds as well

4   Results

Table 2 summarizes the performance of the different NLP components in the pipeline. 71% of the NLR requirements were successfully formalized by the

Req2Spec pipeline, leading to significant decrease in the time spent on manual formalization. Further, we believe that even though 29% of the requirements had formalization errors, they still provide a head start to the engineer who can make minor edits before feeding them to HANFOR. The error rate can be attributed to the following reasons:

1. Irreducible errors of the machine learning models.
2. Syntactic components of the pipeline such as Test Intent Extraction and Triplet Extraction are impacted by the quality of grammatical correctness and ambiguities in the requirements. For example, consider the requirement: *When cruise control is activated and speed is above 60 kmph or wiper is activated then lamp turns on.* It is unclear which of the following Test Intent pre-conditions combination is valid:
   - (cruise control is activated AND speed is above 60 kmph) OR (wiper is activated)
   - (cruise control is activated) AND (speed is above 60 kmph OR wiper is activated)
3. As the pipeline is linear, the failure of even a single component causes the error to cascade till the end, thereby leading to an incorrect formal specification.

Table 2. Performance (%) of the Syntactic (Syn) and Semantic (Sem) NLP components used in Req2Spec pipeline.

Component	Algorithm	Type	Precision	Recall	F-1	Accuracy
Scope classification	SciBERT	Syn+Sem	93	93	93	98
Pattern classification	SciBERT	Syn+Sem	95	96	96	96
Named entity recognition	SciBERT	Syn+Sem	83	83	83	88
Test intent extraction	CPT	Syn	–	–	–	79.27
Triplet extraction	CPT	Syn	–	–	–	88.73
Expression generation	SBERT	Sem	–	–	–	93.24
Formal specifications	–	–	–	–	–	71.61

5   Conclusion and Future Work

In this paper we have proposed Req2Spec, a NLP based pipeline that performs syntactic and semantic analysis to formalize software requirements into HANFOR compliant formal specifications, which can then be used to perform tasks like requirements analysis and test specification generation. We demonstrated our pipeline on 4 different types of requirements (2 scopes and 2 patterns), out of which 71% of the requirements resulted in the correct formal specifications, giving strong confidence on the feasibility of the pipeline. We believe that this can lead to productivity gains for the various stakeholders of the SDLC and overall improve the software quality, as the manual interventions required will decrease significantly. Our future work will focus on including datasets beyond the automotive domain and also extending the pipeline to handle additional scopes and patterns to increase coverage on different types of requirements.

References

1. IEEE: IEEE Recommended Practice for Software Requirements Specifications. IEEE Std 830-1998, pp. 1–40 (1998). https://doi.org/10.1109/IEEESTD.1998.88286
2. Fatwanto, A.: Software requirements specification analysis using natural language processing technique. In: 2013 International Conference on QiR, pp. 105–110. IEEE (2013)
3. Dalpiaz, F., van der Schalk, I., Lucassen, G.: Pinpointing ambiguity and incompleteness in requirements engineering via information visualization and NLP. In: Kamsties, E., Horkoff, J., Dalpiaz, F. (eds.) REFSQ 2018. LNCS, vol. 10753, pp. 119–135. Springer, Cham (2018). https://doi.org/10.1007/978-3-319-77243-1_8
4. Zhao, L., et al.: Natural language processing (NLP) for requirements engineering: a systematic mapping study. arXiv preprint arXiv:2004.01099 (2020)
5. Gervasi, V., Riccobene, E.: From English to ASM: on the process of deriving a formal specification from a natural language one. Integration of Tools for Rigorous Software Construction and Analysis, p. 85 (2014)
6. Becker, S., et al.: Hanfor: semantic requirements review at scale. In: REFSQ Workshops (2021)
7. IBM Engineering Requirements Quality Assistant tool. https://www.ibm.com/in-en/products/requirements-quality-assistant. Accessed 13 Oct 2021
8. QRA QVscribe tool. https://qracorp.com/qvscribe/. Accessed 13 Oct 2021
9. Dwarakanath, A., Sengupta, S.: Litmus: generation of test cases from functional requirements in natural language. In: Bouma, G., Ittoo, A., Métais, E., Wortmann, H. (eds.) NLDB 2012. LNCS, vol. 7337, pp. 58–69. Springer, Heidelberg (2012). https://doi.org/10.1007/978-3-642-31178-9_6
10. Nayak, A., et al.: Knowledge graph from informal text: architecture, components, algorithms and applications. In: Johri, P., Verma, J.K., Paul, S. (eds.) Applications of Machine Learning. AIS, pp. 75–90. Springer, Singapore (2020). https://doi.org/10.1007/978-981-15-3357-0_6
11. Nayak, A., Kesri, V., Dubey, R.K.: Knowledge graph based automated generation of test cases in software engineering. In: Proceedings of the 7th ACM IKDD CoDS and 25th COMAD, pp. 289–295 (2020)
12. Kesri, V., Nayak, A., Ponnalagu, K.: AutoKG-an automotive domain knowledge graph for software testing: a position paper. In: 2021 IEEE International Conference on Software Testing, Verification and Validation Workshops (ICSTW), pp. 234–238. IEEE (2021)
13. Böschen, M., Bogusch, R., Fraga, A., Rudat, C.: Bridging the gap between natural language requirements and formal specifications. In: REFSQ Workshops (2016)
14. Fatwanto, A.: Translating software requirements from natural language to formal specification. In: 2012 IEEE International Conference on Computational Intelligence and Cybernetics (CyberneticsCom), pp. 148–152. IEEE (2012)
15. Giannakopoulou, D., Pressburger, T., Mavridou, A., Schumann, J.: Generation of formal requirements from structured natural language. In: Madhavji, N., Pasquale, L., Ferrari, A., Gnesi, S. (eds.) REFSQ 2020. LNCS, vol. 12045, pp. 19–35. Springer, Cham (2020). https://doi.org/10.1007/978-3-030-44429-7_2
16. Langenfeld, V., Dietsch, D., Westphal, B., Hoenicke, J., Post, A.: Scalable analysis of real-time requirements. In: 2019 IEEE 27th International Requirements Engineering Conference (RE), pp. 234–244. IEEE (2019)

17. Moitra, A., et al.: Towards development of complete and conflict-free requirements. In: 2018 IEEE 26th International Requirements Engineering Conference (RE), pp. 286–296. IEEE (2018)
18. Fifarek, A.W., Wagner, L.G., Hoffman, J.A., Rodes, B.D., Aiello, M.A., Davis, J.A.: SpeAR v2.0: formalized past LTL specification and analysis of requirements. In: Barrett, C., Davies, M., Kahsai, T. (eds.) NFM 2017. LNCS, vol. 10227, pp. 420–426. Springer, Cham (2017). https://doi.org/10.1007/978-3-319-57288-8_30
19. Post, A., Hoenicke, J.: Formalization and analysis of real-time requirements: a feasibility study at BOSCH. In: Joshi, R., Müller, P., Podelski, A. (eds.) VSTTE 2012. LNCS, vol. 7152, pp. 225–240. Springer, Heidelberg (2012). https://doi.org/10.1007/978-3-642-27705-4_18
20. Konrad, S., Cheng, B.H.: Real-time specification patterns. In: Proceedings of the 27th International Conference on Software Engineering, pp. 372–381 (2005)
21. HANFOR tool. https://ultimate-pa.github.io/hanfor/. Accessed 13 Oct 2021
22. Beltagy, I., Lo, K., Cohan, A.: SciBERT: a pretrained language model for scientific text. In: Proceedings of the 2019 Conference on Empirical Methods in Natural Language Processing and the 9th International Joint Conference on Natural Language Processing (EMNLP-IJCNLP), pp. 3615–3620 (2019)
23. Kingma, D.P., Ba, J.: Adam: a method for stochastic optimization. arXiv preprint arXiv:1412.6980 (2014)
24. Nayak, A., Timmapathini, H.P.: Wiki to automotive: understanding the distribution shift and its impact on named entity recognition. arXiv preprint arXiv:2112.00283 (2021)
25. Angeli, G., Premkumar, M.J.J., Manning, C.D.: Leveraging linguistic structure for open domain information extraction. In: Proceedings of the 53rd Annual Meeting of the Association for Computational Linguistics and the 7th International Joint Conference on Natural Language Processing (Volume 1: Long Papers), pp. 344–354 (2015)
26. Del Corro, L., Gemulla, R.: ClausIE: clause-based open information extraction. In: Proceedings of the 22nd International Conference on World Wide Web, pp. 355–366 (2013)
27. Manning, C.D., Surdeanu, M., Bauer, J., Finkel, J.R., Bethard, S., McClosky, D.: The Stanford CoreNLP natural language processing toolkit. In: Proceedings of 52nd Annual Meeting of the Association for Computational Linguistics: System Demonstrations, pp. 55–60 (2014)
28. Reimers, N., Gurevych, I.: Sentence-BERT: sentence embeddings using siamese BERT-networks. arXiv preprint arXiv:1908.10084 (2019)

FRETting About Requirements: Formalised Requirements for an Aircraft Engine Controller

Marie Farrell$^{(\boxtimes)}$, Matt Luckcuck$^{(\boxtimes)}$, Oisín Sheridan, and Rosemary Monahan

Maynooth University, Maynooth, Ireland
valu3s@mu.ie

Abstract. [**Context & motivation**] Eliciting requirements that are detailed and logical enough to be amenable to formal verification is a difficult task. Multiple tools exist for requirements elicitation and some of these also support formalisation of requirements in a way that is useful for formal methods. [**Question/problem**] This paper reports on our experience of using the Formal Requirements Elicitation Tool (FRET) alongside our industrial partner. The use case that we investigate is an aircraft engine controller. In this context, we evaluate the use of FRET to bridge the communication gap between formal methods experts and aerospace industry specialists. [**Principal ideas/results**] We describe our journey from ambiguous, natural-language requirements to concise, formalised FRET requirements. We include our analysis of the formalised requirements from the perspective of patterns, translation into other formal methods and the relationship between parent-child requirements in this set. We also provide insight into lessons learned throughout this process and identify future improvements to FRET. [**Contribution**] Previous experience reports have been published by the FRET team, but this is the first such report of an industrial use case that was written by researchers that have not been involved FRET's development.

Keywords: Formal requirements · FRET · Traceability

1 Introduction

Formal verification uses mathematically-based techniques to guarantee that a system obeys certain properties, which is particularly useful when developing safety-critical systems like those used in the aerospace domain. Developing a correct set of requirements necessitates discussion with people who have expertise in the system under development, who may not have skills in formal methods.

The authors thank Georgios Giantamidis, Stylianos Basagiannis, and Vassilios A. Tsachouridis (UTRC, Ireland) for their help in requirements elicitation; and Anastasia Mavridou (NASA Ames Research Center, USA) for her help with FRET. This research was funded by the European Union's Horizon 2020 research and innovation programme under the VALU3S project (grant No. 876852), and by Enterprise Ireland (grant No. IR20200054). The funders had no role in study design, data collection and analysis, decision to publish, or preparation of the manuscript.

V. Gervasi and A. Vogelsang (Eds.): REFSQ 2022, LNCS 13216, pp. 96–111, 2022.
https://doi.org/10.1007/978-3-030-98464-9_9

In which case, it can be beneficial to the requirements elicitation process to write the requirements in an intermediate language. Tools like NASA's Formal Requirements Elicitation Tool (FRET) provide a gateway for developing formal requirements with developers who are not familiar with formal languages [7].

In this paper, we examine how FRET can be used in an industrial case study of an aircraft engine controller that has been supplied by our industrial partner, United Technologies Research Center (Ireland). FRET has previously been used to formalise the requirements for the 10 Lockheed Martin Cyber-Physical Challenges [11]. However, to the best of our knowledge this paper provides the first experience report on FRET's use on an industrial case study, by a team not involved in FRET's development.

Our approach provides external and internal traceability. Using a tool like FRET to develop the requirements provides a link between natural-language requirements and formally verified artefacts. FRET also enables the user to describe a link between requirements at different levels of abstraction, which means that this traceability is maintained within the developing set of requirements. We also use FRET to collect information about the rationale behind a requirement, further improving the traceability; either back to a natural-language requirement, or forward to a more concrete requirement. These traceability features encourage better explainability of a requirement's source, and the intermediate language improves the explainability of the requirements themselves.

The rest of the paper is laid out as follows. Sect. 2 outlines the relevant background material pertaining to FRET and the aircraft engine controller use case. Then, we describe our requirements elicitation process and present detailed requirements in Sect. 3. These requirements are analysed in Sect. 4. We discuss the lessons that were learned through this work in Sect. 5 and Sect. 6 concludes. We also make an extended version of this paper available that contains a detailed appendix showing the full set of requirements, test cases, Simulink model and FRETISH requirements[1].

2 Background

This section provides an overview of FRET and the aircraft engine controller use case for which we were developing requirements.

FRET: is an open-source tool that enables developers to write and formalise system requirements [7]. FRET accepts requirements written in a structured natural-language called FRETISH, in which requirements take the form:

scope condition **component** shall timing **response**

The condition, **component**, and **response** fields are mandatory; scope and timing are optional fields. This allows **responses** that are tied to a scope, are triggered by conditions, relate to a system **component**, and may have timing constraints.

The underlying semantics of a FRETISH requirement is determined by the scope, condition, timing, and **response** fields. There is a template for each possible

---

[1] This Paper Extended Version: https://arxiv.org/abs/2112.04251.

combination of a requirement's fields, currently FRET provides 160 such templates [8]. The selected template is used to generate formalisations of the associated requirement in both past- and future-time metric Linear-time Temporal Logic (LTL). FRET displays a diagramatic semantics for each requirement, which shows: the time interval where it should hold, and its triggering and stopping conditions (if they exist). Both versions of the requirements are helpful for sanity-checking what has been written in FRETISH.

The user must give each FRETISH requirement an ID, which can be used to create a many-to-many, hierarchical link between requirements: a *parent* requirement may have many *child* requirements, and one child may have many parents. While this link facilitates traceability, FRET does not define this relationship (formally or otherwise). For example, a child requirement does not inherit definitions from its parent. We discuss possible improvements to this link in Sect. 4.2. FRET also allows the user to enter 'Rationale' and 'Comments' for a requirement, which further supports traceability and encourages explainability of requirements.

FRET can automatically translate requirements into contracts for a Simulink diagram, written in CoCoSpec, which are checked during Simulink simulations by the CoCoSim tool, using the Kind2 model checker [4]. FRET can also generate runtime monitors for the Copilot framework [6].

Aircraft Engine Controller: Our use case is a software controller for a high-bypass civilian aircraft turbofan engine, provided by our industrial partner on the VALU3S [2] project, based on existing controller designs [13,14]. It is an example of a Full Authority Digital Engine Control (FADEC) system, which monitors and controls everything about the engine, using input from a variety of sensors. The engine itself contains two compressors (high-pressure and low-pressure) turning a central spool, which drives the engine.

As described in our prior work [9], the controller's high-level objectives are to manage the engine thrust, regulate the compressor pressure and speeds, and limit engine parameters to safe values. It should continue to operate, keeping settling time, overshoot, and steady state errors within acceptable limits, while respecting the engine's operating limits (e.g. the spool's speed limit), in the presence of:

- sensor faults (a sensor value deviating too far from its nominal value, or being unavailable),
- perturbation of system parameters (a system parameter deviating too far from its nominal value), and
- other low-probability hazards (e.g. abrupt changes in outside air pressure).

The controller is also required to detect engine surge or stall and change mode to prevent these hazardous situations.

Our industrial partner has supplied us with 14 English-language requirements (Table 1) and 20 abstract test cases, which provide more detail about the controller's required behaviour. The naming convention for requirements is:

<*use case id*>_R_<*parent requirement id*>.<*child requirement id*>

For example, because this is Use Case 5 in the VALU3S project[2], requirement one is named UC5_R_1. Note, we use a similar naming convention for test cases. Table 2 shows the abstract test cases for UC5_R_1. Our industrial partner also designed the controller in Simulink[3], shown in the extended version of this paper[4].

For our Use Case, we collaborated with scientists in the System Analysis and Assurance division of an aerospace systems company. The hour-long requirements elicitation meetings were held monthly, over a period of 10 months, with additional meetings as needed. In these meetings, our collaborators reviewed the FRETISH versions of their natural-language requirements, validating our formalisation and clarifying ambiguities for us. Since our collaborators were already familiar with other formal tools we were able to introduce them to FRET quite quickly. However, we produced a training video for other members of the project consortium[5].

3 Our Requirements Elicitation Process Using FRET

In this section we describe our requirements elicitation process. We begin by outlining how this fits into our larger approach to verification for the aircraft engine controller use case. We then describe our journey from natural-language requirements to formalised FRETISH requirements.

3.1 Requirements-Driven Methodology

As part of the three-phase verification methodology outlined in our prior work [9], we used FRET to elicit and formalise requirements for the aircraft engine controller. Focussing on Phase 1, this paper includes the full set of FRETISH requirements and presents lessons learnt, which were not discussed in [9]. Figure 1 shows a high-level flowchart of our methodology, with an exploded view of the relationship between the artefacts involved in Phase 1. The methodology takes the natural-language requirements (Table 1), test cases, and Simulink diagram of the engine controller as input, and enables the formal verification of the system's design against the requirements.

Phase 1 of our methodology involves formalising natural-language requirements using FRET, eliciting further detail as we progress. Phase 2 consists of two, potentially parallel, phases. Phase 2A uses FRET's built-in support for generating CoCoSpec contracts that can be incorporated into a Simulink diagram for verification with the Kind2 model-checker. In Phase 2B, the formalised requirements drive a (manual) translation into other formal methods, as chosen by the verifier. These tools typically require the construction of a formal model of the system, which is verified against the translated requirements. This step

---

[2] The VALU3S project: https://valu3s.eu/.
[3] Simulink: https://mathworks.com/products/simulink.html.
[4] This Paper Extended Version: https://arxiv.org/abs/2112.04251.
[5] "Formalising Verifiable Requirements" Presentation: https://www.youtube.com/watch?v=FQGKbYCbxPY&list=PLGtGM9euw6A66ceQbywXGjVoTKEhP-Of7&index=9.

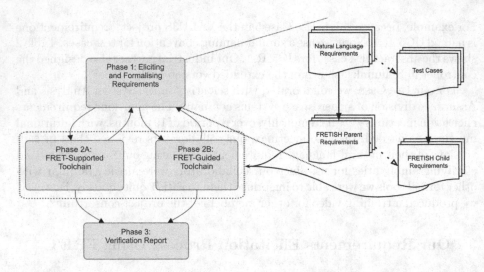

Fig. 1. Flowchart of our three-phase requirements-driven verification methodology [9] (left) with an exploded view of Phase 1's artefacts (right). The solid lines and arrowheads show direct information flow between artefacts (and back into Phase 2A and 2B), the dashed lines and open arrowheads show an artefact being implemented by another.

requires translation of the FRETISH requirements into the formalism of the chosen verification tool. Finally, Phase 3 produces a report collecting the verification results and other useful artefacts, such as formal models, Simulink diagrams, various versions of the requirements, counter-examples, proofs, etc. This supports tracing the requirements through the system's development lifecycle.

The following subsections describe the requirements elicitation process (Phase 1) in more detail. Figure 1's exploded view, shows how natural-language requirements are translated into FRETISH parent requirements (solid arrow), and the test cases are translated into child requirements. Since we view the test cases as implementations of the natural-language requirements (dashed arrow), the child requirements are similarly viewed as implementations of their corresponding parent requirements. The left-hand side of Fig. 1 shows how the work in this paper fits within our development and verification methodology; the solid arrows from the FRETISH parent and child requirements, to Phases 2A and 2B, show how the output of this work is consumed by the next phase.

3.2 Speaking FRETISH: Parent Requirements

The inputs to our requirements elicitation process were the Simulink diagram, 14 natural-language requirements (Table 1), and 20 abstract test cases that were supplied by our industrial partner. We elicited further information about the requirements through regular team discussions with our industrial partner.

We started by translating the natural-language requirements into FRETISH, producing the set of 14 FRETISH requirements in Table 3. The correspondence

Table 1. Natural-language requirements for the aircraft engine controller as produced by the aerospace use case in the VALU3S project. These 14 requirements are mainly concerned with continued operation of the controller in the presence of sensor faults (UC5_R_1–UC5_R_4), perturbation of system parameters (UC5_R_5–UC5_R_8) and low probability hazards (UC5_R_9–UC5_R_12). There are also requirements for switching between modes if engine surge/stall is detected (UC5_R_13–UC5_R_14).

ID	Description
UC5_R_1	Under sensor faults, while tracking pilot commands, control objectives shall be satisfied (e.g., settling time, overshoot, and steady state error will be within predefined, acceptable limits)
UC5_R_2	Under sensor faults, during regulation of nominal system operation (no change in pilot input), control objectives shall be satisfied (e.g., settling time, overshoot, and steady state error will be within predefined, acceptable limits)
UC5_R_3	Under sensor faults, while tracking pilot commands, operating limit objectives shall be satisfied (e.g., respecting upper limit in shaft speed)
UC5_R_4	Under sensor faults, during regulation of nominal system operation (no change in pilot input), operating limit objectives shall be satisfied (e.g., respecting upper limit in shaft speed)
UC5_R_5	Under mechanical fatigue conditions, while tracking pilot commands, control objectives shall be satisfied (e.g., settling time, overshoot, and steady state error will be within predefined, acceptable limits)
UC5_R_6	Under mechanical fatigue conditions, during regulation of nominal system operation (no change in pilot input), control objectives shall be satisfied (e.g., settling time, overshoot, and steady state error will be within predefined, acceptable limits)
UC5_R_7	Under mechanical fatigue conditions, while tracking pilot commands, operating limit objectives shall be satisfied (e.g., respecting upper limit in shaft speed)
UC5_R_8	Under mechanical fatigue conditions, during regulation of nominal system operation (no change in pilot input), operating limit objectives shall be satisfied (e.g., respecting upper limit in shaft speed)
UC5_R_9	Under low probability hazardous events, while tracking pilot commands, control objectives shall be satisfied (e.g., settling time, overshoot, and steady state error will be within predefined, acceptable limits)
UC5_R_10	Under low probability hazardous events, during regulation of nominal system operation (no change in pilot input), control objectives shall be satisfied (e.g., settling time, overshoot, and steady state error will be within predefined, acceptable limits)
UC5_R_11	Under low probability hazardous events, while tracking pilot commands, operating limit objectives shall be satisfied (e.g., respecting upper limit in shaft speed)
UC5_R_12	Under low probability hazardous events, during regulation of nominal system operation (no change in pilot input), operating limit objectives shall be satisfied (e.g., respecting upper limit in shaft speed)
UC5_R_13	While tracking pilot commands, controller operating mode shall appropriately switch between nominal and surge / stall prevention operating state
UC5_R_14	During regulation of nominal system operation (no change in pilot input), controller operating mode shall appropriately switch between nominal and surge/stall prevention operating state

Table 2. Abstract test cases corresponding to requirement UC5_R_1. Each specifies the preconditions for the test case, the input conditions/steps and the expected results.

Test Case ID	Requirement ID	Description
UC5_TC_1	UC5_R_1	**Preconditions**: Aircraft is in operating mode M and sensor S value deviates at most +/- R % from nominal value **Input conditions/steps**: Observed aircraft thrust is at value V1 and pilot input changes from A1 to A2 **Expected results**: Observed aircraft thrust changes and settles to value V2, respecting control objectives (settling time, overshoot, steady state error)
UC5_TC_2	UC5_R_1	**Preconditions**: Aircraft is in operating mode M and sensor S value is not available (sensor is out of order) **Input conditions/steps**: Observed aircraft thrust is at value V1 and pilot input changes from A1 to A2 **Expected results**: Observed aircraft thrust changes and settles to value V2, respecting control objectives (settling time, overshoot, steady state error)

between the FRETISH requirements and their natural-language counterparts is clear. For example, requirement UC5_R_1 states that:

Under sensor faults, while tracking pilot commands, control objectives shall be satisfied (e.g., settling time, overshoot, and steady state error will be within predefined, acceptable limits).

This became the corresponding FRETISH requirement:

```
if ((sensorfaults) & (trackingPilotCommands)) Controller shall
satisfy (controlObjectives)
```

Producing this initial set of requirements enabled us to identify the ambiguous parts of the natural-language requirements. For example, the phrase "*sensor faults*" simply becomes a boolean in our FRETISH requirements, highlighting that we need to elicit more details. We captured these additional details as child requirements, as described in Sect. 3.3.

3.3 Adding Detail: Child Requirements

Once the FRETISH parent requirements (Table 3) were complete, we added more detail to make the requirements set more concrete. We paid particular attention to ambiguous phrases translated from the natural-language requirements. These extra details were drawn from the abstract test cases and from detailed discussions with our industrial collaborators, who clarified specific ambiguities.

We captured the extra details in 28 child requirements. As mentioned in Sect. 2, a child requirement does not inherit definitions from its parent(s). However, we use this hierarchical link to group the detail in the child requirements under a common parent, which enables the detailed child requirements to be traced back to the more abstract parent requirements.

For example, UC5_R_1 was distilled into three requirements (UC5_R_1.1, UC5_R_1.2 and UC5_R_1.3), shown in Table 4. These three child requirements each

Table 3. FRETISH parent requirements corresponding to the natural-language requirements outlined in Table 1. The correspondance is clear to see and we have used booleans to represent the ambiguous terms from the natural-language requirements.

ID	FRETISH
UC5_R_1	if ((sensorfaults) & (trackingPilotCommands)) `Controller` shall satisfy (`controlObjectives`)
UC5_R_2	if ((sensorfaults) & (!trackingPilotCommands)) `Controller` shall satisfy (`controlObjectives`)
UC5_R_3	if ((sensorfaults) & (trackingPilotCommands)) `Controller` shall satisfy (`operatingLimitObjectives`)
UC5_R_4	if ((sensorfaults) & (!trackingPilotCommands)) `Controller` shall satisfy (`operatingLimitObjectives`)
UC5_R_5	if ((mechanicalFatigue) & (trackingPilotCommands)) `Controller` shall satisfy (`controlObjectives`)
UC5_R_6	if ((mechanicalFatigue) & (!trackingPilotCommands)) `Controller` shall satisfy (`controlObjectives`)
UC5_R_7	if ((mechanicalFatigue) & (trackingPilotCommands)) `Controller` shall satisfy (`operatingLimitObjectives`)
UC5_R_8	if ((mechanicalFatigue) & (!trackingPilotCommands)) `Controller` shall satisfy (`operatingLimitObjectives`)
UC5_R_9	if ((lowProbabilityHazardousEvents) & (trackingPilotCommands)) `Controller` shall satisfy (`controlObjectives`)
UC5_R_10	if ((lowProbabilityHazardousEvents) & (!trackingPilotCommands)) `Controller` shall satisfy (`controlObjectives`)
UC5_R_11	if ((lowProbabilityHazardousEvents) & (trackingPilotCommands)) `Controller` shall satisfy (`operatingLimitObjectives`)
UC5_R_12	if ((lowProbabilityHazardousEvents) & (!trackingPilotCommands)) `Controller` shall satisfy (`operatingLimitObjectives`)
UC5_R_13	if (trackingPilotCommands) `Controller` shall satisfy (`changeMode(nominal)`) | (`changeMode(surgeStallPrevention)`)
UC5_R_14	if (!trackingPilotCommands) `Controller` shall satisfy (`changeMode(nominal)`) | (`changeMode(surgeStallPrevention)`)

have the same `condition` and **component**, but differ in their **responses**. Each child requirement specifies one of the *"control objectives"* (settling time, overshoot and steady state error) mentioned in the natural-language version of UC5_R_1. During elicitation discussions, it was revealed that these were actually the *only* control objectives that were of concern for this use case. Here, using FRET encouraged us to question exactly what the phrase *"control objectives"* meant.

Each of these requirements includes the condition when (diff(r(i),y(i)) > E) and the timing constraint until (diff(r(i),y(i)) < e), which were initially overlooked in the natural-language requirements but revealed during elicitation discussions with our industrial partner. The **response** must hold when the difference between the reference sensor value, $r(i)$, and the observed sensor value, $y(i)$, falls between specific bounds (E and e). This important detail was missing from the parent requirement but was uncovered during our requirements elicitation.

The "**Preconditions**" of test cases UC5_TC_1 and UC5_TC_2 (Table 2) showed us that the phrase "*Under sensor faults*" meant a period where a sensor value deviates by $\pm R\%$ from its nominal value or returns a `null` value. To represent this, the child requirements use the function `sensorValue(S)` where `S` is a parameter representing each of the 4 sensors for the engine controller. These requirements are thus applied to all of the sensors in the model.

In UC5_TC_1 and UC5_TC_2, the "**Input conditions/steps**" refer to the aircraft thrust and a change in the pilot's input. We encoded this as the condition and response pair `(pilotInput => setThrust = V2) & (observedThrust = V1)` and satisfy (**observedThrust = V2**), where `V1` and `V2` are thrust variables and `=>` is logical implication. During elicitation discussions we found that this pair corresponds to the `condition`, `trackingPilotCommands`. This was a particularly important clarification because `trackingPilotCommands` models the phrase "*while tracking pilot commands*", which the natural-language requirements use extensively. This underlines that it is possible for an ambiguous statement to have a very precise meaning that was lost while drafting the requirements.

The thrust variables `V1` and `V2` in our FRETISH requirements correspond to variables **V1**, **V2**, **A1**, and **A2** in the test cases. During elicitation discussions, we found that **V1** and **V2** alone were sufficient to capture the requirement. **V1** and **A1** are used interchangeably as the initial thrust value, which we label `V1`. Similarly, **V2** and **A2** refer to the updated thrust value, which we label `V2` for consistency. This is another ambiguity that our translation from natural-language to FRETISH helped to clarify.

Our industrial partner checked the child requirements to ensure that there were no errors or omissions. The intuitive meaning of FRETISH constructs simplified this check, and features like the requirements' diagramatic semantics provided quick feedback when we edited the requirements during elicitation discussions. The act of formalising the requirements helped us to identify ambiguities in the requirements, prompting elicitation of further detail from our industrial partner.

4   An Analysis of Elicited Requirements

This section provides an analysis of the FRETISH requirements that we produced for the aircraft engine controller use case. We note that the requirements only refer to one component, the `Controller`, but this could be decomposed to refer to specific blocks in the use case Simulink design.

4.1   Requirement Templates

Each of the 14 FRETISH parent requirements (Table 3) uses the same pattern: `condition` **component** shall **response**. As described in Sect. 2, FRET maps each requirement into a semantic template so that it can generate the associated LTL

Table 4. We have three distinct child requirements for UC5_R_1 that capture the correct behaviour concerning each of settling time, overshoot and steady state error.

ID	Parent	FRETISH
UC5_R_1.1	UC5_R_1	`when (diff(r(i),y(i)) > E) if((sensorValue(S) > nominalValue + R)` | `(sensorValue(S) < nominalValue - R)` | `(sensorValue(S) = null) & (pilotInput =>` `setThrust = V2) & (observedThrust = V1))` **Controller** shall until `(diff(r(i),y(i)) < e)` satisfy **(settlingTime >= 0) & (settlingTime <= settlingTimeMax) & (observedThrust = V2)**
UC5_R_1.2	UC5_R_1	`when (diff(r(i),y(i)) > E) if((sensorValue(S) > nominalValue + R)` | `(sensorValue(S) < nominalValue - R)` | `(sensorValue(S) = null)& (pilotInput =>` `setThrust = V2) & (observedThrust = V1))` **Controller** shall until `(diff(r(i),y(i)) < e)` satisfy **(overshoot >= 0) & (overshoot <= overshootMax) & (observedThrust = V2)**
UC5_R_1.3	UC5_R_1	`when (diff(r(i),y(i)) > E) if((sensorValue(S) > nominalValue + R)` | `(sensorValue(S) < nominalValue - R)` | `(sensorValue(S) = null)& (pilotInput =>` `setThrust = V2)& (observedThrust = V1))` **Controller** shall until `(diff(r(i),y(i)) < e)` satisfy **(steadyStateError >= 0) & (steadyStateError <= steadyStateErrorMax) & (observedThrust = V2)**

specification. Our parent requirements all correspond to the template [*null, regular, eventually*], which specifies the *scope-option*, *condition-option* and *timing-option*, respectively (if the *timing-option* is omitted, then *eventually* is the default). Specific details about templates in FRET are given in [8].

We introduced `until` clauses into all of the 28 child requirements, although with different timing constraints. The introduction of the `until` clauses was identified through a combination of the information in the test cases and from extensive discussions with our industrial parter. However, the specific timing constraints required in-depth discussion with our industrial partner to identify. Most of the child requirements correspond to the template [*null, regular, until*]. However, some child requirements differed slightly as outlined below.

UC5_R_13 and UC5_R_14 generated a lot of discussion, because they differ so much from the other requirements; here, the system changes between modes of operation, so we use the `scope` clause. This produced the child requirements shown in Table 5. The `when` and `until` clauses differ from the other requirements, because here the mode change is triggered by comparing the set value of the low-pressure compressor's spool speed (`setNL`) to the value produced by the sensor (`observedNL`). It is necessary to differentiate between the cause of the difference, i.e. whether it was directly caused by `pilotInput` or by external factors (`!pilotInput`). In either case the system must change modes, but our industrial partner felt that it was important that the requirements distinguish the difference.

Table 5. Child requirements corresponding to UC5_R_13 and UC5_R_14. These differ from the previous requirements because we use the **scope** field to assert which mode of operation the controller is in.

ID	Parent	FRETISH
UC5_R_13.1	UC5_R_13	in **nominal** mode when (diff(setNL, observedNL) > NLmax) if (pilotInput => surgeStallAvoidance) **Controller** shall until (diff(setNL, observedNL) < NLmin) satisfy (**changeMode(surgeStallPrevention)**)
UC5_R_13.2	UC5_R_13	in **surgeStallPrevention** mode when (diff(setNL, observedNL) < NLmax) if (pilotInput => !surgeStallAvoidance) **Controller** shall until (diff(setNL, observedNL) > NLmin) satisfy (**changeMode(nominal)**)
UC5_R_14.1	UC5_R_14	in **nominal** mode when (diff(setNL, observedNL) > NLmax) if (!pilotInput => surgeStallAvoidance) **Controller** shall until (diff(setNL, observedNL) < NLmin) satisfy (**changeMode(surgeStallPrevention)**)
UC5_R_14.2	UC5_R_14	in **surgeStallPrevention** mode when (diff(setNL, observedNL) < NLmax) if (!pilotInput => !surgeStallAvoidance) **Controller** shall until (diff(setNL, observedNL) > NLmin) satisfy (**changeMode(nominal)**)

Figure 2 contains the semantics diagram produced by FRET for UC5_R_14.2. The semantic template that was used is [*in, regular, until*]. In a recent study using FRET to formalise the 10 Lockheed Martin Cyber Physical Challenge problems, the most commonly used semantic template was [*null, null, always*] [11]. Of these 10 problems, the autopilot system is the closest to our case study, and it was the only requirement set to use the *in* scope-option. The timing-option in their requirements was different to ours; but we use until, which was introduced into FRETISH after that study.

We used all of the fields available in FRETISH in our use case, although a lot of our individual requirements used a subset of them. We only used **scope** in the four child requirements of UC5_R_13 and UC5_R_14. FRET provides many ways of specifying modes, but we only used in mode for this; there are many ways to specify a condition, but we only used when and if. There are also multiple ways to specify timing, but in this case study we only used until clauses.

Despite until providing timing constraints, we did not use explicit times (e.g. ticks/timesteps/seconds) in our requirements. This is because the natural-language requirements (Table 1) do not mention timing, and our introduction of timing constraints came from elicitation discussions. However, time points are implicit in some of the child requirements, e.g. comparing r(i) and y(i) in the child requirements of UC5_R_1(Table 4), or the T1 and T2 variables in UC5_R_11.1 (Table 6). The timing clause was not intentionally avoided, but we felt that the implicit time constraints better suited the requirements and was closer to the description agreed with our industrial partner.

in surgeStallPrevention mode when (diff(setNL, observedNL) < NLmax) if (!pilotInput =>
!surgeStallAvoidance) Controller **shall** until (diff(setNL, observedNL) > NLmin) satisfy
(changeMode(nominal))

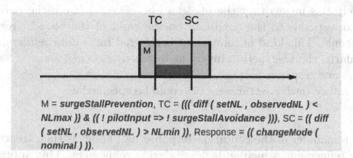

M = *surgeStallPrevention*, TC = *(((diff (setNL , observedNL) <
NLmax)) & ((! pilotInput => ! surgeStallAvoidance)))*, SC = *((diff
(setNL , observedNL) > NLmin))*, Response = *((changeMode (
nominal)))*.

Fig. 2. FRETISH and semantics diagram generated for UC5_R_14.2. Here, 'M' indicates
the mode, 'TC' the triggering condition, and 'SC' the stopping condition.

Table 6. Child requirement of UC5_R_11 which has timing implicit through the use
of the timestamp variables T1 and T2.

ID	Parent	FRETISH
UC5_R_11.1	UC5_R_11	when (diff(r(i),y(i)) > E) if (outsideAirPressure(T1) != outsideAirPressure(T2) & (diff(t2,t1) < threshold) &(abs(outsideAirPressure (T1) - outsideAirPressure(T2)) > pressureThreshold) &(observedThrust = V1) &(pilotInput => setThrust = V2)) **Controller** shall until (diff(r(i),y(i)) < e) satisfy (shaftSpeed >= operatingLowerBound) & (shaftSpeed <= operatingUpperBound) & (observedThrust = V2)

4.2   Parent-Child Relationship in Our Use Case

As previously mentioned, FRET allows a requirement to be related to another
as a 'parent' or a 'child', but this relationship is not well defined, formally or
otherwise. The parent-child relationship in FRET could be viewed as formal
refinement [1]: a concept supported by a variety of formal methods that enable
formal specifications to be gradually made more concrete, while proving that
they still obey a more abstract version of the specification. Similar approaches
exist in the literature on refactoring goal-driven requirements [5,15].

If viewed through the lens of refinement, we would need to introduce *abstraction invariants* to relate the abstract and concrete specifications. These invariants facilitate the proof that the concrete specification does not permit any
behaviours that the abstract specification forbids.

Here, we investigate whether FRET's parent-child relationship can be
expressed as formal refinement. In particular, it is possible to formalise the following abstraction invariant in relation to sensorfaults:

sensorfaults $\iff$ (sensorValue(S) > nominalValue + R) | (sensorValue(S) < nominalValue - R) | (sensorValue(S) = null)

Intuitively this means that the boolean sensorfaults (from the parent requirement) corresponds to the condition on the right of the '$\iff$' (from the child requirement). This kind of refinement is referred to as *data refinement*.

Similarly, the abstraction invariant between trackingPilotCommands and the condition and response pair (pilotInput => setThrust = V2) & (observedThrust = V1) and satisfy (observedThrust = V2) could be specified as:

$$trackingPilotCommands \iff pilotInput$$

The remainder of the condition-response pair above is then treated as *superposition* refinement, which adds detail during refinement. This approach is used because of the update of the observedThrust variable which is difficult to express in an abstraction invariant because it provides a behavioural update rather than a simple match between booleans. The additional when and until clauses in the child requirement are also superposition refinements.

The parent-child relationship in FRET appears to us to be formal refinement, at least for our set of requirements. In which case UC5_R_1 is refined by its three child requirements (UC5_R_1.1, UC5_R_1.2, UC5_R_1.3). We will examine this further in future work, where we will seek to translate these requirements into a formalism that supports refinement, and then examine whether the appropriate proof obligations can be discharged by theorem provers.

4.3   Translatable Requirements

As mentioned in Sect. 1, our aim is to formally verify the aircraft engine controller system described in Sect. 2. It is often difficult to identify what properties a system should obey, for example what does it mean for the system to operate 'correctly'. Identifying the properties to verify often causes difficulties for non-domain experts. FRET helped to guide conversations with the domain experts to facilitate the formalisation of the requirements.

FRET currently supports translation to the CoCoSim [4] and Copilot [12] verification tools. We are particularly interested in using CoCoSim since it works directly on Simulink diagrams. Thus, we have started to generate CoCoSim contracts for these requirements automatically using FRET [10]. This is described in [9] and corresponds to Phase 2A of the methodology outlined in Fig. 1.

As described in Sect. 4.1, we didn't rely heavily on timing constraints that specified specific time steps, rather we used until constraints that could potentially be translated into boolean flags in other formalisms. As such, we believe that the vast majority of the requirements that we formalised in FRET could be used by other formal methods. For example, we may need to model the aircraft engine controller in an alternative formalism if some of these properties fail to verify using CoCoSim due to the state space explosion. This approach has been taken, manually, in previous work [3].

5   Lessons Learnt and Future Improvements

This section summarises some of the lessons that we learnt from this case study.

Communication Barrier: We found that FRET and FRETISH provided a useful conduit for conversation with our industrial partner. Formalising natural-language requirements is often time-consuming because of contradictions and ambiguities. FRETISH provides a stepping-stone between readable natural-language requirements and their fully-formal counterparts, and helped us to step-wise reduce ambiguity. This process produced requirements that are easier to read than if they had been fully-formal, but which FRET can still automatically formalise.

We used FRET during elicitation discussions to explain and update our requirements, alongside our industrial partner. The diagramatic semantics gave a useful visualisation of the requirements, helping both us and our industrial partner to sanity-check updates. FRET also enabled our documentation of information for each natural-language requirement, recording the reasoning for any changes, alongside each FRETISH requirement, thus facilitating requirements explainability.

Parent-Child Relationship: While not a formal relationship, the link between parent and child requirements enabled us to gradually make the requirements more concrete, by adding details and removing ambiguities. For example, the term `sensorfaults` in UC5_R_1 was replaced with `(sensorValue(S) > nominalValue + R) | (sensorValue(S) < nominalValue - R) | (sensorValue(S) = null)` in its child requirements (Table 4). Documenting these links, via the 'Parent ID' and 'Rationale' fields in FRET, provides a structuring mechanism that enables traceability within the requirement set. However, a more concrete definition of this link would be beneficial. We have suggested a definition using formal refinement, but an object-oriented inheritance relationship could also provide structure here.

Limitations of FRETISH: While a useful language, we note some limitations of FRETISH. Logical quantifiers ($\forall$, $\exists$) would be a welcome addition to FRETISH. For example, in UC5_R_1.1, we used `sensorValue(S)`, where the parameter S indicates that this condition applies to all sensors. This is slight *abuse of notation*, it would have been more accurate to use a $\forall$ quantifier.

We also suggest that highlighting assignments to variables (which hold *after* the requirement is triggered) would be beneficial. For example, in UC5_R_1.1 we use the **observedThrust** variable in both the `condition` and the **response**. We expect that **observedThrust** has been updated by the **response** but this is not obvious, and may have implications when translating to other verification tools.

An Industrial Perspective: Our industrial partner had not used FRET before, so we asked them about their experience with it. They felt that the FRETISH requirements were '*much more clear*' than the natural-language requirements, and that using a '*controlled-natural language with precise semantics is always better than natural-language*'. When asked if FRET was difficult to use or understand they said that FRET was '*very easy to use; interface is intuitive; formal language is adequately documented inside the tool (along with usage examples)'.* Overall, they found that FRET was useful *'because it forces you to think about the actual meaning behind the natural-language requirements'.*

Having installed FRET, our industrial partner found some usability improvements that could be made. Some were problems with the GUI, which have a low impact but happen very frequently. Other issues related to FRETISH; for example, they would like to be able to add user-defined templates and patterns, such as specifying timing within the condition component. Finally, to aid interoperability they *'would like to be able to export to a format where the formalised requirements are machine readable (e.g. parse tree)'.*

Impact: Formalising the requirements made them more detailed and less ambiguous; crucially much of the detail came from elicitation discussions, not from existing documents. FRET captures the links between requirements, and explanations of their intent (which was often more detailed than what already existed). These two things mean that the FRET requirements are a valuable development artefact. We are currently pursuing Phase 2 of our methodology (Fig. 1), in which we will assess the impact of the FRETISH requirements on verification.

We believe that FRET can scale to larger requirements sets, with the parent-child relationship providing a grouping function. However, for large sets of requirements it might be necessary to modularise or refactor the requirements so that they are easier to maintain. We are currently examining how FRETISH requirements can be refactored for our use case.

6   Conclusions and Future Work

This paper provides an experience report of requirements elicitation and formalisation of an aircraft engine controller in FRET. Our industrial partner provided a set of natural-language requirements, test cases, and a Simulink diagram. In close collaboration with our industrial partner, we clarified ambiguous text in the requirements and test cases. This was essential, as we had originally misunderstood some of the text. This iterative process produced a set of detailed FRETISH requirements that we, and our industrial partner, are confident correspond to the intent of the natural-language requirements. The FRETISH requirements are now ready for use in formal verification activities.

During this work we identified improvements that could be made to FRET, which we plan to investigate in future work. First, our FRETISH requirements contain quite a lot of repetition, so if changes were needed we often had to make the change manually in several places. This was very time-consuming, so we propose adding automatic requirement refactoring. Second, we plan to investigate how to introduce globally-declared variable types. This would improve the readability of requirements; clarifying what operations are valid for a particular variable, while encapsulating definitions that might change in the future. This could be made optional, to retain the ability to write very abstract initial requirements. Finally, we would like to improve the interoperability of FRET with other formal verification tools. For example, adding a translator to the input language of a theorem prover to avoid the state-explosion faced by model checkers (like Kind2, which is used to verify CoCoSpec contracts); or outputting the requirement to a parse tree, as suggested by our industrial partner.

References

1. Back, R.J., Wright, J.: Refinement Calculus: A Systematic Introduction. Springer, Cham (1998)
2. Barbosa, R., et al.: The VALU3S ECSEL project: verification and validation of automated systems safety and security. In: Euromicro Conference on Digital System Design, pp. 352–359. IEEE (2020)
3. Bourbouh, H., et al.: Integrating formal verification and assurance: an inspection rover case study. In: Dutle, A., Moscato, M.M., Titolo, L., Muñoz, C.A., Perez, I. (eds.) NFM 2021. LNCS, vol. 12673, pp. 53–71. Springer, Cham (2021). https://doi.org/10.1007/978-3-030-76384-8_4
4. Bourbouh, H., Garoche, P.L., Loquen, T., Noulard, É., Pagetti, C.: CoCoSim, a code generation framework for control/command applications An overview of CoCoSim for multi-periodic discrete Simulink models. In: European Congress on Embedded Real Time Software and Systems (2020)
5. Darimont, R., Van Lamsweerde, A.: Formal refinement patterns for goal-driven requirements elaboration. ACM SIGSOFT Softw. Eng. Notes 21(6), 179–190 (1996)
6. Dutle, A., et al.: From requirements to autonomous flight: an overview of the monitoring ICAROUS project. In: Workshop on Formal Methods for Autonomous Systems, pp. 23–30. EPTCS (2020)
7. Giannakopoulou, D., Mavridou, A., Rhein, J., Pressburger, T., Schumann, J., Shi, N.: Formal requirements elicitation with FRET. In: International Conference on Requirements Engineering: Foundation for Software Quality (2020)
8. Giannakopoulou, D., Pressburger, T., Mavridou, A., Schumann, J.: Automated formalization of structured natural language requirements. Information and Software Technology 137, 106590 (2021)
9. Luckcuck, M., Farrell, M., Sheridan, O., Monahan, R.: A methodology for developing a verifiable aircraft engine controller from formal requirements. In: IEEE Aerospace Conference (2022)
10. Mavridou, A., Bourbouh, H., Garoche, P.L., Giannakopoulou, D., Pessburger, T., Schumann, J.: Bridging the gap between requirements and simulink model analysis. In: International Conference on Requirements Engineering: Foundation for Software Quality (2020)
11. Mavridou, A., et al.: The ten lockheed martin cyber-physical challenges: formalized, analyzed, and explained. In: International Requirements Engineering Conference, pp. 300–310. IEEE (2020)
12. Perez, I., Dedden, F. and Goodloe, A.: Copilot 3. Technical report, NASA/TM-2020-220587, National Aeronautics and Space Administration (2020)
13. Postlethwaite, I., Samar, R., Choi, B.W., Gu, D.W.: A digital multimode H∞ controller for the Spey Turbofan engine. In: European Control Conference (1995)
14. Samar, R., Postlethwaite, I.: Design and implementation of a digital multimode H∞ controller for the Spey Turbofan engine. J. Dyn. Syst. Measur. Control 132(1), 011010 (2010)
15. Zave, P., Jackson, M.: Four dark corners of requirements engineering. ACM Trans. Softw. Eng. Methodol. (TOSEM) 6(1), 1–30 (1997)

User Stories

Case Stories

Invest in Splitting: User Story Splitting Within the Software Industry

Emanuel Dellsén[1], Karl Westgårdh[1], and Jennifer Horkoff[1,2]

[1] University of Gothenburg, Gothenburg, Sweden
jennifer.horkoff@gu.se
[2] Chalmers, University of Gothenburg, Gothenburg, Sweden

Abstract. Context and Motivation: Requirements as captured in user stories often must be split to facilitate further work. There are many different theoretical descriptions on how user story splitting should be conducted in agile software development. However, current research does not give insight into how teams and team members conduct user story splitting in practice. **Question/problem:** Our research aims to decrease the gap between the theory and the practice by exploring why, how, and what the impact is of user story splitting for the participants within the context. **Principal ideas/results:** Through interviews and observations, we see indications of purposes which the majority of the participants have in common. Their practices are similar to those found in the literature but not specifically prescribed from any specific source. As a result of their practices, many participants describe that they receive an understanding that they previously did not have. The participants are also able to deliver results incrementally and estimate their work with higher precision. **Contribution:** We use our results to provide guidelines on user story splitting and to guide further research on the topic.

Keywords: User story splitting · Requirements decomposition · Work item breakdown · Vertical split · Agile methodology

1 Introduction

Agile is a term used for a set of practices and ceremonies widely used within today's software development teams and companies. Some of these ceremonies involve user story splitting, which is described as the process "of breaking up one user story into smaller ones while preserving the property that each user story separately has measurable business value" [1].

In the context of this research paper, whenever we mention "User story splitting" we do not exclusively refer to the splitting of User stories with the familiar format, *As a <role>, I want <goal>, [so that <benefit>]* [2]. Many agile teams define their user stories in terms of a hierarchy containing different user stories or work items. There can be epics, features, user stories, and tasks, and many other options in a hierarchy [3]. We are instead referring to the process of splitting or breaking down any large item into smaller pieces within agile software

V. Gervasi and A. Vogelsang (Eds.): REFSQ 2022, LNCS 13216, pp. 115–130, 2022.
https://doi.org/10.1007/978-3-030-98464-9_10

development. Examples of names for the practice of user story splitting found in the literature are "user story decomposition" and "user story breakdown". Variations also exist of what type of work item is the focus of the practice, such as "feature splitting" or "epic splitting".

There are several purposes described for the practice of user story splitting. Cohn describes the need of splitting user stories that are too large (for example, epics) so that the user story can fit into an iteration (a work period) of a software development team [4], also mentioned in [5]. As described in [5], when splitting user stories, it is still required to consider that the user story in itself should also have value, which implies that there could be user stories that are too small and are not valuable by themselves. Other purposes for user story splitting are to make user stories more understandable as well as estimatable [5], and to make them easier to work with [6].

Multiple techniques and practices for user story splitting exist. Visual Paradigm describes both horizontal and vertical splitting [7]. The horizontal technique splits large user stories into smaller ones by separating the architectural layers (e.g., one user story for UI, one for backend, and one for persistent storage). Vertical splitting focuses on one function that uses each of these parts and thereby provides value in itself. There is also a user story estimation technique, "Expected Implementation Duration" (EID) [5]. EID is used to validate split user stories to see whether a user story is correctly sized.

However, the literature does not reveal how participants in the industry implement user story splitting nor the reasons and impacts of said practice. This research is important to provide insight and decrease the gap between theoretical information and practical adaptation regarding user story splitting as a practice.

The purpose of this case study is to explore why, how, and what the impact is of user story splitting for the participants of agile software development teams. This helps us to produce recommendations for better splitting practices grounded in empirical findings. The study was conducted by interviewing members of agile software development teams and observations of meetings where user story splitting took place. We interviewed 12 participants in various roles across five companies and performed three observations.

We have selected the following research questions to guide our study:

RQ1: What is the purpose of user story splitting for the participants?

RQ2: How is user story splitting conducted by the participants?

RQ3: What is the impact of user story splitting for the participants?

With these questions, we aim to understand user story splitting in practice, improve current practices by providing guidelines, and to direct further research.

The paper is structured as follows: Sect. 2 describes related work. We describe the research methodology in Sect. 3, and present our findings related to the research questions in Sect. 4. Sect. 5, discusses our findings and future work. We conclude our study in Sect. 6.

2 Related Work

User Stories: The User Story is an artifact used in agile methodology. This artifact can both represent the functionality and requirements of the system [8]. A user story often follows a particular format, *As a <role>, I want <goal>, [so that <benefit>]*, to capture and represent requirements of a system, from a user or customer perspective [6]. Even though the agile methodology focuses on individuals and interactions over processes and comprehensive documentation [9], requirements engineering and specification through documentation still play a significant part in agile development [10]. According to [11], 90% of companies claim to use user stories to capture requirements, but only 70% follow the specific template found in [12]. This claim implies that there could be different implementations within different companies.

Techniques for Splitting: User story splitting is not a single specific approach. There exist multiple techniques and practices for splitting user stories. In agile environments, one of the most frequently mentioned techniques is vertical splitting or slicing [13,14]. Vertical splitting produces work items or user stories that "include changes to each architectural layer sufficient to deliver an increment of value" [15]. A vertical slice is a user story that contains work on all layers, the user interface, the API, and the database as an example. In contrast to vertical splitting, horizontal splitting also exists. Horizontal splitting means working with an entire layer, for example, the entire user interface. Therefore, several layers must be completed to deliver value to a user or customer.

Many other variations of vertical splitting are available in internet articles, such as splitting by user personas, by capabilities offered, by acceptance criteria, by CRUD (CREATE, READ, UPDATE, DELETE) operations and by business rules [16–18] among many others. Lawrence and Green provide a story splitting flowchart to determine which technique to use when [15].

Benefits of User Story Splitting: To split a user story into smaller pieces has, according to the literature, practical benefit and positive impact(s). Moreover, there are also defined purposes behind this approach, e.g., one user story should be split so that it can fit into one iteration [4]. This approach is echoed in [5] where the author(s) mention the importance of having one user story be complete within one iteration of a software development team. It is important not to split them too much so that each smaller part still provides business value [5]. Lucassen et al. also highlights that a split user story can become more understandable and estimable. Additionally, splitting user stories can improve the agile workflow since they become more manageable and easier to work with [6].

In terms of impact, a user story with the "incorrect" granularity can affect the quality features, such as having acceptance tests, of the user story. The quality is affected regardless of the user stories being too fine or too coarse [5]. Liskin et al. suggest that user story splitting can improve clarity, but more research into the subject is required to validate this suggestion.

The INVEST (Independent, Negotiable, Valuable, Estimable, Small, Testable) criteria address user story quality and are frequently mentioned in different sources, in literature, research papers, and internet articles. INVEST relates to both stories in general and specifically to user story splitting, especially considering the S, which stands for "Small", as in user story size. Related initially to XP (Extreme programming) [19], the INVEST criteria are frequently in use in agile environments. Application of the INVEST criteria is presented in [20] for improving the measurement technique of User Stories. When a user story in this application is either revealed as not independent from another user story, this could indicate that the user story should be split into smaller parts. If the user story does not provide any value, this could suggest that it is now too fine in terms of granularity. Therefore, the INVEST criteria can measure user stories and act as a general guideline in creating good user stories [21].

Requirements Refinement. Another line of work explores the refinement of requirements, e.g., [22]. However, most such approaches focus on refinement into formal representations, with different aims from user story splitting in agile.

3   Research Methodology

To study user story splitting in the software development industry, we chose to conduct an exploratory case study. We made this choice considering that this methodology is used "to study complex phenomena within their contexts" [23]. We chose to conduct qualitative interviews and observations with the participants to answer our research questions. We have followed the guidelines from the paper ACM SIGSOFT Empirical Standard for the interviews [24].

Participants: Our participants were selected depending on whether they and their teams perform some kind of user story splitting in their development process. We have not compared how one team treats user stories to one another in order to make sure that they are comparable. The sampling method is convenience sampling. We contacted the participants by e-mail with a general description of the topic of our study and a description of how we would like them to participate in the study. Some participants only took part in interviews, and some participating teams invited us for observations. We interviewed a total of 12 participants from five different companies and performed three observations where some of the interviewees also were participatants. The participants worked in both large and small companies a variety of domains. The interviewees were mainly from teams based in Sweden, even though two of the interviewees themselves were located in Latvia.

Data Collection: In order to achieve data triangulation and broaden our understanding of the topic, we performed data collection using both interviews and observations [25]. *Interviews:* The data was mainly collected through the use of semi-structured interviews. The interviews were done with one team member at a time from each team. The interviews took between 30 to 50 min and were conducted online between March and April of 2021 over Zoom. We recorded audio

Table 1. Interview participants

ID	Experience	Role	Company	Company information	Team	Team age	Team size
1	20+ years	Product manager	1	American company, data analysis software, 4000+ employees	1	5+ years	4–6 persons
2	40+ years	Software developer	2	Swedish company, tourism and hospitality software, 10+ employees	1	2+ years	4–6 persons
3	3+ years	Requirement analyst	3	Nordic company, financial industry, 5000+ employees	1	3+ years	7–10 persons
4	15+ years	Software developer	2	Swedish company, tourism and hospitality software, 10+ employees	2	2+ years	4–6 persons
5	10+ years	Product owner	3	Nordic company, financial industry, 5000+ employees	2	4+ years	7–10 persons
6	3+ years	Product owner	2	Swedish company, tourism and hospitality software, 10+ employees	2	2+ years	4–6 persons
7	10+ years	Scrum master	3	Nordic company, financial industry, 5000+ employees	2	4+ years	7–10 persons
8	5+ years	Scrum master	4	Swedish company, IT subcontractor, 20+ employees	1	2+ years	4–6 persons
9	3+ years	Product owner	3	Nordic company, financial industry, 5000+ employees	3	2+ years	7–10 persons
10	5+ years	Software developer	4	Swedish company, IT subcontractor, 20+ employees	1	2+ years	4–6 persons
11	5+ years	Quality assurance engineer	2	Nordic company, financial industry, 5000+ employees	3	2+ years	7–10 persons
12	10+ years	Software realization manager	5	European company, logistics solutions, 2000+ employees	1	5+ years	7–10 persons

of all the interview sessions with the permission of the interviewees. We conducted the interviews in English regardless of the participant's native language. The questions asked during the interviews can be found in our online repository https://github.com/Synoecism/user-story-splitting.

We performed one interview pre-test with an individual at a company in Gothenburg, Sweden, in a similar role to that of our interviewees and adjusted the protocol based on feedback. The audio files of the interviews were transcribed using a digital tool (www.rev.ai). The quality of the transcription was good but we had to compare the transcription to the audio recording and correct mistakes made by the tool. After the interviews, the transcript was sent to the respective participant for member-checking to receive additional feedback and allow the participant to remove any information they wished to remove.

Observations: We observed two sprint planning sessions and one epic refinement meeting. All of the observations were performed in the same team in one

Table 2. Conducted observations

Observation	Company/Team	Performed	Type of meeting	Roles involved	Length
1	C1/T1	Early March 2021	Sprint planning	Product Owner, Scrum Master, Developers (3)	45+ min
2	C1/T1	Mid March 2021	Epic refinement	Scrum Master, Developers (2)	60+ min
3	C1/T1	Early April 2021	Sprint planning	Product Owner, Scrum Master, Developers (3), Support technician	45+ min

company. All of the observations were performed in a passive manner where we did not interact with anyone and/or interrupt the natural flow of the meeting/sessions. The reasoning behind this being that we did not want to influence the data. We did this to observe the interaction of the team members in their natural state and increase the number of data sources for the research. The data collection was made through taking notes, these notes was later analyzed which is described further in the next section.

Data Analysis: We analyzed the data using inductive and deductive thematic coding [26], suitable for an exploratory case study with initial research questions. The first two authors coded the transcripts and notes from the interviews and the observations individually, then discussed these codes with the third author. Based on these initial codes, the first two authors derived a list of sub-themes together to align our view of the sub-themes. Then we separately applied the sub-themes to the codes. Whenever a sub-theme was missing or a sub-theme from the list could not be applied to the code, we constructed new ones for that specific code. We then compared the choices of sub-themes, and we discussed each selection before settling on one sub-theme for each code. For example, the sub-theme "Team" comes from the codes "Team culture" and "Defined by the team leader".

The sub-themes were then grouped into themes related to the research questions. Similar to the previous step, the first two authors did so separately and then discussed our individual choices. In the end, we selected one theme for each sub-theme based on each code. Codes that had no occurrences or a single occurrence were dismissed.

4   Results

We start by describing the work environment of the interviewees and their teams' way of working. We also cover the hierarchy of the teams' backlog board. The remaining results section is separated into themes and sub-themes derived from the codes of the interviews and observations. The sub-themes are presented in order of the most frequently occurring codes, we have chosen to present sub-themes with more codes occurring more than five times. An overview of the sub-themes connected to the themes can be seen in Fig. 1.

A complete overview of the codes and sub-themes per theme can be found in the tables available in our online repository (https://github.com/Synoecism/user-story-splitting). Sub-themes are found to the far left of the tables, followed by the codes and the sum of the occurrences of that specific code from the observations and the interviews. With "O1", we refer to Observation 1, and with "I1", we refer to Interview 1. The tables include the frequencies of a specific code in a specific interview or observation. Throughout the rest of this section, there will be text highlighted in *italics* and **bold**, where italics reflects to the sub-themes (see Fig. 1) and bold text reflects the codes under the sub-theme.

Work Environment: All participants worked in an agile environment but used different ceremonies such as Sprints, Sprint Planning, and backlog grooming. The teams used a combination of practices from agile methodology, kanban, and scrum to structure their development and way of working.

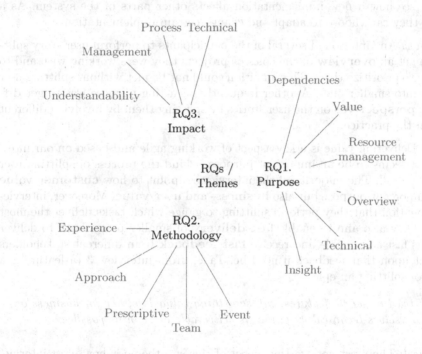

Fig. 1. Themes and sub-themes

We found that all participants use a digital tool to assist their work board and user story splitting. One of the teams used "Jira"[1], but other work board products were also used by the other teams such as "Trello"[2] or "Azure DevOps"[3]. One of the main purposes of tool use was to trace tasks to user stories.

---

[1] https://www.atlassian.com/software/jira.
[2] https://trello.com/en.
[3] https://azure.microsoft.com/en-us/services/devops.

RQ1: What is the purpose of user story splitting for the participants?

Insight: The majority of the interviewees describe how their development process would encounter more problems if they did not split large items into smaller ones. They mention how the process of user story splitting forces them to think and reason about what to include in the scope of a user story and therefore **reveal the scope**. Apart from revealing a scope for different tasks, there is also an explicit idea to promote **understandability** for everyone involved in the process. In terms of one purpose of splitting user stories taken from interview 7:

> "*I think my colleagues appreciate things being split into smaller tasks, because it reduces the uncertainty for everybody*"

Another mentioned purpose of user story splitting is to **identify dependencies**. By identifying these dependencies, the teams say how they can more clearly see how a new implementation affects other parts of the system. As a result, they can choose to adapt and change certain implementations.

Overview: An ambition of several of the participants to perform user story splitting to get an **overview** of the epics or projects they were working with and to be able to prioritize them. This ambition could not be met without splitting user stories into smaller ones. Another frequently occurring purpose was to get **different perspectives** on the user stories by splitting them by involving different roles in the practice.

Value: Delivering value is a key aspect of working agile and based on our interviews, it seems to be an important purpose behind the process of splitting user stories as well. The majority of the interviewees point to how **customer value** is an important purpose but also **business-** and **user value**. Moreover, interviewees mention that they perform splitting to gauge which tasks deliver the most value. They also aim to enable **fast delivery** of smaller pieces both to deliver value as fast as possible and receive **fast feedback** from different stakeholders and act upon that feedback if need be. Taken from interview 3 (a feature is a result of splitting an epic):

> "*we tried to set up features with something valuable either for business or for ourselves technical wise, that is deliverable as soon as possible*"

Technical: The most noteworthy aspect of this sub-theme is how most interviewees mention that one of many purposes behind their splitting process is to have their products **testable**. Interview 4 describes:

> "*if we can split it into smaller parts, then that is much better than to have like two big tests*".

The quote highlights how having smaller parts makes testing less complicated than writing more extensive but fewer tests. From one interview, we could derive the conscious purpose of having **reusability** in mind. This purpose stemmed from actively delivering products that are reusable by other users.

Resource Management: The participants that worked in teams that used sprints to structure their way of working mentioned that they used user story splitting to split their stories to **fit into the sprint**. Projects or larger tasks could rarely fit directly into a sprint, and therefore splitting was necessary to achieve this. It was also mentioned several times that user story splitting was conducted to **distribute workload** and for **resource management**. This was especially apparent for developers because working with smaller stories made them both more focused on the task at hand, and it was easier to divide tasks between them within the teams.

Dependencies: We discussed identifying dependencies in the sub-theme "Insight". Some interviewees point out that they make a conscious effort to split their user stories to **reduce dependencies** found. The majority of the interviewees who mention this as a purpose have a managerial role. Apart from reducing dependencies, we had one interviewee who noted that they aim to **reduce stakeholders**. The number of dialogues necessary to have if more stakeholders are involved in each task could be reduced and hopefully increase productivity.

RQ2: How is user story splitting conducted by the participants?

Team: All participants mentioned that it was natural and important to have **different roles involved** in user story splitting. During the observations, it was apparent where many different roles were involved during both sprint planning and the product meeting. Every role ranging from product owners to scrum masters, to UX designers, to support staff, and last but not least, developers, were involved in the process. Even though different roles involved, scrum masters, product owners, and team lead were more responsible for user story splitting within the participating teams. There were also different roles involved depending on when user story splitting was performed. In interview 9, the interviewee described that developers were not involved in the pre-planning stage:

> "*I guess we don't have the time when we are kind of in those kinds of pre-planning phases, to drill down on all the technical details.*"

Team culture played a large part in how the teams conducted user story splitting. It was described several times as a team effort, and the involvement of all team members was an important factor in the success of splitting. The participants also favored **dialogue over documentation** and emphasize the importance of **involvement and commitment** to the practice. Several participants mentioned that the way of working was **defined by the team lead**.

Event: Some of the interviewees point out that they have specific times where they perform user story splitting, some of them being that they **split at start of Epic, split at sprint planning**, etc. Moreover, the most frequently mentioned event is to **split when necessary** which seems to highlight that this process is not always a ceremony like a "sprint planning", but more when they find the need. One example of such a necessity is when a developer, while developing a task, reveals some aspect previously unknown, such as a need to evaluate what the next step should be. Interview 5 said:

"... it's the expectation, but now we see that it's really hard to do this, or it requires a lot of effort to do it. Then we need to evaluate, should we exclude it, or find another solution or how to treat it."

Experience: The participants had mostly a rather **nonprescriptive** approach to how they conducted user story splitting. In general, they used **experience** from earlier assignments or previous teams they belonged to alongside fragments of specific approaches to splitting. Several interviewees placed a great deal in the experience of especially scrum masters and product owners, for successful splitting. Some of them also mentioned that they performed user story splitting according to **industry knowledge** without being able to derive where they've learned a specific way of working or technique.

Approach: Even though the participants said they relied heavily on experience and team dialogue in conducting user story splitting, the participants mentioned specific techniques. **Vertical splitting** was the most frequent one, and there were also mentions of variations of vertical splitting such as splitting by feature, component, and functionality. Some teams also performed **horizontal splitting**, but the interviewees of those teams said it was rather because of an old way of working than a preferred technique. Another non-voluntary way of splitting was **splitting by expertise** and **by department**. They used this approach because some developers were much more experienced than others and that some parts of the user stories could only be completed by them. **Splitting by size** or **story points** were in use in some teams.

Prescriptive: The concept of this sub-theme is to address the ideas and concepts adopted from outside of the team, it could be literature, courses, etc. Some of the interviewees mention how their team has an approach to only produce items that are **small** based on criteria such as "smallest possible but still deliver value". Two interviewees described how they had been part of agile **educational course(s)** through their companies which prescribes how specific processes "should" be which have influenced their way of working. One of the interviewees who attended an agile course describes how she always keeps the **INVEST**-criteria to a user story in mind when she does her splitting. We will further discuss the INVEST criteria in Sect. 5.

RQ3: What is the impact of user story splitting for the participants?

Understandability: The difference between "understandability" as a purpose and an impact is whether the participant aims to achieve understandability or as a consequence of user story splitting. In eight of the interviews, we were told that splitting large items into smaller, a project **scope became revealed**. Some of the teams noticed that even **non-coding tasks were revealed**, for example, documentation tasks or contacting a customer. Additionally, eight interviewees described that when they previously did not split user stories, they **overlooked** things that needed to be done. Several participants also mentioned that the lack of a process of user story splitting would have resulted in a **lack of overview** of a project, and a **lack of understandability** of what needed to be done.

Process: As an impact of user story splitting, the participants said that it enabled or enhanced their ability to have **incremental deliveries** of features and stories. Interview 7 shows this:

> *"...user stories split the data in a, in a chunk that can be easily, for example, deployable, it can be, it has a life of itself."*

According to some interviewees, user story splitting also made it easier to work with changes to requirements, thereby promoting their **adaptability**. By working with smaller stories, changes in requirements could be isolated and mapped to specific stories rather than large epics. For two interviewees, the user story splitting process increased their ability to promote **correct delivery** since they could with less difficulty visualize what to deliver.

Management: **Estimation** is the most frequently occurring code in this sub-theme. This code describes that splitting user stories is a positive impact because the team members can estimate how long time certain tasks will take, which management valued. Some interviewees mention how this is possible because they know what is included in a certain task with a higher certainty. Another impact mentioned was that user story splitting enabled **comparability** between user stories. Large user stories were described as difficult to compare to other stories, but smaller ones, easier to compare to one another. Comparability also played a part in estimation. Two interviewees mentioned that it became easier to **manage risk** due to the continuous delivery of smaller stories.

Technical: The practice of user story splitting had some impact on technical issues. By splitting stories into smaller pieces, it increased **testability** since it was easier to test them as small individual pieces instead of one big block. Two interviewees said that **code reviewing** was done more easily since it was easier to understand code about the stories when the stories were smaller. Two interviewees told us that user story spitting resulted in **increased code quality** because it was easier to write good code for a small story than a large one. Additionally, these two interviewees said one of the reasons behind increased code quality was that it **reduced the complexity** of the resulting code.

5   Discussion

We see that user story splitting is an integral part of the agile development team's way of working. There are different but logical reasons why certain interviewees split stories in a certain way and, to them, both known and unknown impacts of user story splitting. In terms of the user story splitting literature, our study has verified some of our initial assumptions, but we also found aspects that point to things previously unknown to us.

INVEST: What we have found seems to indicate that several of the qualities prescribed by the INVEST [20] acronym are interwoven in the practice of user story splitting for the participants. Only one participant specifically mentioned

INVEST during the interview, but several other participants mentioned qualities from INVEST without directly connecting to that concept. For example, producing testable items independent of each other and small in size to deliver value faster. Estimation is one key aspect of INVEST, and we have found that this is a positive impact of user story splitting, based on several interviews.

In [20], the authors present the INVEST grid, which is a practical template for evaluating user stories in terms of INVEST criteria. We believe that a study into how teams could apply the INVEST grid in practice, both considering [20], and our findings related to the qualities of INVEST, would be interesting.

Vertical Splitting: The results we have presented indicate that most of the participants use vertical splitting. However, some of the participants are only using horizontal splitting, and some horizontal splitting in addition to vertical splitting. Vertical splitting is a more commonly discussed topic in the literature and articles [15],[18] while splitting horizontally is a less favored approach in an agile environment [27], as it does not focus on the user or customer value but rather on the technical or architectural solution. Vertical splitting seems to be a good approach when you want to focus on delivering user functionality independently. In contrast, based on our impression from several interviews, horizontal splitting seem to result in both longer development time before delivery and potentially developing things that might be unused. Further research to validate efficiency of vertical splitting over horizontal splitting would be valuable.

Work Split: Some of the teams mentioned that they split user stories an additional time both for distribution of workload and depending on expertise. An example of this additional split was when a user story was split into one for frontend work and one for backend work. With this additional split, the new parts lacked independent value and needed to be delivered together, but the two developers were able to separate their work. Three of the developers we interviewed mentioned a different kind of additional split, in order to create a checklist for themselves, which they used to ensure that nothing was forgotten. The same developers did not find it necessary to have these individual checklists connected to the workboard of the team. This might be connected to the idea mentioned by another interviewee, a scrum master, that it is important to trust the developers within his team to do their job. It would be interesting to further explore why these additional splits occur and to see if there are any consequences.

Insight and Overview: All of the participants mentioned that gaining insight and getting an overview of what they were working with was a significant part of the goal of user story splitting. Insight and overview were also mentioned as an impact of the process and understanding the project's scope. There was an indication of this as well in [5], and further strengthened by our findings. Through the process of splitting, the teams are presented with more concrete items. These items could consist of aspects that have been previously unknown but are now known. Moreover, the impression we have got is that the participants find it easier to see dependencies between tasks more clearly, but this impression is worth further investigating in future research.

Another positive impact of user story splitting is that it reveals tasks that are not directly related to producing code. The interviewees that describe this indicate the importance of deriving such tasks. This can be tasks related to understanding other parts of the business, or, for example, contacting a customer and discussing a suggested way to implement one of their requirements.

Different Roles Involved: We find that different roles were involved in various stages and differed significantly between teams, specifically at what granularity level the team was currently splitting. Some teams involved only the product owner or the scrum master when working with epics, and some only involved developers when splitting user stories.

Our findings seem to indicate that it is beneficial for user story splitting to involve many different roles in the process, as each of the different roles provides unique perspectives, which decreases the risk of encountering later problems. Involving more than one type of role is supported by [28], who says that user story splitting should not be the sole responsibility of the product owner, and neither be left completely alone to the development team.

Another aspect of this relates to both gaining insight and overview as well as conducting vertical splitting. Two participants said that the problem with vertical splitting is that an architectural overview might get lost when using horizontal splitting. Involving the architect in the splitting process seems to mitigate this issue while still working with vertical splits.

Recommendations: We believe that our findings suggest a set of recommendations for new teams and practitioners aiming to perform user story splitting or improve their current practice.

- Involve different team roles when splitting, to get different perspectives.
- Split vertically, to focus on delivering value.
- Use the INVEST criteria as a guideline to increase the quality of splitting.
- Actively evaluate the user story splitting practice retrospectively to suit your teams way of working.
- Focus on discussing and splitting epics rather than detailing them upfront.
- Use a digital workboard to support traceability between user stories.

Although these recommendations are in line with many recommendations in the literature, we believe is it helpful to conduct studies such as ours to report evidence which confirms these practices. A future study could further evaluate these recommendations by following teams that apply them to their practice.

Threats to Validity: We discuss the validity threats for an exploratory case study and our data collection techniques. *Construct.* At the beginning of each interview, we made sure to explain our interpretation of terminologies such as "user story splitting", this was necessary given that similar practices do not share the same name. After the interviews, we performed member checking, which helped shed light on confusing comments. On occasions where interviewee(s) have misunderstood our questions or confused user story splitting with agile methodology in general, we have tried to guide them back to the topic at hand. This process also allowed the interviewee(s) to add information to clarify things they read in the transcript and apply corrections to their statements.

Internal. Observing people's work always risks them acting in a way that deviates from how they usually act. Performing the observations through digital tools such as Zoom and turning off our cameras and microphones was a way for us to try and reduce this internal threat. The research should also be seen in the light of the COVID-19 situation occuring during the interviews and observations. Some interview answers may have been affected or not representative of the typical situation due to the work situation during the pandemic.

External. The goal of this research is not to generalize our findings. However, we generate themes derived from the interviews and observations conducted with several teams within different companies, we can point towards a similarity between the various sources. There is also a chance that our findings apply in other contexts since we interviewed and observed teams from different companies and, therefore, different contexts. To validate the claim, more research is necessary.

6   Conclusions

In this paper, we have performed interviews and observations to find what purpose(s) the participants have for user story splitting, how they conduct this process, and its impact. We found that even though there are many strategies and techniques available in the literature, the participants did not base their practice of user story splitting on any specific source or technique. However, the participants did use practices that were similar and shared properties of practices found in the literature. To reveal the scope of a project was both mentioned as a purpose and impact of user story splitting. The other most frequently mentioned reasons were to understand what needed to be done to complete a story to get an overview of the work that needed to be done. We also found that an impact of user story splitting is that it makes it easier to deliver user stories incrementally. We have produced a set of recommendations for the practice of user story splitting based on our findings, and these recommendations can be used by teams and team members to assist or improve their practice. This research can be used as a foundation for further studies into the topic of user story splitting.

Acknowledgement. We express their sincere gratitude and appreciation to: the participating companies and participants, and Abdul Bari, for the mathematical explanations.

References

1. Wirfs-Brock, R.: What is user story splitting? Alliance, A., Ed. (2021).https://www.agilealliance.org/glossary/split/

2. Patton, J.: User story mapping: discover the whole story, build the right product. O'Reilly (2014)
3. Rehkopf, M.: Epics, stories, themes, and initiatives. Atlassian, Ed. (2021). https://www.atlassian.com/agile/project-management/epics-stories-theme
4. Cohn, M.: User stories applied: For agile software development. Addison- Wesley (2004)
5. Liskin, O., Pham, R., Kiesling, S., Schneider, K.: Why we need a granularity concept for user stories. In: Cantone, G., Marchesi, M. (eds.) XP 2014. LNBIP, vol. 179, pp. 110–125. Springer, Cham (2014). https://doi.org/10.1007/978-3-319-06862-6_8
6. Lucassen, G., Dalpiaz, F., Werf, J.M.E.M., Brinkkemper, S.: The use and effectiveness of user stories in practice. In: Daneva, M., Pastor, O. (eds.) REFSQ 2016. LNCS, vol. 9619, pp. 205–222. Springer, Cham (2016). https://doi.org/10.1007/978-3-319-30282-9_14
7. Visual Paradigm. User story splitting - vertical slice vs horizontal slice, (2021). https://www.visual-paradigm.com/scrum/user-story-splitting-vertical-slice-vs-horizontal-slice/
8. Wautelet, Y., Heng, S., Kolp, M., Mirbel, I.: Unifying and extending user story models. In: Jarke, M., Mylopoulos, J., Quix, C., Rolland, C., Manolopoulos, Y., Mouratidis, H., Horkoff, J. (eds.) CAiSE 2014. LNCS, vol. 8484, pp. 211–225. Springer, Cham (2014). https://doi.org/10.1007/978-3-319-07881-6_15
9. Beck, K., et al.: Manifesto for agile software development (2001).https://agilemanifesto.org/
10. Wang, X., Zhao, L., Wang, Y., Sun, J.: The role of requirements engineering practices in agile development: an empirical study. In: Zowghi, D., Jin, Z. (eds.) Requirements Engineering. CCIS, vol. 432, pp. 195–209. Springer, Heidelberg (2014). https://doi.org/10.1007/978-3-662-43610-3_15
11. Dalpiaz, F., Brinkkemper, S.: Agile requirements engineering with user stories. In: 2018 IEEE 26th International Requirements Engineering Conference, pp. 506–507. IEEE (2018)
12. Cohn, M.: User stories. Software, M.G., Ed. (2020). https://www.mountaingoatsoftware.com/agile/user-stories
13. Ratner, I.M., Harvey, J.: Vertical slicing: smaller is better. In: 2011 Agile Conference, pp. 240–245(2011). https://doi.org/10.1109/AGILE.2011.46
14. Lowe, D.: Slicing stories vertically. Kanban, S., Ed. (2013). https://scrumandkanban.co.uk/slicing-stories-vertically/
15. Lawrence, R., Green, P.: The humanizing work guide to splitting user stories. H. Work, Ed. (2020).https://www.humanizingwork.com/the-humanizing-work-guide-to-splitting-user-stories/
16. Balbes, M.J.: A practical guide to user story splitting for agile teams. Beacon, T., Ed. (2021). https://techbeacon.com/app-dev-testing/practical-guide-user-story-splitting-agile-teams
17. Poole, D.: User stories and story splitting. Group, E., Ed. (2015). https://raleigh.iiba.org/sites/raleigh/files/userstoryminibook.pdf
18. Leffingwell, D.: "A user story primer" Tech. Rep. (2009)
19. Wake, B.: Invest in good stories, and smart tasks - xp123 (2003). https://xp123.com/articles/invest-in-good-stories-and-smart-tasks/
20. Buglione, L., Abran, A.: Improving the user story agile technique using the invest criteria. In: Proceedings of the 8th International Conference on Software Process and Product Measurement, pp. 49–53. IEEE (2013)
21. Hartmann, B.: New to agile? invest in good user stories [agile for all] (2009). https://agileforall.com/new-to-agile-invest-in-good-user-stories/

22. Darimont, R., Van Lamsweerde, A.: Formal refinement patterns for goal-driven requirements elaboration. ACM SIGSOFT Softw. Eng. Notes **21**(6), 179–190 (1996)
23. Baxter, P., Jack, S.: Qualitative case study methodology: study design and implementation for novice researchers. Qual. Rep. **13**(4) (2008)
24. Ralph, P.: ACM SIGSOFT empirical standards released. ACM SIGSOFT Softw. Eng. Notes **46**(1), 19–19 (2021)
25. Carter, N., et al.: The use of triangulation in qualitative research. In: Oncol Nurs Forum, p. 545 (2014)
26. Soiferman, L.K.: Compare and contrast inductive and deductive research approaches. In: ERIC (2010)
27. Ramirez, R.: Advantages of vertical slice over horizontal slice in ag- ile software development. T. Technologies, Ed. (2018). https://www.teravisiontech.com/advantages-vertical-slice-horizontal-slice-agile-software-development/
28. Cohn, M.: Five story-splitting mistakes and how to stop making them. M. G. Software, Ed. (2017).https://www.mountaingoatsoftware.com/blog/five-story-splitting-mistakes-and-how-to-stop-making-them

Guided Derivation of Conceptual Models from User Stories: A Controlled Experiment

Maxim Bragilovski[1]([✉])(iD), Fabiano Dalpiaz[2](iD), and Arnon Sturm[1](iD)

[1] Ben-Gurion University of the Negev, Beer Sheva, Israel
maximbr@post.bgu.ac.il, sturm@bgu.ac.il
[2] Utrecht University, Utrecht, The Netherlands
f.dalpiaz@uu.nl

Abstract. **[Context and Motivation]** User stories are a popular notation for representing requirements, especially in agile development. Although they represent a cornerstone for developing systems, limited research exists on how user stories are refined into conceptual design. **[Question/Problem]** We study the process of deriving conceptual models from user stories, which is at the basis of information systems development. We focus our attention on the derivation of a holistic view of structural and interaction aspects, represented via class diagrams and use case diagrams, respectively. In this paper, we examine whether providing *guidelines* has an effect on the ability of humans to derive complete and valid conceptual models. **[Principal Ideas/Results]** We design example-based guidelines for the derivation of class and use case diagrams from user stories. Then, we conduct a two-factor, two-treatment controlled experiment with 77 undergraduate students serving as subjects. The results indicate that the guidelines improve the completeness and validity of the conceptual models in cases of medium complexity, although the subjects were neutral on the usefulness of the guidelines. **[Contribution]** The guidelines may assist analysts in the refinement of user stories. Our initial evidence, besides showing how the guidelines can help junior analysts derive high-quality conceptual models, opens the doors for further studies on the refinement of user stories, and to the investigation of alternative guidelines.

Keywords: Requirements engineering · Conceptual modeling · Use cases · Derivation process · Guidelines · Class diagram · User stories · Controlled experiment

1 Introduction

User stories are a popular technique for expressing requirements from a user perspective [8]. Through their simple notation, they represent who expresses a need, what feature is requested, and the rationale behind the feature. The so-called Connextra notation [8] "*As a ⟨role⟩ I want to ⟨feature⟩ so that ⟨benefit⟩*" is widely used for the representation of the elicited requirements in agile development projects [16,21].

User stories are a central artifact for the subsequent stages of software development [2,26]. In particular, user stories may be *refined* into lower-level specifications.

© Springer Nature Switzerland AG 2022
V. Gervasi and A. Vogelsang (Eds.): REFSQ 2022, LNCS 13216, pp. 131–147, 2022.
https://doi.org/10.1007/978-3-030-98464-9_11

One way to do so is to derive *conceptual models*; this is at the basis of model-driven engineering [5] and, in general, of information systems development.

Conceptual models may represent system functionality; for example, use case diagrams [6] define the roles and the functionality they expect when interacting with the system. Conceptual models can also depict structural aspects by summarizing the major entities and relationships that are referred to in the high-level requirements [15,25,34]. In addition to their use in model-driven engineering [19], conceptual models have been employed in requirements engineering to provide a holistic overview of the product domain and functionality [1,23], for the identification of potential ambiguity [11], and for analyzing quality aspects such as security and privacy [24].

In previous research, we have conducted empirical studies in which we compared user stories and use cases as a starting point for the derivation of structural conceptual models [10,12]. Our results revealed that user stories are better in time-constrained settings [12], while in absence of time constraints, the notations are equivalent and other factors have shown to have a large(r) impact [10], including the complexity of the domain and the use of a systematic derivation process.

Based on these premises, we investigate whether a human analyst's ability to derive conceptual models is influenced by guidelines that illustrate how to construct such models from user stories. While following a systematic derivation process was an emerging factor in previous research [10], here we foster such a systematic approach by providing guidelines. Like in previous research, we study the derivation of a functional conceptual model (use case diagram) and of a structural conceptual model (class diagram). Our research question is as follows: *MRQ. How does the provisioning of guidelines to information systems developers affect the quality of the derived conceptual models?*

In particular, we are going to investigate guidelines that are expressed in the form of examples [14]. Also, we use information systems developers as a general term for system analysts, designers and programmers. To measure the quality, we used the previously adopted metrics of model validity and completeness [10,13].

We answer the MRQ via a controlled experiment in which senior undergrad students were asked to derive conceptual models starting from the user stories for two systems. Half students were provided with the guidelines, half were not. These students serve as a proxy for our target population, which consists of analysts, designers, and developers of information systems. As already mentioned, we assess model quality by measuring the validity and completeness of the models [10,13]. To enable that, the researchers built gold standard conceptual models prior to the experiment's conduction. Furthermore, we assess the students' opinion on the usefulness of and need for guidelines. The results show that the guidelines lead to improved results in terms of validity and completeness, although this is mainly visible in the more complex specification.

Thus, this paper makes two contributions to the literature: (i) we propose example-based guidelines for the derivation of structural and functional conceptual models from user stories; and (ii) we assess the effectiveness and perceived appreciation of the guidelines through an experiment that compares to a baseline group without guidelines.

Organization. In Sect. 2, we set the background for this research and we review related studies. In Sect. 3, we present our devised guidelines. In Sect. 4, we describe the design of our experiment. In Sect. 5, we elaborate on the experiment results whereas in Sect. 6 we interpret and discuss those results. In Sect. 7, we evaluate the threats to validity. We conclude and set plans for future research in Sect. 8.

2 Background and Related Work

User stories are a widespread notation for expressing requirements [16,21], especially in agile development projects [8]. They are simple descriptions of a feature written from the perspective of the stakeholder who wants such a feature. Multiple templates exist for representing user stories [31], among which the Connextra format is the most common [21]: *As a ⟨role⟩, I want ⟨action⟩, so that ⟨benefit⟩*. For example, a user story for a learning management system could be "As an enrolled student, I want to access the grading rubrics, so that I know how my assignments will be evaluated". The 'so that' part, despite its importance in providing the rationale for a user story [20], is often omitted in practice. We consider user stories that are formulated using the Connextra template, and we group related user stories into epics.

Just a few methods exist that derive conceptual models from user stories. Lucassen *et al.* [23] propose an automated approach, based on the Visual Narrator tool, for extracting structural conceptual models (i.e., class diagrams) from a set of user stories. Their work relies on and adapts natural language processing heuristics from the literature. The approach is able to achieve good precision and recall, also thanks to the syntactic constraints imposed by user stories, although perfect accuracy is not possible due to the large variety of linguistic patterns that natural language allows for. Furthermore, the Visual Narrator is limited to the identified lexicon and, unlike humans, is unable to perform the abstraction process that is a key issue in conceptual modeling [27].

Wautelet *et al.* [30] introduce a process for transforming a set of user stories into a holistic use case diagram, which integrates the user stories by using the granularity information obtained through tagging the user stories. Their work focuses on the joint use of two notations, one textual and one diagrammatic.

The same research group [32] proposed one of the few studies on the construction of diagrams from user stories. In particular, they investigate the construction of a goal-oriented model (a rationale tree) that links the who, what, and why dimensions of a user story. Their research shows differences depending on the modeler's background and other factors. While their work is highly related, we focus on a different task, which concerns the derivation of structural and functional conceptual models.

The extraction of conceptual models from natural language description requirements is one of the four types of NLP tools described by Berry *et al.* [3] and a long-standing research thread. We refer the reader to a recent literature review [35] for a comprehensive view; our focus is on humans' ability to derive models, rather than on automated techniques, without over-constraining the humans in the way they specify their requirements or by imposing computer-alike rules for the derivation process.

Very few attempts that test human's ability to extract conceptual models exist. España and colleagues [13] studied the derivation of UML class diagrams from either textual requirements or a requirements model; unlike them, we fix our notation and only study user stories. Some studies compare the effectiveness of automated tools with that of humans. Sagar *et al.* [28] propose a tool that outperforms novice human modelers in generating conceptual models from natural language requirements. This result is achieved thanks to the notational constraints that facilitate the tool; we do not set such constraints in this research.

3   Guidelines for Deriving Models from User Stories

In our earlier experiments on the derivation of conceptual models from requirements (both user stories and use cases) [10, 12], we gave limited guidance to the human partici-pants regarding the way conceptual models should be generated from user requirements. The obtained and compared results, therefore, could have been affected by different interpretations of the derivation task. In earlier work [10], we found out that following a systematic derivation process (self-defined by the subjects) results in higher-quality models. To better control the derivation process, in this work, we set off to define a set of guidelines, with the aim of investigating their effect on the derivation process.

First, we dealt with the issue of what should be the form of the guidelines. We started with a set of linguistic rules, so that one can apply the rules easily by just following them. Our initial aim was to identify effective rules that could later be embedded into an algorithm that could automate their application. This approach was inspired by previous research on the automated derivation of conceptual models, especially the work on the Visual Narrator [23], which employs and adapts NLP heuristics from the conceptual modeling literature in order to derive domain models from user stories. For example, a rule to identify a class diagram entity was "As a ROLE, I want to ACTION on NOUN", where the NOUN would define an entity.

However, after applying the guidelines to some datasets, we encountered several cases in which the rules could not be applied correctly, due to the linguistic variety of natural text. For example, the rule "As a ROLE, I want to ACTION on NOUN" is hard to apply to a user story such as "As a teacher, I want to have an overview of the grades": the verb "to have" does not really represent an action. One could introduce an increasing number of rules, but then the guidelines would become impractical. Furthermore, we realized that applying linguistic rules requires major cognitive efforts.

Therefore, we looked for an alternative way to present the guidelines that will cover many cases, offer flexibility, and require minimal cognitive efforts. We opted for an example-based learning approach [14], which requires less cognitive effort and increases learning outcomes in less time. Such an approach best fits domains in which the tasks are highly structured [14] (such as the task of model derivation), and some background knowledge is required for making learning-by-examples effective. This is also the case we are dealing with, as the guidelines are aimed at developers who are familiar with all artifacts. We built on the principles for designing examples [14], which include focused attention, redundancy avoidance, planning the sub goals, and including a high-level explanation. For more complex cases, for instance, we split the example to have focused rules, with minor repetitions, and with some explanations.

Table 1 presents a few examples of such guidelines, both for use case diagrams and for class diagrams. For example, the first example shows how the role of the user story becomes an actor in a use case diagram, but also that some entity in the rest of the user story can be an actor; here, "researcher". The entire set of guidelines, which consists of 9 examples for use case diagrams and 13 examples for class diagrams, can be found in the experiment forms in the online appendix [4].

Table 1. Some of our example-based guidelines for the derivation of use case diagrams and class diagrams from user stories. The complete guidelines are online [4].

Use Case Diagrams		
Example	*Outcome*	*Remarks*
As an administrator, I want to have researchers reset their own passwords, so that I don't have to send passwords in cleartext.	Actors: administrator, researcher	"researcher" is an actor, although not the role of the user story
As an assistant archivist, I want to upload and tag staff generated working papers, so that staff and researchers are able to easily access them.	UCs: (1) upload staff generated working papers; (2) tag staff generated working papers	Two desired actions in the I want part. The so that part does not lead to a use case, as it represents a non-functional property (easily access)
Class Diagrams		
Example	*Outcome*	*Remarks*
As an archivist, I want to apply a license or rights statement, so that I know what I can do with a file.	Class: License, Rights statement, File	There may be multiple classes in one user story, also in the so that part
As a researcher, I want to check whether a document has a citation information, so that I can cite accurately in a publication.	Class: Document, Citation Association: Document, Citation.	The "has" verb denotes the association

Note that, for class diagrams, we did not provide guidelines for fine-grained aspects such as multiplicity, association types, and navigation, because we are primarily interested in the derivation of high-level models rather than low-level data models.

4 Experiment Design

We investigate how user stories can be translated into conceptual models with and without providing guidelines. We refer to the manual/human derivation of two types of conceptual models: use case diagrams and class diagrams.

Hypotheses. To compare the differences among the two experimental conditions (i.e., with and without provided guidelines), we measure *validity* and *completeness* [13, 18] with respect to gold standard solutions. Furthermore, we collect and compare the perceptions of the subjects with respect to the guidelines (desired or missing).

Although working with guidelines is expected to be easier than using linguistic rules based, e.g., on part-of-speech tags (as per the Visual Narrator heuristics [23]), our example-based guidelines cannot cover all cases: they are incomplete and the analysts using them will have to decide how to adapt them to unseen cases. These observations lead us to the following hypotheses:

- Deriving a use case diagram from user stories with and without guidelines results in equal diagram completeness ($H_0^{UC\text{-}Completeness}$) and validity ($H_0^{UC\text{-}Validity}$)
- Deriving a class diagram from user stories with and without guidelines results in equal diagram completeness ($H_0^{CD\text{-}Completeness}$) and validity ($H_0^{CD\text{-}Validity}$)

Independent Variables. The first variable indicates whether the guidelines were provided (*IV1*). The second independent variable is the case used (*IV2*). It has two possible values: Data Hub (DH) and Planning Poker (PP). These cases are obtained from a publicly available dataset of user story requirements [9]. DH is the specification for the web interface of a platform for collecting, organizing, sharing, and finding data sets. PP are the requirements for the first version of the *planningpoker.com* website, an online platform for estimating user stories using the Planning Poker technique. Table 2 presents a few metrics that characterize the size of the cases.

Table 2. Metrics concerning the user stories and the models.

		Data hub	Planning Poker
User stories	Number of user stories	22	20
Class diagram	Number of entities	15	9
	Number of relationships	16	13
Use case diagram	Number of actors	3	2
	Number of use cases	24	20
	Number of use case relationships	24	22

Dependent Variables. There are two dependent variables, taken from conceptual modeling research [13, 18], that we use for measuring the quality of a generated conceptual model. These variables are specified by comparing the elements in the *subject solution* (the conceptual model derived by a subject) against the *gold standard solution*:

- *Validity (DV1)*: the ratio between the number of elements in the subject solution that are in the gold standard (true positives) and the true positives plus the number of elements in the subject's solution that do not exist within the gold standard solution (false positives). In information retrieval terms, validity equates to precision. Formally, $Validity = |TP|/(|TP| + |FP|)$.
- *Completeness (DV2)*: the ratio between the number of elements in the subject solution that also exist in the gold standard (true positives) and the number of elements in the gold standard (true positives + false negatives). In information retrieval terms, completeness is recall. Formally, $Completeness = |TP|/(|TP| + |FN|)$.

To measure completeness and validity, we use various ways of counting the elements of a model. For the *use case diagram*, we count the number of use cases and actors, and we ignore the number of relationships. For the *class diagram*, we first count only the number of classes. Next, we count the classes and the attributes. In all these metrics, we consider the importance of the appearance of each element equally to avoid bias: we did not favor a class or an attribute. Since relationships can only be identified when the connected entities are identified, we use an *adjusted* version of validity and completeness for the relationships [10], which calculates them with respect to those relationships in the gold standard among the entities that the subject has identified.

Subjects. In an optimal setting, we would have used experienced analysts, designers, and developers of information systems as subjects. However, this is a practically challenging task. Thus, we followed convenience sampling and we involved third-year undergraduate students taking a project workshop that follows a course on *Object-Oriented Analysis and Design* at Ben-Gurion University of the Negev. The course teaches how to analyze, design, and implement information systems based on the object-oriented paradigm. In the course, the students-subjects were taught about modeling techniques, including class and use case diagrams. The instructor of the course was the third author of this paper. The students learned user stories and use cases for specifying requirements as part of the development process. They also practiced class diagrams, use cases, and user stories through homework assignments, in which they achieved good results, indicating that they understood the concepts well. All subjects were taught the same material and the guidelines were not included as part of the course. Recruiting the subjects was done on a volunteering basis. Nevertheless, they were encouraged to participate in the experiment by providing them with additional bonus points to the course grade based on their performance. Before recruiting the subjects, the research design was submitted to and approved by the department's ethics committee.

Task. We designed the experiment so that each subject would experience the derivation of the two conceptual models following one case (either with or without provided guidelines). For that purpose, we designed four forms (available online [4]), in which we alternate the treatment and the case.

The form has three parts: (1) a pre-task questionnaire that checks the subjects' background and knowledge; (2) the task, in which subjects receive the user stories of one application (DH or PP), with or without the guidelines and were asked to derive the conceptual models - one class diagram and one use case diagram for the entire set; We asked the subjects to derive a use case diagram and a class diagram that would serve as the backbone of the system to be developed, as taught in the course. (3) questions about the subjects' perception regarding the task they performed.

To create the gold standard (in the online appendix), the second and third authors applied the guidelines and independently created four conceptual models: a class diagram and a use case diagram for either case. Then, these authors compared the models and produced the reconciled versions, involving the first author for a final check.

Execution. The experiment took place in a dedicated time slot and lasted approximately 1 hour, although we did not set a time limit for the subjects. The assignment of the groups (i.e., the forms) to subjects was done randomly. The distribution of groups was as follows: (i) DH, guided: 19 students; (ii) DH, not-guided: 18 students; (iii) PP, guided: 21 students; and (iv) PP, not-guided: 19 students. Note that the students that were provided with the guidelines have seen them for the first time in the experiment.

Analysis. The paper forms delivered by the students were checked against the gold standard by one researcher who was unaware of the purpose of the experiment, so to avoid confirmation bias. When checking the forms we were flexible regarding the alignment with the gold standard. In essence, the gold standard served as a proxy for the examination. For example, we allowed for synonyms and related concepts. This led to the spreadsheet in our online appendix; there, each row denotes one subject, while each column indicate elements in the gold standard; we also count how many additional elements were identified by the subjects. The statistical analysis was conducted mostly using Python, while the effect size was calculated using an online service at https://www.socscistatistics.com/effectsize/default3.aspx.

5   Experiment Results

We present the results by comparing the groups through their responses in the background questionnaire in Sect. 5.1. We statistically analyze the validity and completeness of the models in Sect. 5.2, then present the students' opinion in Sect. 5.3. Finally, in Sect. 5.4, we provide additional qualitative insights by reviewing in depth the results.

5.1   Background Questionnaire

We run a series of analyses over the results (all materials are available online [4]). In order to determine whether the groups are balanced, we compare their background. Table 3 compares the groups according to four criteria. For each criterion, it presents the arithmetic mean ($\bar{x}$), the standard deviation (σ), the number of participants (N) that responded to the pre-questionnaire, and whether the groups are significantly different. We adopt this structure also for all the following tables. In some rows, the number of participants differs from what was listed earlier because some participants did not complete all the tasks in the experiment. With respect to the background questionnaire, all the responses were self-reported. Familiarity questions were ranked using a 5-point Likert-type scale (1 indicates low familiarity and 5 indicates high familiarity), while the (up to date) GPA is on a scale from 0 to 100. For the familiarity criteria, since they deviate from the normal distribution (following Kolmogorov-Smirnov test), we perform the Mann-Whitney test while for the GPA we perform the T-Test.

Table 3. Pre-questionnaire results: mean, standard deviation, significance.

| | PP | | | | | | DH | | | | | |
| | GUIDED | | | !GUIDED | | Sig. | GUIDED | | | !GUIDED | | Sig. |
	$\bar{x}$	σ	N	$\bar{x}$	σ	N	$\bar{x}$	σ	N	$\bar{x}$	σ	N
CD Familiarity	2.15	0.67	21	2.26	0.65	19	0.926	2.44	0.62	18	2.17	0.62	18	0.177
UCD familiarity	2.75	0.72	21	3.00	0.67	19	0.203	2.89	0.76	18	3.06	0.94	18	0.530
US familiarity	2.80	0.52	21	2.53	0.77	19	0.144	2.74	0.73	19	2.33	0.69	18	0.100
GPA	82.30	5.05	21	82.63	3.98	19	0.759	83.00	4.88	19	80.00	3.74	16	0.052

The results of the statistical tests evidence that the random assignment of the subjects to the four groups, as explained in Sect. 4, does not yield any statistically significant difference that may influence the validity of the results.

5.2   Completeness and Validity of the Derived Models

We analyze the completeness and validity of the conceptual models derived by the students. To do so, we perform the analysis for each case separately due to the different complexity of the domains and of the conceptual models. Table 4 and Table 5 present the results of the DH and PP cases, respectively. For each group, we report the mean, the standard deviation, and the number of responses for the related metric. Bold numbers indicate the best results for a given metric. We also report statistical significance (applying T-Test) and denote statistically significant results (with $p < 0.05$) via gray rows. Finally, we report effect size using Hedges' g. For the qualitative interpretation, we refer to Cohen [7]: small effect when $g > 0.2$, medium effect when $g > 0.5$, large effect when $g > 0.8$.

Table 4. Data hub results.

	GUIDED			!GUIDED			sig.	Effect size (Hedges' g)
	$\bar{x}$	σ	N	$\bar{x}$	σ	N		
UC Completeness	**0.76**	**0.14**	**19**	0.58	0.14	16	p<0.001	1.296
UC Validity	**0.89**	**0.08**	**19**	0.87	0.09	16	0.473	0.250
CD Class Completeness	**0.37**	**0.12**	**18**	0.36	0.09	18	0.917	0.038
CD Class Validity	**0.67**	**0.18**	**18**	0.62	0.19	18	0.454	0.253
CD Class+Att Completeness	**0.31**	**0.16**	**18**	0.29	0.09	18	0.698	0.131
CD Class+Att Validity	**0.58**	**0.18**	**18**	0.44	0.15	18	0.012	0.880
CD Class+Att+relationships Completeness	**0.36**	**0.13**	**18**	0.33	0.10	18	0.425	0.272
CD Class+Att+relationships Validity	**0.50**	**0.12**	**18**	0.37	0.12	18	0.002	1.083

Table 5. Planning poker results.

	GUIDED			!GUIDED			sig.	Effect size (Hedges' g)
	$\bar{x}$	σ	N	$\bar{x}$	σ	N		
UC Completeness	**0.64**	**0.21**	**21**	0.53	0.23	18	0.132	0.494
UC Validity	0.84	0.12	21	**0.87**	**0.14**	18	0.524	0.208
CD Class Completeness	0.53	0.15	20	**0.57**	**0.19**	19	0.480	0.226
CD Class Validity	**0.78**	**0.14**	**20**	0.74	0.11	19	0.279	0.357
CD Class+Att Completeness	0.49	0.13	20	**0.51**	**0.19**	19	0.622	0.161
CD Class+Att Validity	**0.60**	**0.12**	**20**	0.53	0.12	19	0.073	0.585
CD Class+Att+relationships Completeness	0.57	0.13	20	**0.59**	**0.18**	19	0.695	0.129
CD Class+Att+relationships Validity	**0.59**	**0.12**	**20**	0.56	0.10	19	0.435	0.251

For the DH case (Table 4), the conceptual models derived by the subjects who had the guidelines outperformed those derived by those subjects who did not have the guidelines, for all metrics. The difference was statistically significant in the case of UC completeness and in the cases of class diagrams validity including also attributes and relationships. Furthermore, the effect sizes for DH statistically significant differences indicate *a large effect* [7].

For the PP case (Table 5), the results are mixed and statistical significance is never achieved. Therefore, we cannot reject $H_0^{UC\text{-}Completeness}$ nor $H_0^{CD\text{-}Validity}$. While the guided subjects outperformed the non-guided ones for UC completeness, the non-guided ones had higher validity for the use case diagrams. The opposite situation occurs for class diagrams: completeness is higher for the non-guided ones, validity is higher for the guided subjects.

Based on the results, we can conclude that for the Data Hub case we can reject $H_0^{UC\text{-}Completeness}$ and $H_0^{CD\text{-}Validity}$ hypotheses on the equality of having guidelines or not for deriving conceptual modes for the metrics defined above (the grey rows in Table 4). In that case, introducing the guidelines resulted in better conceptual models. For the other metrics, we accept the H_0 hypotheses and can infer that no difference exists when providing the guidelines or not for deriving conceptual models.

5.3 Subjects' Opinion

Table 6 presents the participants' opinions on the performed task, which we collected via a post-questionnaire. The participants were asked to use a 5-Likert scale to rank their agreement with the various statements. With respect to deriving the conceptual model elements, no statistically significant differences were found (applying T-Test) between the guided and the non-guided groups in most cases. For PP, which has simpler models, the provided guidelines did not contribute and even blurred the process. In the case of DH, with a more complex model, the guidelines are perceived as supportive, to some

Table 6. Post-questionnaire results: mean, standard deviation, significance. We use the following abbreviations: Der. for Deriving, Guid. for Guidelines

	PP							DH						
	GUIDED			!GUIDED			Sig.	GUIDED			!GUIDED			Sig.
	$\bar{x}$	σ	N	$\bar{x}$	σ	N		$\bar{x}$	σ	N	$\bar{x}$	σ	N	
Der. UC is easy	2.95	0.76	20	3.00	0.77	18	0.851	2.95	1.03	19	2.94	0.87	18	0.987
Der. actors is easy	1.65	0.93	20	1.72	0.67	18	0.429	1.68	0.67	19	1.89	0.96	18	0.678
Der. classes is easy	2.26	0.65	19	2.72	0.57	18	0.021	3.11	0.57	19	2.78	0.65	18	0.131
Der. class att. is easy	2.75	0.79	20	3.00	0.91	18	0.334	3.47	0.84	19	3.39	0.92	18	0.923
Der. relationships is easy	3.40	0.94	20	3.11	0.68	18	0.381	3.44	0.86	18	3.17	0.99	18	0.390
Guid. for UC are required				1.83	0.62	18					2.72	1.02	18	
Guid. for actors are required				2.83	1.15	18					3.17	1.34	18	
Guid. for classes are required				2.94	1.00	18					2.71	0.85	17	
Guid. for class att. are required				2.89	1.08	18					2.56	1.20	18	
Guid. for relationships are required				2.00	0.69	18					2.33	0.97	18	
Guid.for UC were useful	2.00	0.92	20					2.32	0.95	19				
Guid. for actors were useful	2.75	1.12	20					2.00	0.82	19				
Guid. for classes were useful	2.65	0.81	20					2.58	1.02	19				
Guid. for class att.were useful	2.40	1.14	20					3.00	1.05	19				
Guid. for relationships were useful	2.40	1.19	20					3.16	1.07	19				

extent, for the derivation process. As for the usefulness of the guidelines (lines 11–15 in the table), the subjects indicate limited satisfaction (ranging from 2–3.16 out of 5) and the subjects who did not get the guidelines (lines 6-10 in the table) thought that these are of limited importance (ranging from 1.83–3.17 out of 5)

5.4   Qualitative Insights

We provide qualitative observations by drilling down into the derived conceptual models and by analyzing the alignment of the individual elements (each use case, class, relationship, attribute) with the gold standard solution. To do so, we used the spreadsheet in our online appendix that reports on the alignment of individual elements.

Data Hub. For this first case, with respect to the system functionality via the use case diagram, we observe the following:

1. As expected, all subjects were able to identify all actors in both groups.
2. It seems that the subjects who received the guidelines were able to better identify the use cases. This might be because the guidelines demonstrate the derivation of use cases from the *so that* part. See, e.g., user story E2.5: "so that I can validate the data I am about to publish". Another contribution of the guidelines is that it explicates the important role of the *I want* part. This allows to systematically analyze the user stories without judging their perceived importance; for example, see E3.1: "see real examples of published packages" where the average completeness of the group provided with the guidelines was 0.632 whereas for the other group it was 0.125 or E3.4: "download the data package in one file" the average completeness of the group provided with the guidelines was 1 and for the other group it was 0.75.

With respect to the system structure via the class diagram:

1. The classes Site, Pricing plan, Account, Consumer, Data Package, and Publisher were identified by both groups to a medium-to-large extent (44%–94%). These are core classes in the domain, which are easy to identify even without guidelines.
2. The classes Site Deployment, Key Metric, Billing System, and Configuration Parameter were identified to a limited extent both by the subjects who received the guidelines and those who did not (0–22.2%). Our conjecture is that the subjects considered them to be technical issues; also, they appear only in epic 4.
3. The classes Data, Tag, Single download file, Example, and Published Data Package were also identified to a limited extent by both groups (0–28%). Here again, it seems that the subjects found those classes of limited importance to the domain.
4. With respect to the identification of attributes, completeness was limited in both groups. This is probably due to the fact that the subjects consider those of limited importance, focusing on giving a higher-level overview of the domain.
5. With respect to relationships, it seems that the students who received the guidelines were able to better identify the relationships between the classes when referring to the classes that were identified. This might be attributed to the provided guidelines.

Planning Poker. For the PP case, with respect to the use case diagram:

1. All the actors were identified by all subjects in both groups.
2. Use cases were identified to a satisfactory level. The subjects using the guidelines better identified use cases that appear in the *so that* part. For example, this happened for the user stories, and corresponding use cases, regarding starting the game. Another difference between the groups concerns the user stories that refer to presenting information, e.g., "show all estimates"(the completeness of the group that was provided with the guidelines was 0.571 and for the other group it was 0.157) or "accept the average of all estimates" (the completeness of the group that was provided with the guidelines was 0.619 and for the other group it was 0.389).

With respect to the system structure via the class diagram:

1. The subjects in both groups were able to identify important classes such as Game, Estimator, and Item.
2. For some reason, the class Round was not always identified ($\sim$80%), although it appears five times in the user stories.
3. The Policy class (referring to the estimation policy) and its sub-classes defining specific policies were identified to a very limited extent, probably as they were not explicated in the user stories and appeared only once.
4. The class Estimate was less frequently identified by the subjects that received the guidelines. This may have happened since, although a concept, the user stories were often referring to this notion using the verb *to estimate*, rather than a noun.
5. Attributes were derived to a certain extent, but only limited.
6. Relationships were identified to a satisfactory level. No significant differences can be observed between the two groups.

6 Discussion

The results indicate that the guidelines support the derivation process only to some extent. It seems that, as the complexity of the derived models increases (because of their size, or because of specificity of the domain), the guidelines further improve the validity and completeness of the models.

> **Finding 1**
> *The guidelines seem to lead to increased validity and completeness for more complex domains, while they do not seem effective for more straightforward domains.*

As partially highlighted in Table 2, the DH models were more complex than those of the PP case. For DH, the complexity emerges due to various factors: the number of entities, the number of relationships, the introduction of an external system (for billing) with which the system under design interacts, the multiple interactions among the roles/actors, and the existence of several related roles/actors with similar names. In the DH case, in all metrics, the subjects who got the guidelines achieved better results than those who did not get the guidelines. Although only some of the results are of statistical significance, the trend is clear. In the PP case, those who received the guidelines delivered better models, but the difference was of lower magnitude. These results are in line with our previous experiments [10], in which we found complexity to be a more significant factor than the notation used as a starting point for the derivation of a conceptual model. Also, our previous research [10] pointed out how the students who followed a systematic derivation process obtained better results; here, we fostered (but could not enforce) the adoption of such a process by providing guidelines.

Finding 2

Despite leading to better results in more complex settings, the guidelines are not perceived as useful by the subjects.

The derivation of a conceptual model requires mental effort. While the guidelines create awareness about the expected output, the participants may see the guidelines as a constraining mechanism that limits their ability to analyze the requirements, to identify the relevant concepts, and to assemble those concepts into a model. In addition, the subjects were introduced to the guidelines for the first time during the experiment. They could have ignored some of these while focusing on the actual task based on their own skills. Nevertheless, the example-based guidelines shed light on parts of the user stories that might be neglected by just reading them. For example, the guidelines point to several possibilities: a role can appear in the $\langle action \rangle$ part, multiple functions may be present in the $\langle action \rangle$ part, a function can emerge from the $\langle so\ that \rangle$ part, consider a generalization of several user stories, multiple entities may exist in one user story, etc.

Finding 3

The inclusion of a type of concept/element in a conceptual model does not depend only on the guidelines, but also on its perceived importance for the model.

Our guidelines included references to all major concepts: use cases, actors, and associations for the use case diagram, and classes, attributes, and relationships for the class diagram. However, *attributes* were included only to a limited extent both in the PP and in the DH cases, with or without guidelines. Since the subjects were already filtering the concepts based on the perceived importance, they have probably ranked the attributes as less important than the classes, and, therefore, they could be excluded. The inclusion or exclusion of attributes depends on the task at hand: if we had specified that the class diagram would be used as a blueprint for detailed design (e.g., data structures or a database schema), perhaps they would have paid attention to attributes too. Alternatively, we could have used specific guidelines which could convey the importance of certain concept types, rather than leaving the choice to the subject's perception.

7 Threats to Validity

Our results need to be considered in view of threats to validity. We follow Wohlin *et al.*'s classification [33]: construct, internal, conclusion, and external validity.

Construct validity concerns the relationships between theory and observation and these threats are mainly due to the method used to assess the outcomes of the tasks. We examined if the use of guidelines improves conceptual model derivation. The domains selection may affect the results; our choice is justified by our attempt to provide domains that would be easy to understand. Also, in the experiment, we adopt a fixed set of guidelines. Other sets of guidelines may lead to different results. The subjects have seen the guidelines for the first time during the experiment. Thus, it might be that they were able to absorb the guidelines only to a limited extent, and the positive effect that we identified in the experiment could be larger if the guidelines were learned beforehand. Finally, for practical reasons, we purposefully selected a small set of user stories to be analyzed by the subjects: this may not be representative of real-world tasks. Yet, earlier research has shown that generating conceptual models from many user stories may just transfer the cognitive complexity from text to models [22]. Thus, the manual derivation of such models is better suited for relatively small, cohesive collections of requirements.

Internal validity threats, which concern external factors that might affect the dependent variables, may be due to individual factors, such as familiarity with the domain, the degree of commitment by the subjects, and the training level the subjects underwent. These effects are mitigated by our experiment design. It is unlikely that the subjects were already familiar with the two chosen domains (although they were familiar with the notion of agile development, they were not taught the planning poker procedure). The random assignment that was adopted should eliminate various kinds of external factors. Although the experiment was done on a voluntary basis, the subjects were told that they would earn bonus points based on their performance, and thus we increased the motivation and commitment of the subjects, which could have led them to increase the time on task. Eventually, all subjects received the entire bonus points based on their participation (this was approved by the ethics committee).

Conclusion validity concerns the relationship between the treatment (the notation) and the outcome. We followed the various assumptions of the statistical tests (such as normal distribution of the data and data independence) when analyzing the results. In addition, we used a predefined solution, which was established before the experiment, for grading the subjects' answers; thus, only limited human judgment was required. In addition, as we allow flexibility with respect to the gold standard, it might be that further subjectivity was involved. Another matter the requires attention is that an alternative gold standard could be presented. To mitigate that threat, we discussed the used gold standard among the research team.

External validity concerns the generalizability of the results. The main threats are the choice of subjects and the use of simple experimental tasks. The subjects were undergraduate students with little experience in software engineering, in general, and in modeling in particular. Kitchenham *et al.* argue that using students as subjects instead of software engineers is not a major issue as long as the research questions are not specifically focused on experts [17]. Our main research question studies a task (the derivation of conceptual models) that is part of the educational path of students, and we, therefore, consider the students as an appropriate proxy. Nevertheless, experiments with experienced developers should be conducted to test our assumption. In addition, the presentation of the guidelines may have affected the results (for example, presenting the guidelines as a list and not as a table, maybe also with different examples). Generalization should be taken with care, as our cases are small and might differ from specifications in industry settings.

8 Summary

We provided initial evidence on the effect of providing guidelines for deriving conceptual models from (user story) requirements. This is an important task in information systems development, and we expect the task's importance to grow with the increasing interest in low-code development platforms that embrace the model-driven development of information systems.

We conducted a controlled experiment with 77 undergraduate students as part of a third-year course. The results indicate that the provision of example-based guidelines may increase validity and completeness in the case of non-trivial specifications, although the subjects were rather neutral on the perceived usefulness of the guidelines.

This work calls for further experimentation that analyzes the effect of domain complexity, involves experienced developers, considers other forms of guidelines (such as explicit rules, other examples), and offers comprehensive training before conducting the experiment. It would be important to investigate the use of refined user stories (e.g., via acceptance criteria) as a basis for the derivation process. Moreover, interactive approaches that combine the automated derivation of a model with human refinement should be considered (for example, see Saini *et al.* [29]). Finally, our research so far has relied on an assessment of a model against a gold standard; future research could consider alternative evaluation methods that measure the *quality-in-use* of the generated conceptual models.

References

1. Arora, C., Sabetzadeh, M., Nejati, S., Briand, L.: An Active learning approach for improving the accuracy of automated domain model extraction. ACM Trans. Softw. Eng. Methodol. **28**(1), 1–24 (2019)
2. Berends, J., Dalpiaz, F.: Refining user stories via example mapping: an empirical investigation. In: Proceedings of RE, Industrial Innovation Track (2021)
3. Berry, D., Gacitua, R., Sawyer, P., Tjong, S.: The case for dumb requirements engineering tools. In: Proceedings of REFSQ, pp. 211–217 (2012)
4. Bragilovski, M., Dalpiaz, F., Sturm, A.: Guided derivation of conceptual models from user stories. Online Appendix (2021). https://doi.org/10.5281/zenodo.5905846
5. Brambilla, M., Cabot, J., Wimmer, M.: Model-Driven Software Engineering in Practice, 2 edn. Morgan & Claypool Publishers, San Rafael (2017)
6. Cockburn, A.: Writing Effective Use Cases. Addison-Wesley Professional, Boston (2000)
7. Cohen, J.: Statist. Power Anal. Current directions in psychological science **1**(3), 98–101 (1992)
8. Cohn, M.: User Stories Applied: for Agile Software Development. Addison Wesley, Boston (2004)
9. Dalpiaz, F.: Requirements Data Sets (User Stories) (2018), Mendeley Data, v1. https://doi.org/10.17632/7zbk8zsd8y.1

10. Dalpiaz, F., Gieske, P., Sturm, A.: On deriving conceptual models from user requirements: an empirical study. Inf. Softw. Technol. **131**, 106484 (2021)
11. Dalpiaz, F., van der Schalk, I., Brinkkemper, S., Aydemir, F.B., Lucassen, G.: Detecting Terminological Ambiguity in User Stories: Tool and Experimentation. Inform, Software Tech (2019)
12. Dalpiaz, F., Sturm, A.: Conceptualizing requirements using user stories and use cases: a controlled experiment. In: Proceedings of REFSQ, pp. 221–238 (2020)
13. España, S., Ruiz, M., González, A.: Systematic derivation of conceptual models from requirements models: a controlled experiment. In: Proceedings of RCIS, pp. 1–12. IEEE (2012)
14. van Gog, T., Rummel, N.: Example-based learning: integrating cognitive and social-cognitive research perspectives. Educ. Psychol. Rev. **22**(2), 155–174 (2010)
15. Insfran, E., Pastor, O., Wieringa, R.: Requirements Engineering-based conceptual modelling. Req. Eng. **7**(2), 61–72 (2002)
16. Kassab, M.: An empirical study on the requirements engineering practices for agile software development. In: Proceedings of EUROMICRO SEAA, pp. 254–261 (2014)
17. Kitchenham, B.A., et al.: Preliminary guidelines for empirical research in software engineering. IEEE Trans. Softw. Eng. **28**(8), 721–734 (2002)
18. Lindland, O.I., Sindre, G., Solvberg, A.: Understanding quality in conceptual modeling. IEEE Softw. **11**(2), 42–49 (1994)
19. Loniewski, G., Insfran, E., Abrahão, S.: A Systematic Review of the Use of *Requirements Engineering Techniques in Model-driven Development*. In: Proceedings of MODELS, pp. 213–227 (2010)
20. Lucassen, G., Dalpiaz, F., van der Werf, J., Brinkkemper, S.: Improving agile requirements: the quality user story framework and Tool. Requir. Eng. **21**(3), 383–403 (2016)
21. Lucassen, G., Dalpiaz, F., Werf, J.M.E.M., Brinkkemper, S.: The use and effectiveness of user stories in practice. In: Daneva, M., Pastor, O. (eds.) REFSQ 2016. LNCS, vol. 9619, pp. 205–222. Springer, Cham (2016). https://doi.org/10.1007/978-3-319-30282-9_14
22. Lucassen, G., Dalpiaz, F., van der Werf, J.M.E.M., Brinkkemper, S.: Visualizing User story requirements at multiple granularity levels via semantic relatedness. In: Comyn-Wattiau, I., Tanaka, K., Song, I.-Y., Yamamoto, S., Saeki, M. (eds.) ER 2016. LNCS, vol. 9974, pp. 463–478. Springer, Cham (2016). https://doi.org/10.1007/978-3-319-46397-1_35
23. Lucassen, G., Robeer, M., Dalpiaz, F., van der Werf, J.M.E., Brinkkemper, S.: Extracting conceptual models from user stories with visual narrator. Requir. Eng. **22**(3), 339–358 (2017)
24. Mai, P.X., Goknil, A., Shar, L.K., Pastore, F., Briand, L.C., Shaame, S.: Modeling security and privacy requirements: a Use case-driven approach. Inform. Softw. Tech. **100**, 165–182 (2018)
25. Maiden, N.A.M., Jones, S.V., Manning, S., Greenwood, J., Renou, L.: Model-driven requirements engineering: synchronising models in an air traffic management case study. In: Proceedings of CAiSE, pp. 368–383 (2004)
26. Müter, L., Deoskar, T., Mathijssen, M., Brinkkemper, S., Dalpiaz, F.: Refinement of user stories into backlog items: linguistic structure and action verbs. In: Proceedings of REFSQ, pp. 109–116 (2019)
27. Parsons, J., Wand, Y.: Choosing classes in conceptual modeling. Commun. ACM **40**(6), 63–69 (1997)
28. Sagar, V.B.R.V., Abirami, S.: Conceptual modeling of natural language functional requirements. J. Syst. Softw. **88**, 25–41 (2014)
29. Saini, R., Mussbacher, G., Guo, J.L., Kienzle, J.: Automated traceability for domain modelling decisions empowered by artificial intelligence. In: Proceedings of RE, pp. 173–184. IEEE (2021)

30. Wautelet, Y., Heng, S., Hintea, D., Kolp, M., Poelmans, S.: Bridging user story sets with the use case model. In: Link, S., Trujillo, J.C. (eds.) ER 2016. LNCS, vol. 9975, pp. 127–138. Springer, Cham (2016). https://doi.org/10.1007/978-3-319-47717-6_11

31. Wautelet, Y., Heng, S., Kolp, M., Mirbel, I.: Unifying and extending user story models. In: Proceedings of CAiSE, pp. 211–225 (2014)

32. Wautelet, Y., Velghe, M., Heng, S., Poelmans, S., Kolp, M.: On modelers ability to build a visual diagram from a user story set: A goal-oriented approach. In: Proceedings of REFSQ, pp. 209–226 (2018)

33. Wohlin, C., Runeson, P., Höst, M., Ohlsson, M.C., Regnell, B., Wesslén, A.: Experimentation in Software Engineering. Springer, Berlin (2012). https://doi.org/10.1007/978-3-642-29044-2

34. Yue, T., Briand, L.C., Labiche, Y.: A systematic review of transformation approaches between user requirements and analysis models. Requir. Eng. 16(2), 75–99 (2011)

35. Zhao, L., Alhoshan, W., Ferrari, A., Letsholo, K.J., Ajagbe, M.A., Chioasca, E.V., Batista-Navarro, R.T.: Natural language processing for requirements engineering: a systematic mapping study. ACM Comput. Surv. (CSUR) 54(3), 1–41 (2021)

From User Stories to Data Flow Diagrams for Privacy Awareness: A Research Preview

Guntur Budi Herwanto[1,2]([✉]), Gerald Quirchmayr[1], and A. Min Tjoa[1,3]

[1] Faculty of Computer Science, University of Vienna, Vienna, Austria
gerald.quirchmayr@univie.ac.at
[2] Universitas Gadjah Mada, Yogyakarta, Indonesia
gunturbudi@ugm.ac.id
[3] Vienna University of Technology, Vienna, Austria
a.tjoa@tuwien.ac.at

Abstract. [**Context and otivation**] The well-established Data Flow Diagrams (DFDs) have proven their value in the field of security and privacy for the realization of processes in models. However, the time and resources required to model the system with DFD, could slow down security and privacy threat analysis. [**Question/problem**] Despite the fact that information required for drawing DFD is available in the textual requirement such as user stories, the current approach to modeling the system using DFD is still done by form/questionnaires or manually drawing the diagram. [**Principal ideas/results**] This study proposes a natural language processing (NLP) model that generates DFD automatically from well-formed user stories. We also detect the presence of personal data in user stories by employing Named Entity Recognition, which allows the personal data to be highlighted in DFD. Our preliminary results show that our model can automatically generate a DFD that highlights the presence of personal data. Finally, the DFD could be expanded to a Privacy-Aware DFD, which incorporates privacy checks into the DFD. [**Contribution**] This is the first attempt at automatically transforming user stories into DFD using an NLP approach. The automatic approach may alleviate the burden placed on privacy analysts during the initial stages of threat modeling or eliciting privacy requirements.

Keywords: Data flow diagram · User stories · Natural language processing · Privacy threat modeling

1 Introduction

Data Flow Diagrams (DFD) are used to visualize the system's process model and data flow. DFD is simple yet expressive enough to be used as a modeling system in the context of security and privacy threat analysis. Identifying threats is an essential step in determining the impact of the system under development.

© Springer Nature Switzerland AG 2022
V. Gervasi and A. Vogelsang (Eds.): REFSQ 2022, LNCS 13216, pp. 148–155, 2022.
https://doi.org/10.1007/978-3-030-98464-9_12

Threat modeling, such as LINDDUN, aims to provide a framework to assist in meeting privacy requirements [14]. The first step of LINDDUN is to model the system with DFD. Risk areas or hotspots can then be identified by examining the DFD elements. Modeling the system, on the other hand, imposes a significant burden on the use of threat modeling [14]. When it comes to threat modeling, DFD is still a popular choice for agile teams [4]. Some agile teams spent more than ten hours designing the DFD, which they believed had a negative effect on productivity [4].

The user's requirements serve as the foundation for modeling the DFD. In ASD, user stories are the primary method of capturing user requirements. User story usually divided into three-part. Lucassen et al. [12], refer to the first part of a user story as the *role*, the second part as the *means*, and the third part as the *end*. For example, "As a parent (*role*), I want to be able to message my child's counselors (*means*), so that I can voice my concerns or check on my child's progress (*end*)". According to recent research, the main limitation for integrating privacy in agile teams is identifying privacy criteria in user stories [5].

Based on the situation we described above, we propose a model that automatically transforms user stories into DFD. We use natural language processing (NLP) to extract privacy-related entities and their relationships. To the best of our knowledge, our work is the first attempt at using NLP to transform user stories into DFD automatically.

2   Related Work

Significant research has been carried out to transform user stories into visual representations. Robeer et al. [13] transform user stories to conceptual diagrams that emphasize the relation between concepts. Elallaoui et al. [7], and Kochpati et al. [11] developed a model that automatically converts user stories to UML use case diagrams. The first three research efforts mentioned above use Part of Speech (POS) and heuristics to determine the actors and their relationship. Gilson et al. [8] built a model to transform user stories to robustness diagrams. Gilson et al. [8] add a dependency tree parser in conjunction with rule-based transformation to accurately predict both the elements and relationships. All of the works mentioned above are aimed at general requirements and are not concerned with representing privacy issues.

Several studies have looked into the use of DFD to represent privacy issues. Antignac et al. [3] expand the standard notation of DFD into PA-DFD, which includes the privacy awareness notation. Alshareef [1] provide the tools to automatically transform the standard DFD (Business-oriented DFD) into the Privacy-Aware Data Flow Diagram (PA-DFD). However, the focus of the aforementioned work is not on generating the DFD from textual requirements.

Our contribution aims to bridge the gap between the textual requirement and PA-DFD. To achieve this, we reuse the work from Gilson et al. [8] to obtain the elements and relationships necessary to construct our DFD. We also make our DFD compatible with the PA-DFD from Alshareef [1].

3   The Proposed Approach

As our goal is to generate a privacy-aware DFD, we can filter out user stories that do not contain privacy entities. This is achieved by applying Privacy Named Entity Recognition (NER) model [10] that is able to identify the privacy-related entities, which are: (1) data subject, (2) processing, and (3) personal data. We used the best model that is available on the repository[1] The NER model was trained on a batch of human-labeled user stories data following annotation criteria in [10].

Then we generate unified elements and relationships based on the work by Gilson [8]. We exclude the user story that does not contain one of those entities. In addition, we discuss how to incorporate the *end* part of the user story (reason/value part) into the generated elements. Finally, we will go over the process of diagram creation in Sect. 3.2. Our work is compatible with Alshareef's [1] work, which adds privacy checks to the DFD in the so-called PA-DFD. The implementation of the model, as well as our preliminary result, is available on our repository[2] Figure 1 depicts the overall DFD generation process.

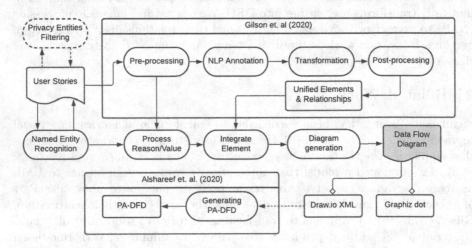

Fig. 1. The workflow of our model to transform user stories into a Data Flow Diagram

3.1   Generating Elements and Relationships from User Stories

To obtain the essential element and relationship from the user stories, we refer to the work from Gilson et al. [8]. The model from Gilson et al. originally intended to generate use case scenarios from user stories. These use case scenarios are depicted in the robustness diagram (RD). The objects in the RD are classified as *actor, boundary, control, entity,* and *property.* This preliminary work is critical

---

[1] https://doi.org/10.5281/zenodo.5801370.

[2] https://doi.org/10.5281/zenodo.5801351.

for understanding the entity dependency used in our DFD. However, Gilson's work [8] omits the *end* part of the user story. According to our observations, the *end* part of our user story data set may contain valuable privacy entities such as personal data and processing that should be considered during threat modeling analysis. When our NER model identifies the existence of verbs or *processing* entity in the *end* part of a user story, it is highly likely to be included as a functional requirement. Thus, we build a rule-based transformation for the *end* part of the user story. We will include it in our DFD whenever the *end* part starts with verbs and targets personal data. Our model will then integrate these results with the element and relationship produced by Gilson's [8] approach.

3.2   Generating Data Flow Diagrams

Given the similarities between the elements of the RD and the DFD, we provide a simple mapping that can be used to map the entities and relationships from the RD to the DFD. Figure 2 illustrates the mapping.

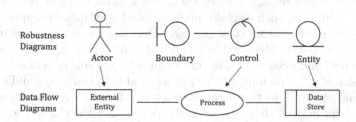

Fig. 2. Element mapping between Robustness Diagram and Data Flow Diagrams

To map the relation between *external entity* to *process* in DFD, we use *boundary* from RD, which bridge *actor* and *control*. The relationship between *control-to-control* and *control-to-entity* is directly mapped into DFD. However, due to the restriction of the rule in DFD, the relation between *entity-to-entity* in RD cannot be directly mapped. To resolve this, we use string matching to locate the *control* that refers to the *entity* which then can be mapped as *process-to-data_store* relation in DFD. Lastly, because our entity contains NER prediction about personal data, we perform simple string matching from the NER prediction with the data store element to highlight its presence in our DFD. Emphasizing can be accomplished in various ways, such as by introducing a new element, as in Antignac [3]. We chose to simply change the color of a data store element to red.

The DFD is generated graphically using Graphiz and in editable XML format. The XML format is compatible with the diagramming software *draw.io*. By enabling the DFD generation in *draw.io* format, our output can be extended to the Privacy-Aware Data Flow Diagram (PA-DFD), which adds privacy checks [1] directly into the DFD.

4   Case Study

We evaluate our model to a set of user stories that we consider privacy-sensitive [10]. In this preliminary evaluation, we chose the camperplus project. Camper-Plus is an Application developed for camp directors and parents who manage camps and monitor their children. The original data of the user stories can be obtained from Dalpiaz [6].

Firstly, we run the NER model to determine the privacy entities in the user stories. Then, we can eliminate the user stories with no privacy entities. Since the Camperplus is a privacy-sensitive project, our NER model able to identify privacy entities in each user story. Based on the ground truth of our previous research [10], these entities can be considered False Positives (FP). In terms of privacy detection, FP is preferable to False Negative (FN) to prevent missing out on the important entities. At the later stage of our approach, the analyst can rule out this FP. For example, in Fig. 3, if analysts consider "Camp" is not personal data, they can change back the color to black.

The NER process can also be used to group the DFD generation based on data subjects. After lemmatization, there are a total of eight data subjects. Several data subjects, such as child, manager, and staff member, appear in the *means* of user stories rather than the *role*. Here are two user stories involving data subjects who were identified as a child: (1) "As a parent, I want to be able to message my child's counselors, so that I can voice my concerns or check on my child's progress". (2) "As a parent, I want to be able to track my child's activity and schedule at camp, so that I can have peace of mind". As can be seen, the primary *role* in both of those stories is the parent, not the child. The grouping of data subjects enables the analyst to conduct a threat analysis posed by each data subject, not just by the primary actor.

The grouped user stories are fed into Gilson's module [8], to be transformed into RD. Then, the RD will be transformed into DFD by the mapping explained in Sect. 3.2. At the same time, we process the *end* part (reason/value) of user stories based on our rule-based algorithm described in Sect. 3.1. Then we integrate both of the elements to be generated in one final DFD.

Figure 3 depicts the DFD generated by our model. The red color of the data store indicates it will likely store personal data. As a result, further threat analysis should be conducted on those data stores. The DFD also demonstrates the model's ability to include and exclude the *end* part of user stories. The *end* part of the first user story is likely to become a functional requirement, whereas the *end* part of the second user story only contains human values of the main functional requirement, which are not suitable with DFD.

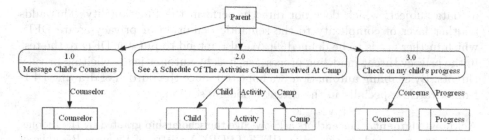

Fig. 3. Data flow diagram that involves *child* as data subject

5   Preliminary Evaluation

To validate our generated DFD, we manually assess the syntactic correctness based on the rules described in [2]. Additionally, we assess whether the labeling inside the element is semantically correct. The semantically correct is an assessment of whether the entity's label and relationship accurately describe the user story's process. This means that we can understand the meaning of each label [9], and the interaction between the entity, process, and data store.

The evaluation conducted on 54 user stories in the *camperplus* project shows that 53 are syntactically correct, resulting in 98% accuracy. Meanwhile, the semantic correctness is 78%, with 12 determined as incorrect. Most of the semantic incorrectness happens in the *process* element of DFD. The example of semantic incorrectness includes an incomplete sentence, failure to capture the negation, and the user story that does not follow the best practice of user story quality criteria such as QUS [12]. This limitation is aligned with the findings in Gilson [8] since our generated element depends on their modules. Nevertheless, the improvement is possible since the project is open source.

We have run our model across all of the Dalpiaz datasets [6]. The complete output is available in our repository (see the output folder). To assure the soundness of the approach, we plan to conduct a more comprehensive evaluation in the near future. In addition, we intend to conduct an expert evaluation on the value of highlighting personal data to raise awareness of privacy within DFD.

6   Conclusion and Future Work

This paper presents a technique for automatically transforming user stories into privacy-aware DFD. Our primary motivation is to accelerate the adoption of privacy threat modeling in the ASD environment. Nevertheless, our model can also be applied to the general purpose of software engineering that requires DFD generation during the requirement or design life cycle. On the other hand, our approach is limited to one DFD level and does not perform the granularity of leveling that is typically enabled when drawn manually.

In the future, we aim for a more comprehensive evaluation in other projects [6]. We also intend to include more privacy-related indicators in the DFD, such as data subject, which does not directly perform the functionality. This adds another layer of complexity to the semantic definition of privacy-aware DFD, which further needs to be defined [9]. We also intend to put our DFD to the test in the privacy threat modeling process, such as by automatically eliciting privacy threats. By enabling automation, we hope to reduce the burden of drawing DFD from scratch, especially in the threat modeling session.

Acknowledgment. The authors acknowledge the scholarship granted by the Indonesia Endowment Fund for Education (IEFE/LPDP), Ministry of Finance, Republic of Indonesia, and the support received from the University of Vienna, Faculty of Computer Science.

References

1. Alshareef, H., Stucki, S., Schneider, G.: Transforming Data Flow Diagrams for Privacy Compliance (Long Version). arXiv preprint arXiv:2011.12028 (2020)
2. Ambler, S.W.: The Object Primer: Agile Model-Driven Development with UML 2.0. Cambridge University Press, New York (2004)
3. Antignac, T., Scandariato, R., Schneider, G.: Privacy compliance via model transformations. In: 2018 IEEE European Symposium on Security and Privacy Workshops (EuroS&PW), pp. 120–126. IEEE (2018)
4. Bernsmed, K., Cruzes, D.S., Jaatun, M.G., Iovan, M.: Adopting threat modelling in agile software development projects. J. Syst. Softw. **183**, 111090 (2022). https://doi.org/10.1016/j.jss.2021.111090, https://www.sciencedirect.com/science/article/pii/S0164121221001874
5. Canedo, E.D., C.A.e.a.: A named entity recognition based approach for privacy requirements engineering. Unpublished Manuscript, presented. In: The 29th IEEE International Requirement Engineering Conference (2021)
6. Dalpiaz, F.: Requirements Data Sets (User Stories). Mendeley Data, V1 (2018)
7. Elallaoui, M., Nafil, K., Touahni, R.: Automatic transformation of user stories into uml use case diagrams using nlp techniques. Procedia Comput. Sci. **130**, 42–49 (2018)
8. Gilson, F., Galster, M., Georis, F.: Generating use case scenarios from user stories. In: Proceedings of the International Conference on Software and System Processes. pp. 31–40. ICSSP 2020, Association for Computing Machinery, New York (2020)
9. Harel, D., Rumpe, B.: Meaningful modeling: what's the semantics of "semantics"? Computer **37**(10), 64–72 (2004)
10. Herwanto, G.B., Quirchmayr, G., Tjoa, A.M.: A named entity recognition based approach for privacy requirements engineering. In: 2021 IEEE 29th International Requirements Engineering Conference Workshops (REW), pp. 406–411 (2021). https://doi.org/10.1109/REW53955.2021.00072
11. Kochbati, T., Li, S., Gérard, S., Mraidha, C.: From user stories to models: a machine learning empowered automation. In: Hammoudi, S., Pires, L.F., Seidewitz, E., Soley, R. (eds.) Proceedings of the 9th International Conference on Model-Driven Engineering and Software Development, MODELSWARD 2021, Online Streaming, February 8–10, 2021. pp. 28–40. SCITEPRESS (2021)
12. Lucassen, G., Dalpiaz, F., Van Der Werf, J.M.E., Brinkkemper, S.: Visualizing user story requirements at multiple granularity levels via semantic relatedness. Lecture Notes in Computer Science (including subseries Lecture Notes in Artificial Intelligence and Lecture Notes in Bioinformatics) pp. 463–478 (2016)

13. Robeer, M., Lucassen, G., Van Der Werf, J.M.E., Dalpiaz, F., Brinkkemper, S.: Automated extraction of conceptual models from user stories via NLP. In: Proceedings - 2016 IEEE 24th International Requirements Engineering Conference, RE 2016 (November 2018), pp. 196–205 (2016)
14. Wuyts, K., Sion, L., Joosen, W.: LINDDUN GO: a lightweight approach to privacy threat modeling. In: Proceedings - 5th IEEE European Symposium on Security and Privacy Workshops, Euro S and PW 2020, pp. 302–309 (2020)

Business, Markets, and Industrial Practice

Requirements Engineering
in the Market Dialogue Phase of Public Procurement:
A Case Study of an Innovation Partnership for
Medical Technology

Gunnar Brataas[1]([⊠]), Geir Kjetil Hanssen[1], Xinlu Qiu[2], and Lisa S. Græslie[1]

[1] SINTEF Digital, Trondheim, Norway
{gunnar.brataas,geir.k.hanssen,lisa.graslie}@sintef.no
[2] NTNU, Trondheim, Norway
xinlu.qiu@ntnu.no

Abstract. *Context and Motivation:* In 2016, the European Union introduced 'innovation partnerships' to facilitate innovative development of the EU through public procurement. Requirements engineering is one of the main challenges in the public procurement of innovative products. Nevertheless, there is little empirical research on public procurement, particularly managing requirements in the pre-tender dialogue phase between potential suppliers and problem owners.

Question/Problem: This paper investigates the market dialogue phase of an innovation partnership project in Norway. We aim to understand critical factors of the dialogue phase that clarify and focus needs and requirements. This leads to the research question: How can we clarify and focus needs and requirements for a new solution in the market dialogue phase?

Principal Ideas/Results: We have conducted a case study at a major Norwegian hospital. The objective of this innovation partnership is to make the emergency room in a Norwegian hospital more efficient. The case study illustrates how requirements have been developed by the joint effort of the procurement team, the active engagement of potential suppliers, and the learning and mutual trust between them. By discussing the vision and getting feedback on opportunities and limitations in existing and projected technologies, the procurement team has refined their ambition and focused on the core of the innovation.

Contribution: This paper contributes to the literature on requirement engineering in public procurement by describing how requirements are focused during the dialogue phase of an innovation partnership facilitated by a cross-functional procurement team with sufficient competencies, resources, and trust.

Keywords: Requirements · Needs · Requirements engineering · Public procurement · Innovation partnership · Innovation · Case study · Market dialogue

V. Gervasi and A. Vogelsang (Eds.): REFSQ 2022, LNCS 13216, pp. 159–174, 2022.
https://doi.org/10.1007/978-3-030-98464-9_13

1 Introduction

Specifying the needs and requirements is the starting point for a procurement project, which is especially challenging for complex and innovative procurements [1, 2]. Even though the agile paradigm with emphasis on incremental requirements management has led to substantial savings and risk reduction in software engineering, the procurement process has been "(o)ne of the most difficult areas to renew." In contrast, requirements must be fixed before the tendering for procurement [1]. Therefore, previous literature on requirements engineering (RE) in procurement calls for dialogues with the vendors to clarify the requirements before tendering [3].

From the procurement management perspective, the literature on RE in public procurement also advocates a pre-tendering dialogue, especially for innovative solutions. Recent studies encourage the public buyers to utilize early-phase market dialogue [4, 5]. Specification of needs and requirements is one of the main challenges in the public procurement of innovation, and suppliers are reluctant to provide innovative solutions with overly rigid requirement specifications [6]. More critically, the procurement entities need to articulate their demands and transform them into requirements, and those requirements must also be matched with supply possibilities within time and budget limits [7]. However, the pre-tender dialogue has attracted very little academic attention [4, 8] and even less for RE during this dialogue. We aim to understand critical factors of the dialogue phase that clarify and focus needs and requirements. Consequently, our research question is: *How can we clarify and focus needs and requirements for a new solution in the market dialogue phase?*

As our case study, we use the dialogue phase before the call for tender in the Autoscore project at St. Olavs Hospital, one of Norway's most prominent hospitals. The objective of the Autoscore project is to procure an innovative solution for contactless measurement of vital signs to simplify the activities in the emergency room (ER).

2 Background

2.1 Innovative Partnership and Market Dialogue

In 2016, the EU introduced *innovation partnerships* to simplify the innovative development of the EU through public procurement. The public authorities in the EU spend around 14% of GDP (approximately €2 trillion per year) on procurement – where software-intensive solutions are a significant part. As stated in the EU directive [9], "public authorities should make the best strategic use of public procurement to spur innovation." The directive "allows contracting authorities to establish a long-term innovation partnership for the development and subsequent purchase of a new, innovative product, service or works provided that such innovative product or service or innovative works can be delivered to agreed performance levels and costs, without the need for a separate procurement procedure for the purchase."

Unlike traditional public procurement, which is strictly regulated by national and international regulations with a strong focus on transparency, fairness, and competition, innovation partnerships allow more interaction between the public purchasers and vendors [5]. Negotiation between the public and private parties during the procurement process enables the public buyers to procure complex contracts with innovative solutions tailored to buyers' specific needs [10].

As exact requirements of the innovative solutions are usually not known by the public buyers, market dialogue is encouraged at the pre-tender stage [11]. This is not unique for the innovation partnership but is recommended for all innovative procurements. The market dialogue is a two-way interaction between suppliers and the public buyers to map needs and improve the requirements specifications prior to a tendering phase, including early market consultation and technical dialogue [8, 12]. This pre-tender market dialogue encourages the purchasers "to write more realistic and 'inspiring,' innovation-driven specifications" [5]. Moreover, market dialogue is an excellent way to interact with the suppliers and inform the market about forthcoming needs [12]. By conducting market dialogues with potential suppliers, the procurers can avoid risks, such as by emphasizing price rather than quality, formulating overly rigid specifications, and specifying without sufficient competencies and knowledge of the innovation solution [12].

2.2 Procurement and Requirements Engineering

The search for literature on experiences with innovation partnerships in RE retrieved no relevant articles. This is not surprising because the EU introduced innovation partnerships in 2016, and only a few empirical studies investigate this new procedure. However, we have found relevant articles on RE in procurement and innovation and outline some key points. Messina and Rogers [1] describe two obstacles to innovation in the procurement process in software engineering. The first obstacle concerns public procurement rules: "(b)ureaucracies, rigidly structured organizations, and formal administrative processes do not like innovation. They kill it." The second obstacle is inadequate commitment: "Leaders and top managers play one of the most relevant roles in introducing innovation by expressing willingness to accept the associated risk and to support and reward innovative ideas and approaches." Similar obstacles are also discussed in [13] by Moe et al. They address the dilemma that public sectors should follow strict procurement regulations while at the same time specifying complex requirements to procure information systems. It is challenging to clarify requirements before talking to vendors [2].

The following literature mentions some proposals to improve the requirements of procurement. Hiisilä et al. [3] describe an iterative process for improving requirements during the procurement phase of acquiring software for a Finnish pension insurance company. As a result of interviews, they present prioritized lessons learned, where this lesson was one of the most important: "Requirements should be discussed with the supplier and refined during the procurement phase." They also explained that "requirements should be improved based on the solutions available on the market. New requirements may also emerge after demonstrations or analyses of the bids."

Moe et al. [14] describe the dilemma when a public entity procures an information system. Procuring an information system requires lengthy dialogues with the vendors to clarify the specification, whereas strict public procurement regulation restricts such dialogues. This article discussed that even though the newly introduced innovation partnership procedure allows more interaction between the public entities and the vendors, this dilemma still exists because the public entities are under strict regulations to limit interaction. Similarly, Moe and Newman show the importance of dialogue meetings with potential vendors to shape the requirement before the tendering phase [15].

3 The Autoscore Case

The Autoscore project started Medio 2020 to simplify the collection of vital signs from patients in the ER at St. Olavs university hospital, as well as other locations where monitoring is essential. Today, monitoring is a time-consuming task for health care workers, connecting sensors and cables to patients, which have little freedom of movement. Health care workers also have a significant cognitive load from working with multiple data sources in a hectic work environment. Consequently, the idea for this innovation partnership was shaped after talks with one vendor with visionary technology for contactless monitoring of vital signs.

The vision for the Autoscore project is to create a solution for contactless measurement of vital signs with no cables and preferably no sensors attached to the patient and where information is well integrated into the health care workers' information systems. The vital signs are related to the National Early Warning Score (NEWS), including respiration rate, oxygen saturation, blood pressure, pulse rate, level of consciousness and awareness, and temperature. Because no medically approved contactless solutions exist, this innovation partnership project was initiated with financial support from Innovation Norway, a state-owned company that stimulates entrepreneurship in Norway.

As described in Fig. 1, Autoscore has five phases: 1) Mapping of needs, user involvement, and planning, 2) Market dialogue with suppliers and experts, 3) Tender competition, 4) Innovation partnership (where the technology is developed jointly), and 5) Distribution and procurement.

#	Phase	2020				2021				2022				2023		
		Q1	Q2	Q3	Q4	Q1	Q2	Q3	Q4	Q1	Q2	Q3	Q4	Q1	Q2	Q3
1	Mapping of needs, user involvment, planning															
2	Market dialogue with suppliers and experts															
3	Tender competition															
4	Innovation partnership															
5	Distribution and procurement															

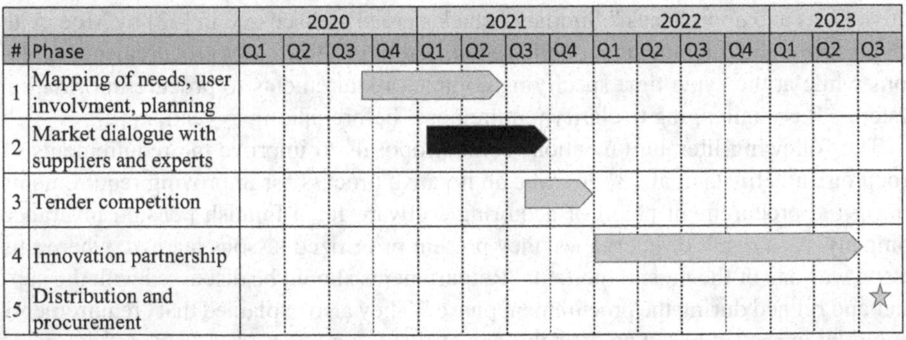

Fig. 1. Case-study timeline.

The focus of our study is phase 2 – the market dialogue. The natural endpoint of this phase is when the needs and requirements in the call for tender are specified.

4 Method

4.1 Research Method

We carried out this research in the form of a case study, collecting information and data about and from the Autoscore case in the market dialogue phase of the innovation partnership process. As a research methodology, the case study can be characterized by at least five aspects commonly mentioned in the literature, e.g., Wohlin, 2021 [16]. Our study relates to these five aspects as follows:

- *Being an empirical inquiry or investigation.* We collected data about the process, covering the entire timespan, including data prior to the process, e.g., plans and data such as observations throughout the process.
- *Studying a contemporary phenomenon:* The case was investigated as it unfolded, e.g., collecting data by observing essential meetings. Collected information was used to identify new observation points, e.g., new meetings. We also collected evolving versions of vital documentation to track developments.
- *Within its real-life context:* Data were collected within the same context as the process we studied. All meetings were online video meetings due to Corona restrictions.
- *Using multiple sources:* We collected both documentation and observations.
- *The boundary between phenomenon and context is unclear:* the focus of our study was to understand the dialogue process, but contextual information was essential to understand the workings of the process, although vague where the boundary was.

4.2 Data Points

Our data points were documentation, observations, and a continuous dialogue with the project manager:

- Documentation was retrieved from the project's public website and shared by the project manager.

  (2020 Q4) "Measurement of Vital Signs in the Emergency Department an Overview of Needs:" a comprehensive slide-set presenting the vision, high-level needs, and relevant context. This document resulted from a needs-mapping process prior to the dialogue phase and may be perceived as initial needs and requirements. This document was openly shared and presented at a dialogue conference in March 2021[1].
  (2021 Q1) "Q&As from the Dialogue conference:" an openly shared document collecting all questions from potential vendors at the dialogue conference and the immediate responses from the Autoscore project group. This document ensures insight and transparency for potential vendors that did not participate in the conference.
  (2021 Q3) The tender documentation: the formal documentation defining requirements that are issued in the request for tenders. A preliminary version was released openly in July for commenting and in the final version in September. We collected different versions throughout the process.

---

[1] Accessed online 31 January 2022: https://bit.ly/3rDFhou.

- Observations of the procurement team's sessions were made by either one or two researchers (first & second author). Notes were taken, as well as screenshots of relevant presentations. Notes transcribed the progress and dialogue of the meetings, including the researcher's evaluation of potentially interesting aspects.

  (2021 Q2) Nineteen one-to-one vendor meetings (five one-hour meetings for three days and four one-hour meetings the final day).
  (2021 Q2–Q3) Seven project group meetings.
  (2021 Q2–Q3) Two steering group meetings.

- Continuous feedback and correspondence between the researchers (first, second, and third author) and the Autoscore project manager (fourth author).
- The three researchers observed but did not influence the procurement process, except that they advised the project manager to discuss the relevant risks with the steering group after making the decision on the requirements.

4.3 Data Analysis

The observation notes and screenshots from the one-to-one, project group, and steering group meetings were coded in 80 nodes in NVivo. To ensure good coverage, codes were not defined up-front but identified by reading the text in multiple passes. Typically, we coded statements, feedback, or discussions related to themes such as requirements or needs, how the team evaluated vendors and reflections of the dialogue process itself. An example of a single code that was applied to several data points is 'Critical view on the project's ambition' – where vendors express doubt or critique (e.g., that the level of ambition is too high). The collected documents were not coded but used to verify notes and provide context for the analysis. After grouping these nodes, three main themes emerged. Sub-themes and representative statements are explored below:

- Maturing the vision and the requirements:

  - Trust or doubts both from the vendors and among the procurement team in the overall contactless vision, e.g., one vendor stated, "It will take at least five years until contactless sensors are mature... In the meantime, ... use available technology." One project team member stated, "If we shall cover all the requirements (for six NEWS parameters), we need both contactless and wireless sensors."
  - Sharpening the requirements, e.g., less than six NEWS parameters.
  - Risks, e.g., the accuracy of contactless measurements, where one vendor stated that they would not be reliable.
  - "Non-functional" requirements, e.g., integration with other hospital IT systems, certification of sensors, and the need for medical competency by vendors.

- Reflections on negative and positive aspects of the procurement process:

  - Negative evaluation from researchers: sometimes, the project meetings were unstructured because key personnel had to focus on their medical work.

– Positive evaluation from the project owner to the steering group 28 May 2021: "I am pleased with the project team … Those who participate have ownership of the project … Get the ambassadors involved from the start, and it will be easier to get the system up and running." Question from the head of the steering group and hospital assistant CEO in the same steering group meeting: "How does the rest of the world compare to this (contactless vision)?… This has great potential." Answer from project manager "A lot happens on the wireless, but we focus on contactless." Replay from assistant CEO: "We do not need to implement what others are doing."

- Assessments of the vendors, e.g., the hospital has good or bad experiences with a given vendor earlier and the willingness of vendors to share future plans (trust).

5 Findings

Based on the data analysis described in Sect. 4.3, this section details how the needs and requirements are managed in the market dialogue phase of an innovation partnership. Market dialogues with different types of vendors are critical to sharpening the requirement, to identify, reduce, and accept the potential risks, and to build trust between the procurer and vendors. A cross-functional procurement team with a safe and inclusive team atmosphere is also fundamental.

5.1 Focusing Requirements Through Vendor Dialogue Meetings

After the dialogue conference, vendors shared input notes that shaped the one-to-one dialogue meetings. Nineteen vendors requested a one-to-one meeting with the project group. During these meetings, the procurement team and the vendor presented themselves, and the vendor presented content from their input notes or suggested solutions for solving the needs. The procurement team had prepared points for dialogue which was shared with the vendor in advance: (1) Necessary competencies, including existing competencies, the need for external competencies or desire for matchmaking with other vendors, and what competencies the vendor needed from the hospital or the procurement team. (2) Technology, including what needs to be developed and what existing technology or infrastructure was thought to be used (or was thought to be lacking). (3) Modularity with other instruments, sensors, and systems. (4) Experience with the development of medical technology. Furthermore, the procurement team requested information on challenges for developing the solution and the solution itself, and they also wanted the vendor to present their future ambitions.

The 19 one-hour dialogue meetings were an efficient learning arena for the project team. By discussing the vision and getting feedback on the opportunities and limitations of existing and projected technologies, the procurement team focused on the kernel of the innovation. In other words, the requirements were focused on the part of the vision that is realizable within time and budget limits. This meant that the ambitious target of contactless monitoring of all six vital signs was reduced to contactless monitoring of the two most critical vital signs—respiration and pulse. Below, we present a variation in how the vendors approached the dialogue meetings in terms of their degree of alignment with the vision:

Vendors Aligned with the Vision: These partners reassured the procurement team of the viability of the bold vision on contactless measurements. However, it became clear that asking for six vital signs as a minimum requirement would not return any tenders because current technology could not reliably measure them all. Accordingly, they focused on two vital signs – respiration rate and pulse rate. Moreover, subsequent dialogues with hospital IT platform representatives revealed that it could cover several aspects of integration and presentation. Finally, the requirement for certification as medical equipment is a complex and time-consuming process with a low probability of reaching full certification within the project period. Hence, a clear strategy for certification became the requirement.

This sharpening of requirements was a significant strategic move to maximize the chances of achieving the core part of the vision, which they learned was very ambitious in this 10 MNOK innovation partnership (approximately 1 million €). The procurement team realized that patient identification was an onerous requirement. This becomes critical with the movement of patients and medical personnel, e.g., patients walking between a bed and a chair or when a nurse bends over a patient in a bed.

Vendors with More Conservative Solutions: These solutions require physical intervention with the patient or restrict their movement. Some of these vendors expressed criticism and argued that the vision was overly ambitious, advising the team to lower the level of ambition to fit their more mature but also more conservative solutions. However, this made it even more apparent to the team that the role of the innovation process was to identify the limits of the technology and not play safe with known solutions requiring tedious cleaning or maintenance tasks.

The interdisciplinary procurement team concluded that the more conservative solutions would not sufficiently increase value compared to today's solutions and would not lead to a contactless future anytime soon. Accordingly, because some of these vendors allowed themselves to understand "contactless" as "wireless," the procurement team clearly defined the term "contactless" in the call for tender as not requiring contact with the patient and as monitoring continuously while moving between furniture.

Vendors with Complementary Offerings: These vendors could complement more innovative vendors so that they together could deliver a more "complete" solution, e.g., by (1) supporting more vital signs with more conservative technology or (2) by offering integration with the hospital IT infrastructure, or (3) with a meaningful presentation of measurements. The initial signal from the project was that either the project or the vendors could propose two or more matching vendors. However, in line with the sharpening of the vision, the procurement team decided on skipping matchmaking altogether.

To summarize, we see that the team made informed decisions in sharpening the vision, the needs, and the requirements as an effect of the dialogues with a large and varied group of vendors, representing an overview of existing technologies, near future innovation opportunities, and limitations of both technologies and project resources.

5.2 Risk Management

The procurement team gradually clarified, understood, accepted, and reduced the project's potential risk by jointly focusing on the requirements while formulating the final needs in the call for the tender. The original vision of the solution requiring all six vital signs would involve high risks in terms of potential loss of time and money by not being able to realize any solution in time. Moreover, in a hospital context, the primary risk is patient harm. Hence, the risks involved in demanding a radical technology were not perceived as high by the clinicians in the procurement team (i.e., the project owner) or the steering group because the solution will not immediately replace existing monitoring technology. On the contrary, *not* being able to explore the possibilities of contactless technology was perceived as a risk by the procurement team because the potential added value would then not be identified. The support from Innovation Norway mitigates the financial risk, and it may be possible to apply for more funding later. Lastly, the innovation partnership procurement instrument aims to co-create innovative solutions instead of a more traditional procurement.

5.3 A Cross-Functional Procurement Team

The cross-functional team was created from the beginning of this innovation procurement project because the project owners recognized that involving ambassadors early was essential for successful change processes. We observed the procurement team through all 19 dialogue meetings, including short recap discussions and several internal meetings. The members of this cross-functional team had complementary competencies and resources relevant to the vision of contactless measurements of vital signs:

- Top-level management: the steering group, led by the hospital assistant CEO, supported the team with the commitment to the sharpened vision and hence supported its risk-taking in focusing on contactless and not wireless technology.
- Medium-level management: Being also the assistant head of the ER, the project owner gave the team members flexibility with their regular work obligations to attend dialogue meetings. The head nurse also contributed to increased commitment among the nurses by being a regular procurement team member.
- End-user level: represented by ER nurses and a patient representative.
- A medical technology and information security expert with deep knowledge of the technological state of the art served as a semantic broker for technology to the rest of the team.
- A procurement expert who understood the innovation partnership instrument.
- Project manager with expertise in innovation and knowledge management (and the fourth author of this paper).

The team atmosphere was safe and inclusive, indicating psychological safety. Experts with natural authority invited other roles with less authority, e.g., the senior medical doctor actively seeking the viewpoints from the patient representative. The team environment enabled discussions on conflicting views without creating conflicts, and varying viewpoints were discussed openly in the team. We observed several cases where, e.g., the medical experts expressed enthusiasm about technologies presented in the dialogue meetings, but the medical expert was able to correct and balance the view based on technical experience and expertise. Thus, the members showed high mutual trust by sharing their knowledge and acknowledging each other's views and knowledge related to different types of requirements. The members had a stronger voice for requirements associated with their competencies, where health care workers were more active in discussions on using the suggested technology and had the last word on focusing such requirements. This was not only with the other members' blessing but by direct encouragement. Therefore, the team was successfully united in the sharpening of the vision.

The bold vision gave a robust commitment to the team. Key members even stated that they would not have participated in the procurement with a less ambitious objective. The team members were all highly engaged throughout the dialogue meetings and able to find time in busy schedules. However, we observed a shift in the engagement when the writing of the call for tender started, and it became harder to involve the team members and verify parts of the documentation. The project manager was the critical author but highly reliant on input and verification of the content by the rest of the team. Hence the writing process became cumbersome but eventually resulted in a complete call for tender. In several minor meetings, the project manager struggled to engage team members with clinical commitments. However, the procurement team often expressed confidence in the shared vision based on the thorough dialogue and inclusive dialogue meetings and argued that they trust the project manager to realize this in written format. In this process, the project manager needed to know "who knows what" to get the correct input and verification during finalization. The procurement expert was also a fundamental part of this process with knowledge about the procurement documents and process, ensuring compliance with the formal procedure and contents.

5.4 Trust from Vendors

Trust between procurer and vendor is vital as an innovation partnership will be an intense R&D cooperation for at least 18 months if both parties agree to continue the collaboration. During the market dialogue phase, the hospital knows that an innovation partnership requires time from critical resources to educate the vendors and to provide access to facilities and users during the development phase. Moreover, because the contract only ensures a purchase option, the vendor can refuse to sell the developed solution. Correspondingly, vendors may have to invest their resources to mature the result, e.g., from a proof of concept to a ready product. The willingness of both the hospital and vendors to commit time and resources shows that their level of trust surpasses the threshold of perceived risk, and they are willing to engage in the relationship [17]. Meanwhile, sensitive information on limitations and plans for future technology development shared by vendors also indicated a high level of trust. To ensure that the market dialogue is an effective and safe process to interact and exchange information, an essential prerequisite for this trust was that the procurement team and the researchers had signed a non-disclosure agreement before the dialogue meetings and reassured the vendors about this before every dialogue meeting.

6 Discussion

Our overall objective was to understand how we can clarify and focus needs and requirements for a new solution in the market dialogue phase. We will discuss how this was achieved below.

6.1 Clarifying and Focusing Needs and Requirements

It was valuable with broad inclusion of vendors spanning from those that propose relatively mature technologies to those willing to discuss innovation and development opportunities. Conservative vendors were eager to discuss technology limitations with contactless sensors, while innovative vendors discussed their opportunities. Suppliers were willing to share ideas and knowledge, including limitations and development challenges. This is in line with Uyarra et al. [6], who found that overly rigid requirements hinder innovative solutions.

An inclusive dialogue phase took time for valuable human resources. However, it has been a vital learning process enabling the team to refine and focus on the vision and clarify and justify requirements. The initial vision was ambitious but open to create interest, and the final sharpened vision was innovative and realistic with acceptable risk, e.g., requiring two vital signs instead of the initial six, with the remaining four signs optional. Other vital requirements were adjusted. For example, the team learned that the user interface would be developed through the planned improvement of existing infrastructure systems – leaving more room to focus on the core part of the vision. Learning points came from the dialogue with a great variety of vendors; some large with experience in medical equipment certification that smaller vendors do not have, some small vendors with specific technologies, and existing hospital's IT system vendors. This sharpening of the needs and requirements is required because the innovation partnership instrument requires the initial specifications of a purchasable solution.

6.2 Understanding of the Innovation Partnership Instrument Among Vendors

The understanding of the innovation partnership instrument varied amongst the vendors. Vendors are accustomed to traditional procurement processes where requirements are specified in detail, and the relationship between the customer and vendor is transactional. In an innovation partnership, the relationship is based on collaboration and co-creation during an innovation process but with a higher risk of not fulfilling the vision [5]. We observed that several vendors took a traditional approach of presenting existing products with less focus on their potential role as an innovation partner. This puzzled us as we expected vendors to more actively describe their potential partner role and abilities to collaborate, e.g., experience in co-creation processes and user involvement. The reason may be that this process is new, unknown, and complex and that the dialogue does not follow established patterns from traditional procurement [1].

Some vendors discussed the innovation potential and their role more as a future development partner than a traditional supplier. Although with a few cases, we suspect there is a sweet spot for good vendors: those with a high level of technological know-how but without being locked by existing products. We believe the *intention* of the innovation partnership instrument should be clarified and that vendors should be challenged to describe their role as development partners explicitly in the dialogue meetings.

6.3 Vendor Matching

Before the dialogue meetings, the initial ambition was to have an open approach to the potential matching of vendors; both vendors and the project team could propose matching to cover the width and complexity of the requirements. Throughout the process, it became clear that the best strategy was to focus on the core of the vision and reduce the need for complementary competencies, covering initial broader requirements like integration, user interface, and certification. Hence, with learning-based justification, they were looking for *one* vendor with a focused innovation process for contactless measurement of vital signs.

6.4 A Well-Aligned Cross-Functional Procurement Team

We see that a well-aligned cross-functional procurement team has been a critical factor with the following characteristics:

- **Cross-functionality:** The cross-functional team represented all stakeholders affected by the innovation process and the envisioned outcome and those with knowledge of innovative procurement processes. This helped to adjust each members' impression from the meetings. In particular, the medical technology expert could inform the doctors and nurses about the realism and technical limitations of a solution that at first glance looked promising.
- **Resources:** The team members had sufficient resources for participation in addition to a hectic schedule. The associate chief of the ER (i.e., the project owner) considered the project and the dialogue process to be of great importance and allowed his medical staff to prioritize the project (at the cost of their regular tasks).
- **Motivation:** The team had a considerable task with a potentially significant impact on the ER and its patients. This ambitious task caused motivation and enthusiasm, compared to the traditional procurement of more conservative technology.
- **Formal procurement competency:** In the dialogue and team meetings, the team was supported by a procurement expert, ensuring compliance with formal procurement routines. This role was crucial for increasing the team members' understanding of what requirements were allowed and what were not (and when), which was a repeated topic during project team meetings and dialogue meetings; and when writing the call for tender. This expertise created safety and order for the project manager and the team.
- **Trustful team dynamics:** Although the team members had varying formal power at the hospital and the ER, the associate chief of the ER and the project manager deliberately sought the viewpoints from all members during the dialogue meetings, especially in the team-internal evaluation at the end of each dialogue meetings.
- **Commitment from top-level management:** The steering group supported the strategic decision to focus on contactless measurement of vital signs.

6.5 Summary of Discussion

In sum, the procurement team has succeeded in using the dialogue phase as intended:

- Limitations and opportunities of the technology have been explored by seeing available technology and getting insight into some vendors' plans and strategies, including R&D.
- The new knowledge of vendors and possible solutions have enabled the team to adjust requirements with confidence (a balance between realism and risk).
- New insight enabled the team to identify the critical risk factor in this case, the risk of not exploring the core of the vision instead of the risk of not getting a fully functional system. The innovations' improvement potential to healthcare workers is too promising not to pursue fully.

From this analysis, we see two main components that have affected the process of prioritizing the core requirement of the vision and adjusting additional requirements: first, a well-functioning learning process, and second, a sufficient level of trust in the team, internally, within the hospital, and towards vendors. This is illustrated in Fig. 2.

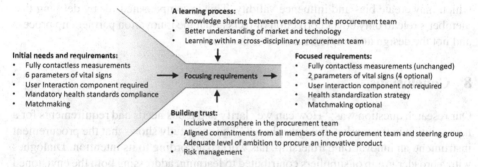

A learning process:
- Knowledge sharing between vendors and the procurement team
- Better understanding of market and technology
- Learning within a cross-disciplinary procurement team

Initial needs and requirements:
- Fully contactless measurements
- 6 parameters of vital signs
- User Interaction component required
- Mandatory health standards compliance
- Matchmaking

Focusing requirements →

Focused requirements:
- Fully contactless measurements (unchanged)
- 2 parameters of vital signs (4 optional)
- User interaction component not required
- Health standardization strategy
- Matchmaking optional

Building trust:
- Inclusive atmosphere in the procurement team
- Aligned commitments from all members of the procurement team and steering group
- Adequate level of ambition to procure an innovative product
- Risk management

Fig. 2. The requirements funnel

7 Threats to Validity

Being a study of a single case, our findings have explorative and explanatory value [18]. We provide insight into a new phenomenon with no previous research available (the dialogue phase in innovation partnerships) by openly collecting and analyzing nearly all available data within the study period. We indicate potential explanations of influencing factors through a thematic analysis (summarized in Fig. 2). However, the study is subject to a set of threats to its validity [18]:

- *Construct validity* (whether we studied the right phenomenon – the dialogue phase): We have sought to ensure construct validity by collecting data through observations of the phenomena itself (dialogue meetings, project group, and steering group meetings), as well as input and output documentation (the vision document, and the resulting request for tender specification). Other potentially influencing sources have been avoided.

- *Internal validity* (whether we have understood casual effects correctly): There is obviously a threat to internal validity with only a single case and no reference cases in the literature. We have, however, sought compensation in building support for claims, combining different aspects in the analysis by openly coding the material (using Nvivo), e.g., several factors explaining the team.
- *External validity* (whether our findings are valid to other cases): This needs to be investigated in other studies, but we have set a restricted scope for the study – the dialogue phase, which is part of a well-defined process, meaning that our findings should have relevance to other cases that are restricted by the same type of process.
- *Reliability* (whether other researchers would reach the same conclusions): This is hard to evaluate, but we have provided a rich insight into findings and how we interpret the findings (discussion). This should enable the reader to assess the reliability of our interpretations.

The project manager of the Autoscore project is the fourth author of this paper, which may create bias and influence validity. This is compensated for by defining that member's role to only cover correction of facts about the innovation partnership process and not the design and implementation of the study.

8 Conclusions

Our research question was: "How can we clarify and focus needs and requirements for a new solution in the market dialogue phase?" The case study shows that the procurement instrument, an innovation partnership, has worked according to its intention. Dialogues with a broader group of suppliers contributed to learning, addressing both the envisioned innovation and the innovation process. New knowledge of opportunities and limitations has helped the procurement team focus their vision and requirements with confidence. Although a costly process, our analysis shows that building an excellent cross-functional team with a high level of trust is a valuable investment.

We believe insights into the Autoscore case are of value both to practice and research, especially as an innovation partnership is a new instrument with sparse empirical experience. This case study has implications for practice and further research:

- *Implications for practice:* (1) A wide range of vendors is valuable for clarifying and focusing initial needs and requirements. Therefore, the initial vision and the initial description of needs and requirements should be so broad that it attracts interest from a variety of vendors. (2) The dialogue phase of the innovation partnership process can benefit from making the vendors' potential role as an innovation *partner* more explicit, both in the initial description of needs and requirements and as a discussion point in the dialogue meetings. (3) Reducing the team's competency and capacity, e.g., to save time for critical stakeholders, pose a significant risk.

- *Implications for research (further work):* (1) The dialogue phase in this case study may be streamlined based on more experience, finding a sweet spot between the quality of the dialogue phase and its cost. This is important since market dialogues are recommended for all public procurements [12]. (2) Apart from observing a procurement team and their interactions with vendors, it would be interesting also to observe vendors and their internal prioritizations and evaluations prior to and after the dialogue meetings. This would give a more complete picture.

Looking into the near future for the Autoscore project, we may ask: how should the innovation partnership phase build on the promising results from the dialogue phase? Based on our experience with innovative software engineering processes, we believe that an agile approach would be fruitful. Iterations and increments simplify development and synchronous clarification of functional and commonly under-focused quality requirements, e.g., as addressed by Brataas et al. [19].

Acknowledgment. The research leading to these results has received funding from the Research Council of Norway in the project SMED: Smarter Innovation with Digital Transformation of Innovative Procurement (grant #285542). We thank St. Olavs university hospital for making this case study possible through access to the Autoscore project.

References

1. Messina, A., Rogers, A.: Using the "Agile" paradigm to support innovation in large organizations. In: Ciancarini, P., Litvinov, S., Messina, A., Sillitti, A., Succi, G. (eds.) SEDA 2016. AISC, vol. 717, pp. 191–203. Springer, Cham (2018). https://doi.org/10.1007/978-3-319-70578-1_18
2. Moe, C.E., Päivärinta, T.: Challenges in information systems procurement in the Norwegian public sector. In: Janssen, M., Scholl, H.J., Wimmer, M.A., Tan, Y. (eds.) EGOV 2011. LNCS, vol. 6846, pp. 404–417. Springer, Heidelberg (2011). https://doi.org/10.1007/978-3-642-22878-0_34
3. Hiisilä, H., Kauppinen, M., Kujala, S.: An iterative process to connect business and IT development: Lessons learned. In: 2016 IEEE 18th Conference on Business Informatics (CBI). IEEE (2016)
4. Holma, A.M., et al. Service specification in pre-tender phase of public procurement-A triadic model of meaningful involvement. J. Purch. Supply Manag. 26(1), 100580 (2020)
5. Torvatn, T., De Boer, L.: Public procurement reform in the EU: start of a new era? IMP J. 11(3), 431–451 (2017)
6. Uyarra, E., et al.: Barriers to innovation through public procurement: a supplier perspective. Technovation 34(10), 631–645 (2014)
7. Edler, J., Uyarra, E.: Public procurement of innovation. In: Handbook of Innovation in Public Services. Edward Elgar Publishing, Cheltenham (2013)
8. Hamdan, H.A., De Boer, L.: Innovative public procurement (IPP)–Implications and potential for zero-emission neighborhood (ZEN) projects? In: IOP Conference Series: Earth and Environmental Science. IOP Publishing, Bristol (2019)
9. EU, On public procurement and repealing (Directive 2014/24/EU). European Parliament (2014)

10. Iossa, E., Biagi, F., Valbonesi, P.: Pre-commercial procurement, procurement of innovative solutions and innovation partnerships in the EU: rationale and strategy. Econ. Innov. New Technol. **27**(8), 730–749 (2018)
11. Godlewska, M.: Innovation partnership in the European union–a chance for successful competition with the USA. Rev. Euro. Aff. **1**, 89–102 (2017)
12. Alhola, K., Salo, M., Antikainen, R., Berg, A.: Promoting public procurement of sustainable innovations: approaches for effective market dialogue. In: Thai, K.V. (ed.) Global Public Procurement Theories and Practices. PAGG, vol. 18, pp. 59–82. Springer, Cham (2017). https://doi.org/10.1007/978-3-319-49280-3_4
13. Moe, C.E., Risvand, A.C., Sein, M.K.: Limits of public procurement: information systems acquisition. In: Wimmer, M.A., Scholl, H.J., Grönlund, Å., Andersen, K.V. (eds.) Electronic Government. EGOV 2006. Lecture Notes in Computer Science, vol. 4084. Springer, Berlin, Heidelberg (2006). https://doi.org/10.1007/11823100_25
14. Moe, C.E., Newman, M., Sein, M.K.: The public procurement of information systems: dialectics in requirements specification. Eur. J. Inf. Syst. **26**(2), 143–163 (2017)
15. Moe, C.E., Newman, M.: The public procurement of IS--a process view. In: 2014 47th Hawaii International Conference on System Sciences. IEEE (2014)
16. Wohlin, C.: Case study research in software engineering—it is a case, and it is a study, but is it a case study? Inf. Softw. Technol. 133, 106514 (2021)
17. Mayer, R.C., Davis, J.H., Schoorman, F.D.: An integrative model of organizational trust. Acad. Manag. Rev. **20**(3), 709–734 (1995)
18. Runesson, P., Höst, M.: Guidelines for conducting and reporting case study research in software engineering. Empir. Softw. Eng. **14**(2), 131–164 (2009)
19. Brataas, G., et al.: Agile elicitation of scalability requirements for open systems: A case study. J. Syst. Softw. **182**, 111064 (2021)

A Business Model Construction Kit for Platform Business Models - Research Preview

Nedo Bartels[1]([⊠])[iD] and Jaap Gordijn[2][iD]

[1] Fraunhofer IESE, Fraunhofer-Platz 1, 67663 Kaiserslautern, Germany
nedo.bartels@iese.fraunhofer.de
[2] Vrije Universiteit Amsterdam, De Boelelaan 1105,
1081 HV Amsterdam, The Netherlands
j.gordijn@vu.nl

Abstract. [**Context and motivation**] In recent years, the Internet has led to new ways of doing business and has spawned new, platform-based business models. For example, Uber and Airbnb offer platforms that enable *broker/mediation* services between parties organized in two-sided markets. [**Question/problem**] To be financially sustainable, platform-specific revenue models are needed to generate cash flows from these intermediation services. Moreover, these revenue models should be revisited over and over again, due to continuous changes in a competitive environment. To a large extent, it is unknown how to continuously (re)design revenue models for platforms efficiently. [**Principal ideas/results**] We propose three research streams with outcomes that should support continuous and efficient platform design: (1) formalization of known platform revenue models, (2) the organization of known platform revenue models into design patterns such that existing knowledge can be reused efficiently, and (3) support for the dynamics of these models, e.g., how they evolve over time. [**Contribution**] In the long term, we propose a novel and tractable approach called the *Business Model Construction Kit* for the continuous and efficient design of platform business models, including the selection of appropriate revenue model(s). The kit will provide a variety of methodologically well-integrated *design*-oriented tools and *accepted knowledge* to quickly (re)design a platform business model with a focus on revenue models. The result is a method aimed at helping practitioners design platform business models.

Keywords: Platform business models · Revenue model · Construction kit · Digital platform

1 Introduction

In this research preview, we consider the problem of how to efficiently and continuously (re)design *revenue models* for IT-enabled *platforms* in a dynamic, and changing business environment. We view the design of revenue models as a form of *early* requirements engineering, e.g., regarding the elicitation of business requirements,

© Springer Nature Switzerland AG 2022
V. Gervasi and A. Vogelsang (Eds.): REFSQ 2022, LNCS 13216, pp. 175–182, 2022.
https://doi.org/10.1007/978-3-030-98464-9_14

and similar to other contextual RE-methods such as i^* [23] and e^3value [11]. We argue that for platforms with IT as an intrinsic part of their value proposition, it is important to have an *inclusive* requirements engineering process, that is, not restricted to information system requirements only, but also taking into account business, financial and market requirements. Platforms such as those offered by Uber, Spotify, Airbnb etc. are more than just IT systems and are able to create digital markets for various stakeholders in dynamic business contexts. As a consequence of this observation, understanding the business context is a prerequisite for finding requirements of the information system that will enable the platform, which should therefore be part of the overall requirements engineering process.

The business context is expressed by means of a *business model*, which explains what kind of value is offered, how this offered value is created, and how the created value is captured through a revenue model. According to [18], a revenue model is part of a business model and describes the mechanism by which a company makes a profit from its value-creating activities. A business model represents the underlying logic of a business, with a focus on how economic value is created, distributed, and consumed in a network of actors that are (non-for-profit) organizations. When a business model bundles several actors via a platform, we consider this kind of a business model a platform business model. A platform business model enables and supports transactions between supply- and demand-side participants [21]. We advocate the logic that, e.g., Uber Ride (platform provider) brokers rides (assets) provided by drivers (provider-side) for passengers (consumer-side) on its platform [22]. Here, the revenue model must clarify which monetization mechanisms are used to generate revenue from the platform's mediation activities. In addition to Uber, there are a number of other platform business models that are established in different domains, including the business models of eBay Marketplace, Spotify Music, or Airbnb Lodging. As each of these platform business models creates value differently, various revenue models are needed to capture value. A revenue model should define appropriate revenue sources and revenue streams to transform the value delivered [21]. Finding a suitable revenue model that contains ideal revenue mechanisms is challenging, as each platform business model deals with its own requirements. Based on this, our research preview is motivated by answering the following questions:

RQ1: How can we formalize and transfer knowledge about the revenue models of existing platform business models?, *RQ2*: How can we formalize accepted, well-known design knowledge with respect to platform business models as patterns, so that they can be used by practitioners in the field?, *RQ3*: How can we provide support for the inherent dynamic nature of business models?.

This paper does not yet present any findings regarding these three research topics; rather, it provides a research preview and lays our plans with respect to these topics. In brief, we plan to develop a Business Model Construction Kit for platform business model that addresses the three above-mentioned directions. This paper is structured as follows. In Sect. 2, we introduce *platform business models* and describe the linkage to *revenue models*. This is followed by a discussion in Sect. 3 about the challenges posed by *business model dynamics* and their significance for platform business models. Section 4 outlines our proposed approach and the importance of *design patterns* for our Business Model Construction Kit. Our next steps are presented through a roadmap in Sect. 5. Based on this, Sect. 6 summarizes our concluding remarks.

2 Revenue Model as a Part of a Platform Business Model

A shared understanding and consent are argued by [13] regarding three core business model dimensions: value creation, value delivery, and value capture. A revenue model is a part of the business model's value capture, and therefore it illustrates how (economic) value is generated. We consider revenue models for platforms as a concept that shows the monetization mechanisms used to capture value from the platform's mediation activities between its two-sided markets. A digital platform is able to connect the supply side and the demand side of a market through an intermediary called the platform provider, which enables the brokering of the core asset under consideration [21, 22]. Consequently, the composition of the revenue streams between (1) platform provider, (2) asset providers, and (3) asset consumers is highly important for shaping a comprehensive revenue model. A platform can be monetized focusing on supply-side participants, demand-side participants, third parties [21], or both market sides. In addition, [5] formulates two monetization references that can be used to place payments: (1) platform participants have to pay fees for participating in a platform or (2) platform participants have to pay fees per transaction. As shown in Table 1 different variants can be used to shape a platform revenue model.

Table 1. Descriptions of revenue models for selected platform business models

Platform business model	Used revenue mechanisms
Uber Ride (brokers rides between drivers and passengers)	Uber generates revenue by charging drivers a 20–25% fee on the total price for each trip performed (monetization of supply-side participants)
eBay Marketplace (brokers items between sellers and buyers)	eBay generates revenue by charging the sellers a 2–13% fee on the total price for each item sold (monetization of supply-side participants)
Spotify Music (brokers music songs between artists and listeners)	Spotify generates revenue by offering an advertising-free platform access for a monthly subscription of $4–11 (monetization of demand-side participants)
Airbnb Lodging (brokers accommodations between hosts and travellers)	Airbnb combines a transaction-based fee and charges, guests a service fee of 5–15%, and hosts a commission fee of 3–5% of the total price for each reservation (monetization of both market-sides)

These different types of revenue models lead to the assumption that monetization mechanisms could be combined to formalize business model patterns. To pursue this, we will conduct a first SLR regarding the notation of 'platform business models' and a second SLR regarding revenue models that currently exist for platforms. Using the SLRs and a series of workshops to be held with parties developing and maintaining platform business models, we will draft a Business Model Construction Kit (a preliminary version for non-platform based business models already exists: see [4]).

3   Dynamics of Evolving Platform Business Models

In recent years, we have seen an increase in the number of digital platforms, e.g., *Salesforce AppExchange* (marketplace for B2B applications) as a redesign and expansion of an already existing service, while others create new platforms by disrupting existing markets (e.g., Spotify or Airbnb). These evolutions and innovations towards platform-oriented business models can be considered as *business model dynamics*, which show the firms' adaptation to a turbulent and changing environment [20]. However, many studies and development approaches look at business models from a static perspective, as snapshots in time [19], and ignore the dynamic evolution of business models [7].

We consider a business model not as a static construct, but as a dynamic concept that evolves over time. For example, as a matching service, Uber initially heavily subsidized taxi rides to create the market, both from a customer and a supplier perspective [8]. Moreover, we argue that we can also take a design perspective on the evolution of the business model *itself*; we can think about how to launch a particular business platform and what that business model should look like a few years after the initial deployment. In fact, this is precisely what Uber (and other platform providers) did to overcome the problem also known as the *chicken-egg problem*. The provider platform must therefore think about how to address both market sides and how to reach a critical mass when setting up a platform business model [17].

Another example of business model dynamics can be seen in the revenue model of Airbnb. Listing a room on Airbnb is free. When a guest rents a room, that person then pays the renter through Airbnb, which takes a fee from both sides [8]. This revenue model has been implemented since August 2008, following the launch of Airbnb's own payment infrastructure [2]. Before that, when Airbnb was called AirBed&Breakfast and fees were only charged if a host charged more than $300/night, a $30 fee was charged by AirBed&Breakfast to list the accommodation [1]. This led to a different revenue stream, without involving the consumer side (or travelers), and thus to a different revenue model.

These dynamics between business model changes should be understood to provide a starting point to raise business model requirements. Designing business models is a continuous task, in the same sense as in agile software development and continuous delivery and integration of software. We argue that this is not only the case for software development, but also for the business models of platforms enabled by such software. Based on the assumption that platform business models and their revenue models can be formalized systematically in patterns, we try to understand business model dynamics by the change from one pattern to another pattern (e.g., the change of AirBed&Breakfast's revenue model to today's Airbnb revenue model). Therefore, our proposed construction kit could be used to analyze the intersection between different patterns and their dynamics and changes.

4   Organizing Revenue Models into Patterns

As argued by Jackson in his book 'Problem Frames' [12], most problems that designers have to solve have been solved before, and often many times. In Information Systems and Software Engineering, the approach of patterns for presenting accepted design knowledge is quite popular. Initiated in the area of building construction [3], patterns are often used in Requirements Engineering and Software Design (see, e.g., the Gang of Four book [9], and Interaction Design [6]). Briefly speaking, a pattern comprises *proven* and *accepted solutions* for recurring *problems* in a particular *context*. The selection of a particular solution may be subject to *forces*. The keyword is 'proven'; the solution should be known to be successful. Previously, we successfully defined patterns for interorganizational controls in networks of enterprises [14]. We intend to use a similar approach in terms of best-practice elicitation and use e^3value as (part of) the pattern description language. Our patterns follow a predefined structure and rules. For this reason, the process can be called a language because, like a natural language, it contains elements, namely patterns and rules of application [16]. The *55 business model patterns* identified by [10] are universally applicable business model strategies based on a comprehensive company analysis performed by the authors. Unfortunately, these patterns are poorly formalized (e.g., in terms of conceptual modeling) which may lead to ambiguity, subjective interpretation and hence confusion. However, we will use these patterns as a point of departure to arrive at a more model-based library of patterns specifically for platform business models. The patterns found will be integrated into our Business Model Construction Kit, as introduced in Sect. 2. As for our Business Model Construction Kit, the identified business model dynamics will result in an ongoing, continuous process with respect to business model development. We see that too often, a business model development project is a single-shot effort, whereas it should be a continuous and ongoing process.

5   Roadmap

The next steps in our roadmap towards developing the Business Model Construction Kit are described in the following.

Conducting an SLR. Existing literature about revenue models for platform business models will be systematically reviewed to identify mechanisms for monetizing platform business models (e.g. Subscription, Pay per Use etc.), and revenue streams between platform provider, asset providers and asset consumers.

Formalizing Platform Revenue Model Patterns. The collected knowledge about revenue models for platform business models will be aggregated and formalized as generic patterns to ensure reusability. Each formalized pattern will contain a textual description and a model-based component. The model-based component will be enabled with e^3value , because it has already been used successfully, as shown in [15] for the formalization of 'control patterns'. With the formalization we will address *RQ1*.

Developing a Pattern-Based Approach for Platform Business Models. The formalized patterns will first be applied to a sample of existing platform business models in order to check their applicability and, if necessary, make adjustments and extensions. Afterwards, the patterns will be used in various research projects dealing with the development of platform business models. Based on individual interviews and group workshops with industry partners, the formalized patterns will be prioritized and a selection will be made to derive insights into, what requirements need to be met in order to run certain platform business models successfully (e.g., what are the requirements for running a pay-per-use revenue model?). Here, we will address *RQ2*, and prove which requirements have to be fulfilled in order to use specific revenue model patterns for certain value propositions and platform' value creation. The findings will be finalized in our Business Model Construction Kit.

Evaluating the Pattern-Based Approach. The evaluation will test whether control groups are able to develop appropriate revenue models for platform business models. To quantify the results for *RQ3*, if the Business Model Construction Kit supports the development of resilient platform business models, our results will be compared to existing approaches such as the *Business Model Canvas*.

6   Conclusion

This research preview presented the current challenges of business model design and its revenue models for platform business models. We outlined a pattern-based Business Model Construction Kit for platform business models to be implemented as a quantification framework in the e^3value business modeling methodology. The aim of this research is to develop a supporting tool, as kind of a software-based and model-based pattern library for platform business models and their dynamics. We believe that with the proposed framework, we can provide an approach that allows systematic and transparent development of novel platform business models.

References

1. Help: Is it free to list? https://web.archive.org/web/20090824205042/http://www.airbnb.com/help/question/33. Accessed 24 Oct 2021
2. News: The airbnb story. https://news.airbnb.com/about-us/. Accessed 24 Oct 2021

3. A Pattern Language: Towns, Buildings, Construction. Oxford University Press, New York, August 1977
4. Bartels, N.: The business model matrix: a kit for designing and innovating business models. J. Bus. Models **9**(3), 14–23 (2021)
5. Becker, F., Gedenk, K.: Optimale nichtlineare tarife auf zweiseitigen medien-märkten. Schmalenbachs Zeitschrift für betriebswirtschaftliche Forschung **72**(4), 423–445 (2020)
6. Borchers, J.O.: A Pattern Approach to Interactive Design. John Wiley Sons Ltd., Chichester (2001)
7. Chen, J., Tang, Y., Yang, J.: A survey of system dynamics in B2C e-commerce business model. Mod. Econ. **9**(4), 830–852 (2018)
8. Cusumano, M.A.: The sharing economy meets reality. Commun. ACM **61**(1), 26–28 (2018)
9. Gamma, E., Helm, R., Johnson, R., Vlissides, J.M.: Design Patterns: Elements of Reusable Object-Oriented Software. Addison-Wesley Professional, Boston (1994)
10. Gassmann, O., Frankenberger, K., Csik, M.: The Business Model Navigator. Pearson PLC, London (2014)
11. Gordijn, J., Wieringa, R.: E3value User Guide - Designing Your Ecosystem in a Digital World. The Value Engineers, 1st edn. (2021)
12. Jackson, M.: Problem Frames: Analyzing and Structuring Software Development Problems. Addison-Wesley Longman Publishing Co. Inc., Boston (2000)
13. Jensen, A.B.: Do we need one business model definition? J. Bus. Models **1**(1), 61–84 (2013)
14. Kartseva, V., Hulstijn, J., Tan, Y., Gordijn, J.: Towards value-based design patterns for inter-organizational control. In: K. Bogataj (ed.) Proceedings of the 19th Bled Electronic Commerce Conference, eValues. University of Maribor (2006)
15. Kartseva, V., Hulstijn, J., Gordijn, J., Tan, Y.H.: Control patterns in a health care network. In: Boella, G., van der Torre, L., Verhagen, H. (eds.) Normative Multi-agent Systems. No. 07122 in Dagstuhl Seminar Proceedings, Internationales Begegnungs- und Forschungszentrum für Informatik (IBFI), Schloss Dagstuhl, Germany, Dagstuhl, Germany (2007). http://drops.dagstuhl.de/opus/volltexte/2007/915
16. Khambete, P.: A pattern language for touch point ecosystem user experience: a proposal. In: IndiaHCI 2011, Association for Computing Machinery, New York, NY, USA, pp. 68–74 (2011). https://doi.org/10.1145/2407796.2407805
17. Navidi, Z., Nagel, K., Winter, S.: Toward identifying the critical mass in spatial twosided markets. Environ. Plann. B Urban Anal. City Sci. **47**(9), 1704–1724 (2019)
18. Osterwalder, A.: The Business Model Ontology. University of Lausanne, Switzerland (2004)
19. de Reuver, M., Bouwman, H., MacInnes, I.: Business model dynamics: a case survey. J. Theoret. Appl. Electron. Commer. Res. **4**(1), 1–11 (2009)
20. Saebi, T.: Business model evolution, adaptation or innovation? A contingency framework on business model dynamics, environmental change and dynamic capabilities. In: Foss, N.J., Saebi, T. (eds.) Business Model Innovation: The Organizational Dimension. Oxford University Press (2014)
21. Täuscher, K., Laudien, S.M.: Understanding platform business models: a mixed methods study of marketplaces. Eur. Manage. J. **36**(3), 319–329 (2017)

22. Trapp, M., Naab, M., Rost, D., Nass, C., Koch, M., Rauch, B.: Digitale Ökosysteme und plattformökonomie Was ist das und was sind die chancen? (2021). https://www.informatik-aktuell.de/management-und-recht/digitalisierung/digitale-oekosysteme-und-plattformoekonomie.html
23. Yu, E.: Towards modelling and reasoning support for early-phase requirements engineering. In: Proceedings of ISRE 1997: 3rd IEEE International Symposium on Requirements Engineering, pp. 226–235 (1997). https://doi.org/10.1109/ISRE.1997.566873

On Testing Security Requirements in Industry – A Survey Study

Sylwia Kopczyńska(✉) ⓘ, Daniel Craviee De Abreu Vieira, and Mirosław Ochodek ⓘ

Poznan University of Technology, Poznan, Poland
{skopczynska,mochodek}@cs.put.poznan.pl, craviee@pm.me

Abstract. [**Context and motivation**] Among all categories of non-functional requirements, requirements concerning security are those that are specified frequently and tackled with care. [**Question/problem**] Constant changes in technologies used to develop software products drive to new and changing security requirements, which requires adapting of the approaches used to investigate if the security requirements are satisfied. And, thus, the question arises if and how security requirements are tested. [**Principal ideas/results**] We conducted an online survey among software development practitioners. 190 respondents from a wide variety of countries shared with us their experience concerning testing security requirements. [**Contribution**] We learned that security requirements are tested in the majority of surveyed projects. However, in some having high impact (economic, human health, environment) the dedicated effort is small or none. There are different techniques used from automated ones like static code analysis, to manual ones like code reviews. Most developers, QAs and DevOps are testing security. The greatest challenges concern culture, knowledge, and difficulty in specifying tests.

Keywords: Security · Security requirements · Survey · Testing

1 Introduction

Numerous cases of software development projects and products provide evidence of how important software requirements are, both functional and non-functional ones. For example, according to the Standish Group [14] among the top factors that make projects successful one concerns requirements [15]. Interestingly, although a great majority of practitioners consider non-functional requirements (NFRs) as critical for their projects [8], NFRs are often neglected or inappropriately managed, which often is traced as one of the root causes of projects' failure (e.g., [13]).

One of the five top-most frequently considered types of NFRs for software systems are security-related requirements [9]. Unfortunately, each year numerous security vulnerabilities are reported [4,12]. Some authors claim that one of the

© Springer Nature Switzerland AG 2022
V. Gervasi and A. Vogelsang (Eds.): REFSQ 2022, LNCS 13216, pp. 183–198, 2022.
https://doi.org/10.1007/978-3-030-98464-9_15

reasons behind this situation is inadequate security testing [11]. However, little is known about how security-related NFRs are really tested in the industry. Therefore, in this study, we embark on a research project to investigate how practitioners test security requirements in their software projects and product teams. In particular, we would like to provide an up-to-date overview of the state-of-practice of security requirements testing and challenges related to this process so that both researchers and practitioners can benefit in their future work in this area.

To achieve our goal, we conducted an online survey among 190 practitioners from all over the world. The main contributions of our study are as follows:

- we investigated what is the effort and perceived value of testing security requirements,
- we studied the approaches used by practitioners focusing on the level of automation, the tools, the roles, and when testing is performed,
- finally, we identified the challenges concerning security testing.

The rest of the paper is organized as follows. In Sect. 2 we discuss the related studies. Next, in Sect. 3, we describe the design of the survey and discuss the validity threats. The results of the survey are presented and discussed in Sect. 4. Section 5 concludes our findings.

2   Related Work

There is a scarcity of information on testing security requirements that provides a general overview of the state of practice. One of the most famous reports that is based on the experience of practitioners is the TOP 10 Web Application Security Risk report [12]. It describes and ranks application vulnerabilities and provides some guidelines on how to protect against them, including testing of security requirements.

Next, in 2014, SANS Institute conducted a survey on application security programs and practices among a large group of respondents (488) that provided some insights in the area [1]. It concerned a broader area—application security programs themselves (including training, challenges to implement an effective program). The respondents were asked about a few details of the security testing practice, i.e., how helpful are several practices like penetration testing, threat modeling, etc.; how frequently security testing is performed, and about the frequency of vulnerability breaches. Neither the work by OWASP nor the survey by SANS Institute provides an overall picture of how security requirements are tested in practice with specific techniques, tools, etc.

The experience of 20 participants of agile software development projects about security and performance requirements testing can be found in the work by Camacho et al. [2]. They conducted semi-structured interviews that identified seven main factors influencing testing of the two categories of non-functional requirements. Since the focus of that study was on exploring these factors, the scope of the study is limited and does not allow understanding of how security requirements are tested (e.g., level of automation, level of testing).

Fedeler et al. [4] provided an overview of security testing techniques based on a thorough analysis of the state-of-art and the industry experience reported in papers and books; both up to 2016. Their focus was to describe and explain the terms, methods, techniques, and the role of security testing in the software development life-cycle.

An overall overview of testing practices could be drawn from the surveys conducted among the respondents from different countries, e.g., Kassab et al. [7] or focusing on certain regions, e.g., Garousi et al. [5]. These studies inspired us while formulating questions for our survey. However, in contrast to our study, the authors of these studies did not investigate testing from the perspective of security requirements.

3   Research Methodology

Our goal is to investigate the practice of testing security requirements in software development projects and product teams (we will refer to them as projects). To achieve the goal, we formulate four research questions:

- RQ1. *Are security requirements tested?*
- RQ2. *How valuable to the project is testing security requirements?*
- RQ3. *What are the challenges of testing security requirements?*
- RQ4. *What are the approaches and tools used to test security requirements?*

These questions could be simplified to three simple questions: if and how security requirements are tested in projects and if it is valuable? In particular, by answering RQ1, we will learn how common the practice of testing security-related NFRs in software development projects. The second research question (RQ2) complements RQ1 by revealing the rationale for spending time and resources on testing such requirements. Finally, the two remaining questions (RQ3 and RQ4) regard the process of testing security requirements by looking at potential difficulties and state-of-the-practice tools and methods.

Research Method. Our research method of choice is questionnaire-based Survey Research. Since the method allows for collecting and analyzing large samples of projects in a cost-effective way, it gave us the possibility to draw an overall picture of testing security requirements. We designed our study by following the guidelines provided by Wohlin et al. [17] and by Molléri et al. [10]. The questionnaire and collected data are available on the website of the research study[1].

Population and Sample Representatives. We define the target population as participants of software development projects and product teams who have experience in testing security. We assume that a representative sample of the target population shall include software-development practitioners and projects that were conducted in recent years in different contexts (country, domain, etc.).

---

[1] https://github.com/skopczynska/securitytesting.

Survey Instrument. We designed an online questionnaire divided into four parts and implemented it using the Survey Monkey platform. The first part consisted of three pages: a welcome page (presenting the goal of the survey, estimated time, and providing the contact information to the researchers conducting the study), a page explaining what non-functional requirements are, including security, and a page asking a respondent to focus on one of their projects or product teams. Also, we asked about the date of the last participation in the project. The second part contained twelve demographic questions asking about organizations, projects, and respondents themselves. The third part regarded the practice of testing non-functional requirements. In this paper, we report the results regarding testing security-related NFRs, however, the survey contained questions regarding other categories of NFRs. First, respondents were asked whether security requirements are tested in their project. If the answer was negative, they were asked about the reasons for such situations. Otherwise, they were asked about the value of testing security and the challenges concerning this practice. More in-depth questions followed, including tools, techniques, and types of tests. The fourth part asked about remarks and comments. Also, every respondent might have provided an e-mail address to get the summary of the results after the survey is completed.

Survey Instrument Validation and Evolution. The prepared questionnaire underwent multiple internal and external reviews. First, it was examined by the authors of this paper and the initial version was subjected to a pilot study with 19 participants (three members of our research group, and IT professionals with experience in testing greater than 5 years—10 people and lower than 5 years—6 people). The feedback from 12 of them allowed us to introduce minor improvements into two demographic questions. The questionnaire was not further modified during the study.

Ethical Considerations. While designing our study, we have considered a series of ethical considerations, especially those discussed by Vinson and Singer [16]. Participation in the study was voluntary (*informed consent*). The invitation letter and the introduction page of the questionnaire form informed potential participants about the goal of the study, the research group conducting the study, the research procedure, the benefits of participating, the estimated time to complete the survey, and the contact e-mail addresses of the research team members. Participation in the study was anonymous (*anonymity*). We did not ask about any personal information or the names of the companies. However, the participants could provide us with their e-mail addresses that might contain their names or surnames. Therefore, we excluded these data from the further analyses. A direct benefit of participating in our study was the early access to the results of the survey before they are officially published (*beneficence*). The online survey was conducted using the Survey Monkey platform, which we consider to be a secured service (*confidentiality*).

Data Collection. We decided to target the respondents using Internet-based channels since no single 'place' provides access to the representatives of the population. Our survey had a form of invitation-based online survey. We sent messages to people we knew to have experience in testing, we posted the request to participate in the survey in social network groups related to testing on LinkedIn and Facebook. We also sent invitations to speakers of testing conferences and those who on GitHub had provided their position as related to testing. The data collection took place between July 17, 2020, and November 21, 2020. The exact response rate cannot be calculated due to the usage of public invitations, but given that we collected 380 responses, the response rate can be interpreted as low, which is typical for online surveys.

We collected 180 complete and 200 incomplete responses plus 11 responses from the pilot study. We decided to include pilot responses as well since there were no important flaws identified during the pilot study that could affect the responses to the main questions. One of the complete responses regarded a project conducted in the year 2000, therefore, the response was rejected as the project did not meet the criteria for sample representativeness. Consequently, *190 complete responses* were included in the analysis

The respondents spent on average ca. 27 min (median) to complete the whole survey (also including other categories of non-functional requirements). The majority of incomplete respondents 52% (100) answered just the first question that is to provide the year of the project and devoted to the survey ca. 1 min (median). Other 16% (30) of incomplete respondents spent ca. 3 min (median) and answered the demographic questions. Finally, 32% (62) of incomplete respondents dedicated ca. 5 min to the survey and left it after sharing their opinion on whether security was tested or not in their projects. Thus, it seems that the major issues that could discourage our respondents were either (1) the topic of the survey that after reading the introduction was not compelling enough to continue, or they did not have experience in the area, (2) answering questions about demographic questions was too exhausting.

Data Analysis Methods. We used frequency analysis for the multi-choice questions and the grounded theory techniques of coding (open and axial coding) and constant comparison as recommended by Charmaz [3] to analyze responses to the open-text questions.

Validity Threats. The analysis of validity threats is based on the guidelines provided by Wohlin et al. [17].

Construct Validity. The first threat relates to the understanding of the term "security" by the respondents. To mitigate this threat, we provided a definition of security in the questionnaire to ensure a common understanding of that term. Since there are numerous tools to test security requirements we asked participants to provide the names of the tools they used to test security requirements in form of an open question. It might have led to not providing all tools as some names might have not come to mind of a respondent at the time of filling the questionnaire in. Also, we made sure that the participants understood the goal of the study by clarifying the goal at the beginning of the questionnaire, so they were motivated to provide comprehensive and true answers to the questions. Next, there is no single accepted list of challenges nor of techniques that we could use in the survey. Our lists come from literature review, and our own experience. We allowed for the option "Other" to let respondents add, if missing, their proposals. Finally, we decided to run the survey anonymously to mitigate the evaluation apprehension threat. Only after respondents completed all the research-related questions they were asked to voluntarily provide their email address to receive a report of the results (still it gave the possibility to stay anonymous).

Content Validity. To mitigate the risk that the questions are not representative of what they aim to measure, we asked our experts (mixture of researchers, senior and junior experts in testing) in the pilot study if they see any necessary changes to introduce to achieve the goals of our study. We need also to accept that we could have added some more questions to the questionnaire.

Internal Validity. Although we did not seek to establish causal relationships, we believe that there are some threats that we can classify as belonging to internal validity. First of all, we partially relied on inviting the members of agile social networks (LinkedIn, Facebook) to participate in our survey. As a result, it limited our control over the response-collection process. Consequently, we were not able to determine neither the response rate nor who received our invitation. Also, there is a question about the trustworthiness of the respondents. However, we cannot identify the reasons to intentionally provide false responses. Also, informing the participants about the results of the study was the only incentive we offered for participating in the study. It could have a double-edged impact on the responses we collected. The use of monetary incentives could have increased the response rate, however, it could also harm the quality of the responses since some of the respondents might have been interested in completing the survey to be rewarded rather than motivated by the will of sharing their opinions with the community. Another threat concerns the skills required to fill in the questionnaire. We assumed that the respondents would not have problems in responding to an online survey which is created using one of the most popular survey tools (Survey Monkey) and consisting of a commonly-used type of questions. Moreover, we assumed that they are fluent enough in English to understand the questions. We conducted a pilot study to ensure that the questionnaire is easy to understand. We continuously monitored the process of filling in the survey (using quick analysis of the answers in the survey tool) and, especially, the time that the respondents spent on answering the questions. We did not observe any disturbing cases and it took ca. 27 min (median) to complete the survey, which seems to be a reasonable duration for this kind of survey (we informed the participants on the first page of the questionnaire about the estimated time – ca. 30 min). We also monitored those who dropped out. Since a significant proportion of respondents left the survey after the first question (see the analysis in Sect. 3) it seems that either the topic was not interesting or providing demographic information was too overwhelming. Thus, we might suspect that those who provided complete answers were those most interested in the topic.

External Validity. The main threat concerns the representatives of the respondents and their projects. As it follows from our study design and the analysis of the demographic data (see Sect. 4) the respondents represent the diverse profiles of software project participants (i.e., they have different experience, work in various industry sectors, projects were developed in different countries, etc.), which is essential to mitigate the risk of skewing the observations towards some particular context. The sample seems appropriate for the goal of our study, which was to get a general overview of testing security requirements. However, a side effect of surveying such a broad population is that we were not able to relate certain characteristics to specific context factors in the projects. Therefore, based on our results, we cannot tell which testing approach one should expect to see in their particular project.

Conclusion Validity. We allowed for providing open-text answers or stating "I don't know"/"Other" to avoid biasing the results by forcing the respondents to answer about the provided sets. We employed a qualitative coding technique to analyze open-text responses. Although two authors of the paper performed a multi-step process of analyzing the responses, such an approach might have introduced some bias to the conclusions.

4   Results and Discussion

4.1   Demographic Information

The 190 survey participants performed a large variety of project roles. The largest group of respondents were involved in testing-related tasks: testers/test engineers/QA engineers (75), test managers (32), QA representatives (23). Many of them were also involved in the design and/or implementation: developers/software engineers (60) and architects (37). The less frequently performed roles related to project management/coaching (Scrum Master (14), coach (12), middle management (15), executive management (6)) or requirements elicitation and management (Product Owner (12), business/requirements analyst (10)).

More than 76% of the participants had 5 or more years of experience and only 2% of them were working in IT for less than a year. Also, 56% of the participants had 5 or more years of experience in testing while 12% of them were involved in testing for less than a year.

The respondents referred to their recent projects since 95% of them were developed within the last three years (83% in 2020, 11% in 2019, and 2% in 2018). Figure 1 presents the countries in which the respondents' projects were developed. The most dominating areas were North America, Europe, India. The most underrepresented region was Central Africa while Central Europe could be over-represented for the Europe region.

As it is presented in Table 1, the projects were developed for different industry sectors, with banking/finance/insurance, information technology, and medical & health care, and Telecommunication as dominating domains. Also, the three most frequently developed types of applications were web applications, services, and mobile applications. We could also see that the responses covered most of the application types. The observed distribution of industry sectors is similar to the one reported by Hill [6] for the ISBSG database.

Fig. 1. Geographic locations of the respondents' projects.

Table 1. Industry sectors in which the respondents' projects were conducted and application types that were developed.

Industry sector	Resp.	%	Application type	Resp.	%
Finance/Banking/Insurance	39	21%	Web application	87	46%
Information technology	24	13%	Web Services/SOA	37	19%
Medical & health care	15	8%	Mobile Application	14	7%
Telecommunication	14	7%	Desktop client-server	10	5%
Government	12	6%	Desktop standalone	8	4%
Traveling	9	5%	IoT system	5	3%
Aviation	6	3%	Embedded	5	3%
Education	6	3%	Library	3	2%
Transportation	6	3%	Database	2	1%
Sales, retail & business development	5	3%	Other	19	10%
Electronics & computer	4	2%			
Energy	4	2%			
Gas and oil	4	2%			
Media, publishing	4	2%			
Security and protective services	4	2%			
Automotive	3	2%			
Entertainment	3	2%			
Gaming	3	2%			
Utilities	3	2%			
Aerospace	2	1%			
Human resources/Payroll	2	1%			
Pharmaceuticals	2	1%			
Services	2	1%			
Manufacturing	1	1%			
Marketing	1	1%			
Sales, retail & business development	1	1%			
Other	11	6%			

The large majority of the project teams worked according to one (or many) agile methods, e.g., Scrum (145), Kanban (55), XP (15), or SAFe (4). There were also 22 respondents whose projects were based on the waterfall process. Finally, there were a few project that followed other project management methodologies such as PRINCE2 (3), RUP (3), PSP (1), or some other/custom methods (20).

The majority of the respondents' projects were developed by large or medium organizations (62%), however, there were also 15% of projects developed by micro organizations (see Table 2). Also, the largest number of project teams consisted between 3–9 people, which is convergent with the fact that most of them were developed according to the agile methods that promote small teams. Most of the teams (75%) worked from different sites or remotely. Finally, we asked about the project duration at the moment a given respondent participated in it for the last time. As it can be seen in Table 2, the sample contains a mix of projects at different stages of their development.

Based on the presented analysis of the demographic information we did not find strong evidence against the sample representatives of the target population (see Sect. 3). However, we can see that our sample of projects developed in Europe could be slightly skewed towards Central Europe.

Table 2. Duration and team/organization sizes of the respondents' projects.

Duration	Resp.	%	Team size	Resp.	%	Organization size	Resp.	%
0–3 months	44	23%	Up to 3	7	4%	Micro (1–10 persons)	29	15%
3–6 months	28	19%	3–9	90	47%	Small (11–50 persons)	43	23%
6–12 months	30	15%	10–18	46	24%	Medium (51–250 persons)	49	26%
1–2 years	37	15%	19–27	16	8%	Large (250+ persons)	69	36%
2–5 years	28	12%	Over 27	31	16%			
5+ years	23	16%						

4.2 RQ1. Are Security Requirements Tested?

According to our respondents, security requirements were tested in 91% of projects (see Fig. 2). The intensity of testing differ between the projects. In 43% of the projects the effort invested in this activity was indicated as definitely high or rather high while in 27% of them it was evaluated by participants as rather low or definitely low. Only 9% (18) of the respondents stated that testing of security requirements was not performed in their projects. The most frequently reported reason for that was lack of security requirements in projects (12). Unfortunately, we were not able to determine whether the lack of security requirements resulted from, e.g., insufficient requirements analysis, the fact that security concerns were irrelevant for the product being developed. Other reasons for omitting this task mentioned by at least two participants were lack of security testing culture (3) or management decision (3).

Unfortunately, as it is presented in Fig. 3, in many projects developing products that could have severe negative consequences on human lives, environment, or cause economic loss in case of their failure testing security requirements is either not performed or performed in a minimal way.

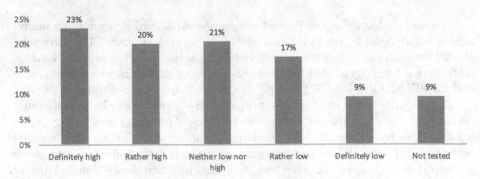

Fig. 2. Effort dedicated to testing security requirements.

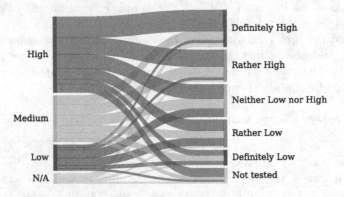

Fig. 3. Sankey diagram presenting the relationship between the potential harmful consequences resulting from the failure of systems, i.e., human life endangered, environment is harmed, economic loss (left) and effort of testing security requirements (right). The width of the arrows are proportional to the number of observations.

4.3   RQ2. How Valuable to the Project Is Testing Security Requirements?

The practice of testing security requirements was perceived as valuable by 72% of the respondents while 15% of them indicated it as not bringing value to their projects. However, as it can be seen in Fig. 5, the benefits come with price. In overall the more effort is invested in the process of testing security requirement, the more visible are the benefits. Still, the figure shows some examples when low investment in security testing brought visible benefits to the project.

4.4   RQ3. What Are the Challenges of Testing Security Requirements?

In ca. one-third of the projects testing security requirements was perceived to rise the following challenges: C1. Lack of security testing culture (47%), C2. Lack of knowledge (34%), C3. Lack of priority, and C4. Difficulties in specifying

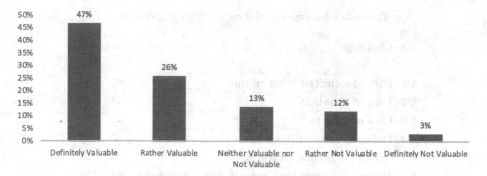

Fig. 4. Benefits from testing security requirements.

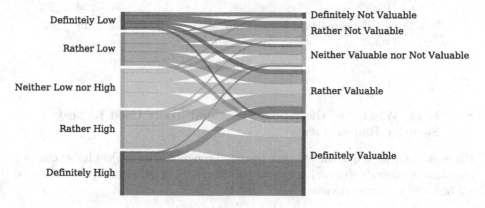

Fig. 5. Sankey diagram presenting the relationship between the effort (left) and value (right) of testing security requirements.

tests (29%) (see Table 3). Challenges C2 to C4 are especially important for the Requirements Engineering (RE) community since their presence might mean that there is a need for education on how to verify security requirements, the need for developing methods of requirements prioritization (some respondents commented that functional requirements were given priority but *"when though the impact of the latter was much higher"* and that *"Low priority except a few req."*) and the need of developing methods that would help in generating or recommending tests for certain requirements. Interestingly, a low percentage of participants identified the existing tools as an obstacle (C9) (only 13%). Other challenges raised by the respondents concerned communication with the testing team, lack of overall strategy, understanding the need for security testing, and the fact that it is a shared responsibility across multiple stakeholders. Finally, 10% of the respondents did not find any challenges in testing security requirements (Fig. 4).

Table 3. Challenges in testing security requirements.

ID	Challenge	Responses	
		Num.	%
C1	Lack of security testing culture	80	47
C2	Lack of knowledge	58	34
C3	Lack of priority	52	30
C4	Difficulty in specifying tests	50	29
C5	Long time needed for testing	45	26
C6	Difficulty in specifying quantifiable requirements	44	26
C7	Conflict between requirements	42	24
C8	High cost	34	20
C9	Available tools did not suit our needs	22	13
	None	18	10
	Other	9	5

4.5   RQ4. What Are the Approaches and Tools Used to Test Security Requirements?

Phases. Security requirements were tested throughout the project life-cycle, but the most intensively during implementation (in 62% of projects) and acceptance (in 50%) of projects outcomes (see Table 4).

Techniques. The three most frequently employed techniques of testing security requirements were code reviews, architecture reviews, and vulnerability scanning (see Table 4) used in 72%, 59%, and 59% of projects, respectively. Also, in over 50% of projects, penetration testing and automated static code analysis were used. It follows from the results that the human factor is still of high value and indispensable. Since the respondents mentioned that security requirements are tested during the requirements specification phases and study design phases in more than one-third of projects, it seems that those human-intensive techniques are then employed.

Level of Tests. Security requirements are tested at different levels, mostly at the acceptance level 26% (see Fig. 6B). Only in 17% of the projects, there was security testing performed at the unit level.

Automation. A low percentage of respondents claimed that the testing was performed fully automatically (see Fig. 6A). Over half of respondents employed a manual approach to a large extent (fully manually or more manually less automated). It shows that either the automated techniques are still far from being perfect or are costly. Also, taking into account that the majority of the tests are acceptance tests (see Fig. 6A), it might suggest the existence of the gap in the methods and tools for security testing at that level.

Table 4. Description of testing security requirements from the perspectives of techniques, planning, roles responsible, phases of project, and planning approaches.

Techniques	Responses		Roles responsible	Responses	
	Num.	%		Num.	%
Code reviews	123	72	Developers	98	57
Architecture reviews	101	59	Internal QA/Testing team	67	39
Vulnerability scanning	101	59	External QA/Testing team	55	32
Penetration testing	93	54	Separate testers in the team	33	19
Automated static analysis	88	51	DevOps	28	16
Risk analysis	83	48	Client	20	12
Source and binary code fault injection	29	17	Other	19	11
Binary code analysis	26	15	User(s)	8	5
Fuzz testing	21	12			

Phases	Responses		Planning	Responses	
	Num.	[%]		Num.	[%]
Study and Concept	33	19	Together with other activities in the total package	67	39
Requirements Specification	58	34	Not planned	29	17
System Design	68	40	For performing QA as a whole	28	16
Implementation	107	62	I don't know	27	16
Acceptance	86	50	For individual QA measures	13	8
Maintenance	51	30	For each req. separately	7	4
Other	7	4	Other	1	1

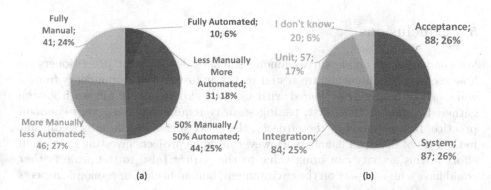

Fig. 6. Automation level (A) and Level of tests (B) in testing security requirements.

Tools. There were 90 different tools named by the respondents that are used to test security requirements. The top three most frequently mentioned are Sonar-Qube (20 respondents), Burp Suite (12), and OWASP ZAP (10). 6 practitioners claimed that they use custom, in-house developed tools, while another 4 respondents claimed that they applied static code analysis tools but could not recall the names of the tools.

The tools used can be divided into several categories: Measurement tools (e.g., Sonar), App Scanners detecting vulnerabilities (e.g., OWASP ZAP, SQL Map, Acunetix), Static code analyzers (e.g., linters, Visual studio, Fortify), Tools to automate the execution of test cases (e.g., Selenium, Apache JMeter), Tools to investigate communication over a network (e.g., Wireshark), API test helpers (e.g., Postman), Repositories and Addons (e.g., Git, GitHub, BitBucket), Tools to document test cases (e.g., Excel), Task management tools (e.g., Azure DevOps).

Roles Responsible. In ca. 57% of projects Developers were those who test security requirements (see Table 4). In 67% projects, there were separated people responsible for this task, in particular, internal QA team (39%), external QA team (32%), or separate testers within the teams (19%). Interestingly, there are also projects in which the client or user(s) tested security requirements. Some respondents mentioned also that Architect (3 projects) or dedicated security teams– Internal (4) or External (3) were responsible for testing.

Planning. In nearly 40% of projects testing security requirements was planned together with other activities without isolating specific tasks (see Table 4). From the RE point of view, it is interesting that rarely the effort is estimated for each security requirement separately (only in 4% of projects) and quite often it is not planned at all (17%). Also, taking into account there were difficulties in specifying quantifiable requirements (C4) present in nearly one-third of projects (see Table 3), the question "how to support specification, documentation, analysis of security requirements to increase their predictability?" might need to be answered in the future.

5   Conclusions

We conducted an online survey among software development practitioners on how security requirements are tested in the industry. 190 respondents from a wide variety of countries shared with us their experience. It follows from the gathered responses that, first, testing security requirements is a very common practice. In nearly half of the projects, the effort spent on testing is significant in the eyes of the team members. However, in some projects investing even small effort in this activity can bring value to the project (also to the projects that could have a high impact on the environment, human health, or economic aspects in case of their failure).

Second, the projects and product teams struggle with several challenges. The challenges concern lack of testing security requirements culture, lack of knowledge on how to test those requirements, and difficulty in specifying tests. Moreover, some respondents raised the issues concerning prioritization, e.g., it appears that testing security requirements has low priority compared to testing functional requirements, or that only when the security-related risks materialize the priorities increase.

Third, there are different techniques used to test security requirements. Mostly, they are tested during the implementation and acceptance phases, and on the acceptance and system levels. The testing is performed mostly manually. Additionally, we identified that the respondents find specifying tests challenging. Thus, it seems that the methods and techniques that support automation—from requirements to test cases—in the area of security would be valuable. Also, the results of our survey raise another question—why effort needed to test security requirements is rarely planned for each requirement or sometimes not planned at all.

The three discussed groups of findings open new directions for future research to investigate the reasons behind them. It would be interesting to conduct more in-depth studies like case study in different organizations to better understand the identified issues.

Moreover, our survey delivers some insights that might be useful for practitioners to compare the practices and tools used for testing security requirements in their organizations and their potential competitors to seek ways for improvement.

Acknowledgments. We thank the participants of the survey for sharing their experience with us.

References

1. Bird, J., Kim, F.: SANS survey on application security programs and practices (2014). https://www.qualys.com/docs/sans-enterprise-application-security-policy-survey-report.pdf. Accessed 21 Oct 2021
2. Camacho, C.R., Marczak, S., Cruzes, D.S.: Agile team members perceptions on non-functional testing: influencing factors from an empirical study. In: 2016 11th International Conference on Availability, Reliability and Security (ARES) (2016)
3. Charmaz, K.: Constructing Grounded Theory: A Practical Guide Through Qualitative Analysis. Sage, London (2006)
4. Felderer, M., Büchler, M., Johns, M., Brucker, A.D., Breu, R., Pretschner, A.: Security testing: a survey. In: Advances in Computers, vol. 101. Elsevier (2016)
5. Garousi, V., Varma, T.: A replicated survey of software testing practices in the Canadian Province of Alberta: what has changed from 2004 to 2009? J. Syst. Softw. **83**(11), 2251–2262 (2010)
6. Hill, P.R.: Practical Software Project Estimation: A Toolkit for Estimating Software Development Effort & Duration. McGraw-Hill Education, New York (2011)
7. Kassab, M., DeFranco, J.F., Laplante, P.A.: Software testing: the state of the practice. IEEE Softw. **34**(5), 46–52 (2017)

8. Kopczyńska, S., Ochodek, M., Nawrocki, J.: On importance of non-functional requirements in agile software projects—a survey. In: Jarzabek, S., Poniszewska-Marańda, A., Madeyski, L. (eds.) Integrating Research and Practice in Software Engineering. SCI, vol. 851, pp. 145–158. Springer, Cham (2020). https://doi.org/10.1007/978-3-030-26574-8_11

9. Mairiza, D., Zowghi, D., Nurmuliani, N.: An investigation into the notion of non-functional requirements. In: Proceedings of the 2010 ACM Symposium on Applied Computing, pp. 311–317 (2010)

10. Molléri, J.S., Petersen, K., Mendes, E.: An empirically evaluated checklist for surveys in software engineering. Inf. Softw. Technol. **119**, 106240 (2020)

11. NIST: The economic impacts of inadequate infrastructure for software testing (2002). www.nist.gov/director/planning/upload/report02-3.pdf. Accessed 31 Oct 2021

12. OWASP: OWASP top 10 (2021). https://owasp.org/www-project-top-ten/. Accessed 31 Oct 2021

13. Piechowiak, A.: Archiwum dokumentów elektronicznych(ADE) (EN: Archives of electronic documents) (2009). http://www.i3conference.net/online/2009/prezentacje/Archiwum_Dokumentow_Elektronicznych.pdf. Accessed 29 Jan 2022

14. Standish Group: Chaos Report (1995). https://www.standishgroup.com/. Accessed 13 Jan 2022

15. Standish Group: Chaos Report (2001). https://www.standishgroup.com/. Accessed 13 Jan 2022

16. Vinson, N.G., Singer, J.: A practical guide to ethical research involving humans. In: Shull, F., Singer, J., Sjoberg, D.I.K. (eds.) Guide to Advanced Empirical Software Engineering, pp. 229–256. Springer, London (2008). https://doi.org/10.1007/978-1-84800-044-5_9

17. Wohlin, C., Runeson, P., Höst, M., Ohlsson, M.C., Regnell, B., Wesslén, A.: Experimentation in Software Engineering. Springer, Heidelberg (2012). https://doi.org/10.1007/978-3-642-29044-2

Setting AI in Context: A Case Study on Defining the Context and Operational Design Domain for Automated Driving

Hans-Martin Heyn[1,2](✉) [iD], Padmini Subbiah[1], Jennifer Linder[1],
Eric Knauss[1,2] [iD], and Olof Eriksson[3]

[1] Chalmers University of Technology, 412 96 Gothenburg, Sweden
hans-martin.heyn@gu.se
[2] University of Gothenburg, 405 30 Gothenburg, Sweden
[3] Veoneer Sweden AB, 103 02 Stockholm, Sweden

Abstract. [**Context and motivation**] For automated driving systems, the operational context needs to be known in order to state guarantees on performance and safety. The operational design domain (ODD) is an abstraction of the operational context, and its definition is an integral part of the system development process. [**Question/problem**] There are still major uncertainties in how to clearly define and document the operational context in a diverse and distributed development environment such as the automotive industry. This case study investigates the challenges with context definitions for the development of perception functions that use machine learning for automated driving. [**Principal ideas/results**] Based on qualitative analysis of data from semi-structured interviews, the case study shows that there is a lack of standardisation for context definitions across the industry, ambiguities in the processes that lead to deriving the ODD, missing documentation of assumptions about the operational context, and a lack of involvement of function developers in the context definition. [**Contribution**] The results outline challenges experienced by an automotive supplier company when defining the operational context for systems using machine learning. Furthermore, the study collected ideas for potential solutions from the perspective of practitioners.

Keywords: Artificial intelligence · Context · Machine learning · Operational design domain · Requirements engineering · Systems engineering

1 Introduction

Automated driving systems (ADS) rely on machine learning (ML) especially for cognition tasks and sensor fusion. Machine learning, as part of artificial intelligence (AI), experiences an advent of methods, tools, and applications, especially due to breakthroughs in applying deep neural networks to machine learning problems.

This project has received funding from the European Union's Horizon 2020 research and innovation program under grant agreement No 957197.

V. Gervasi and A. Vogelsang (Eds.): REFSQ 2022, LNCS 13216, pp. 199–215, 2022.
https://doi.org/10.1007/978-3-030-98464-9_16

The growing interest in the development of systems that can take control of driving is accompanied by concerns regarding safety, i.e., assuring that the ADS is able to operate safely and as expected in the desired operational context [23, 27].

At present, an answer to the safety concern is to keep the context for automated driving very limited, for example to factory sites, harbours, or mining operations. By developing ADS for many different, limited, contexts, the hope is to take the experiences and lessons learned from these limited contexts and apply them to a wider context, such as automated driving on highways. The challenge is, that a wider context will cause a formidable grow in possible scenarios and situations. With the current processes and methods that were developed (or naturally grown) for limited contexts, it will be difficult to capture and describe all the possible scenarios that the vehicle can encounter in a wider context. Another challenge is owed to the way of working in the automotive industry. Much of the product development is done either solely by a supplier company, or in cooperation with the original equipment manufacturer (OEM). This requires efficient and correct processes for communication of information regarding the system context between the customers, the OEM, and the supplier companies.

This case study investigates qualitatively the current challenges and solution ideas of a Tier 1 supplier[1] regarding the definition of context and operational design domain from use cases for systems of automated driving that incorporate machine learning. Interviews with employees in a variety of different positions at the supplier company are the main source of data for this study in addition to data collected at different OEMs and partner companies. The findings were triangulated with background literature and a focus group validated the findings from the interview study. The study finds deficits in the standardisation of context definitions and ODDs, uncertainty and lack of transparency in processes for context definitions, insufficient documentation of context assumptions, and too little participation of function developers in use case interpretation and context definitions.

Section 2 of this paper describes the background and briefly the history of context definitions for computer systems and provides a problem definition and research questions. Section 3 explains the applied methodology. Section 4 presents the validated findings of the study. Section 5 includes the triangulation of findings to the background literature, a summary, and a discussion of the main findings.

2 Background

A system's desired behaviour and responsibilities are often described through textual use cases. They state how a system reacts to different situations with as little text as possible, but also clearly convey the reactions to these situations [3]. The task of a requirement engineer is to translate the use cases into requirements for the system. Different requirements concern different parts of the system: Examples of these are functional requirements, quality requirements,

---

[1] a Tier 1 supplier develops and sells products and solutions directly to an OEM.

safety requirements, etc. However, some of the requirements are linked to a specific context in which they are valid in [16]. At design time, contextual attributes that can change at run time need to be identified in order to avoid uncertain or even undesired behaviour of the system at run time. A contextual requirement then forms a tuple of desired behaviour (requirement) and the required state of the contextual attributes [15]. However, considering every contextual attributes and their changes at design time requires a complete understanding of the operational environment which is not feasible for complex or even chaotic behaving environments [22]. What does it mean to talk about the "context of a system"? The Oxford Learner's Dictionary defines "context" as:

> "[Context is] the situation in which something happens and that helps you to understand it" [30].

For computer systems, Dey provided a more specific definition of context:

> "Context is any information that can be used to characterise the situation of an entity. An entity is a person, place, or object that is considered relevant to the interaction between a user and an application, including the user and applications themselves" [14, p. 4].

Researchers in systems engineering extended the definition of context of a system by including the environment in which the system shall operate [1, 10]. Chen et al. further extended the definition of context by adding system capabilities and the situational roles, beliefs, and intentions of people engaged with the system to the definition of context:

> "[Context is] information about a location, its environmental attributes (e.g., noise level, light intensity, temperature, and motion) and the people, devices, objects and software agents it contains. Context may also include system capabilities, services offered and sought, the activities and tasks in which people and computing entities are engaged, and their situational roles, beliefs, and intentions" [2, p. 1–2].

Nemoto et al. introduces "spatial-temporal elements", and thus adds a temporal dimension to the context [18]. The development in vehicle automation increased the discussion around context definition for computer systems. Because of the temporal dimension, the context is highly dynamic, and it is important to find a systematic way to describe and confine the context of a vehicle automation system [28]. Traditionally, scenarios are created with the aim to represent typical driving situations in a given context. Damak argues that it is difficult to capture all relevant contextual elements in a scenario-based approach. He therefore proposed to build the scenarios in discrete stages based on different context elements, such as use case, environment, road infrastructure, and traffic objects [8].

Besides context definition, the term "operational design domain" (ODD) has become popular when discussing capabilities and limitations of vehicle automation systems. The SAE standard J3016 [24] introduced a widely adopted classification of driving automation into six levels: Level 0 indicates no automation at all, and thus an ODD is not applicable. Level 1 to 4 indicate different levels of automation, from merely driver assistance (Level 1) to full automation in a predefined environment (Level 4). On the highest level of automation (Level 5), the ODD is "unlimited". The standard defines the ODD as:

> "[The ODD describes the] operating conditions under which a given system for driving automation or feature thereof is specifically designed to function, including, but not limited to, environmental, geographical, and time-of-day restrictions, and/or the requisite presence or absence of certain traffic or roadway characteristics" [24, p. 14].

This definition leaves much room for interpretation of what constitutes an ODD and how to argue for completeness. Many proposals for what constitutes an ODD have been put forward in recent years (for example a discrete list of ODD items [19], a detailed ontology of road structures [7], runtime monitoring requirements [4], another categorised list of ODD items [17], or internal system capabilities [9]). Still, there is a lack of a common definition for the ODD, which creates challenges in communication and collaboration between the stakeholders of the system [29].

Problem Definition: A use case assumes a context, and the resulting requirements will only be valid in that assumed context. For safety relevant systems, the dependencies of the requirements on the context is specifically obvious: A specific level of safety is only guaranteed in a clearly specified and tested ODD. Outside of the ODD, the behaviour of the system cannot be guaranteed to any safety level. The problem is, that there is neither a clear understanding of how to define the context in which a system shall operate, nor is there a common definition for an ODD. Ideally, the use cases for a system should include information about the context in which it shall operate within. However, use cases are often quite broad and non-specific, which requires the practitioners to interpret how the context for the requirements needs to be defined from the use case. Especially for adaptive systems, it is important to relate requirements to a specific context, because the context might change while the system is active [15].

2.1   Research Design

The problem of unclear context definitions is especially problematic for the development of functions for automated driving that use some form of AI: Without a clearly outlined context of the desired use case, it will be impossible to refine a testable operational design domain in which performance and safety aspects can be guaranteed or to find the right data sets for training and validation of the AI.

This study investigates and explores the current status, challenges, and possible improvements for deriving context definitions from use cases for automated driving and advanced driver assistance systems. The study is carried out as a case study at a Tier 1 automotive supplier that develops and provides sensor systems for automated driving systems.

The aim of this study is to provide views and information on challenges with deriving context definitions and ODDs from use cases, in the setting of a Tier 1 supplier providing machine learning supported sensor systems for automated driving. This empirical study does not provide a set of solutions for the challenges.

Research Questions: Following the research approach for empirical case studies outlined in [6], the research questions that guide this study are formulated as open-ended questions. They focus on the previously described central phenomenon of deriving context definitions and ODDs from use cases.

Research Question 1 (RQ1): What is the current understanding of context definitions?

Research Question 2 (RQ2): What are the challenges with deriving context definitions from use cases?

Research Question 3 (RQ3): Which support would be appropriate for deriving context definitions from use cases?

3   Methodology

Figure 1 gives an overview of the applied methodology, which consists of four steps: Preparation of interviews, data collection through interviews, data analysis, and result validation.

3.1   Preparation of Interviews

The aim of the data collection was to illuminate the situation and challenges with context definitions as they are experienced primarily from the perspective of a Tier 1 supplier. The reason behind choosing a Tier 1 supplier as site of the investigation is that automated driving functions are part of highly complex

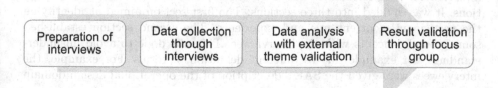

Fig. 1. Overview of the applied methodology

systems that are primarily developed in cooperation between an OEM and its Tier 1 suppliers [21]. Because of the cooperation with OEMs, public authorities and other research organisations in the development of automated driving functions, we chose to collect some of the data from OEMs, a public traffic regulation authority and a research company. All of these parties have worked in collaboration with the Tier 1 supplier in the past on automatic driving projects.

Sampling Strategy: This empirical study follows a maximum variation strategy for sampling [6]. The participants were chosen purposefully to represent a wide variety of experiences and positions involved in the development of automated driving functions that use machine learning [20]. To simplify the filtering of suitable candidates, we defined four position groups:

Positions with a High Level Perspective: system managers, system engineers, system architects, and system designers;

Positions Dealing Primarily with Requirements: requirements engineers and (public) policy makers;

Positions with a Customers/End-User Focus: product owners and function owners;

Positions with a Clear Focus on Development: function developers and system developers which develop the function/system based on given specifications.

The aim of the sampling strategy was to have representation of each of these groups to ensure a view on the entire system development chain. Seven participants from two Tier 1 supplier companies located in the United States and Sweden were interviewed. To add the OEM's perspective to the sampling data, we also interviewed four participants from three different OEMs (one OEM each from Sweden, China, and Japan). In order to increase diversity among the participants and to reduce company induced bias in the results, one additional person could be interviewed from a Japanese automotive technology research company, and one person participated from the Swedish Transport Administration (Trafikverket). Altogether 13 interviewees participated in this study. A full list of participants and their respective roles is given in Table 1[2].

3.2 Data Collection Through Interviews

The interview questions, collected in an interview guide only available to the interviewers, were formulated based on the a-priori formulated research questions. It was divided into three sections: The first section aimed at identifying the participant's current role and experience. The second section established some ground concepts with the interviewee. This was done to avoid misunderstandings, for example due to different definition of terms. For example, the interviewees were given the SAE's description of the operational design domain

---

[2] Note that due to privacy concern, we intentionally chose not to reveal the respective company.

Table 1. Participants of the case study

Interviewee	Role	Experience
A	Group manager	ADAS features and collision avoidance features
B	Functional developer	ADAS features
C	System engineer	Planning and control for safety critical issues
D	Researcher	Innovation for sensors and systems
E	Developer	Algorithms for obstacle detection
F	Functional developer and functional safety engineer	ADAS feature development
G	Project manager	ADAS vehicles
H	Researcher	Data management and computer vision
I	Product owner	Ground truth systems
J	Technical lead	AI and machine learning projects
K	Technical specialist adaptive cruise control	Blind spot detection, lane changing, adaptive cruise control, collision avoidance
L	Functional safety manager	Functional safety work and documentation
M	Researcher	Standardisation of safety methodologies

and providing examples for different context definitions. For each of these examples, the interviewees were asked to provide their opinion on applicability and problems with the provided examples. The third section explored the process of deriving context definitions from use cases. The aim was to investigate the multiple facets of the process, including identifying the main concerns, describing of what works well in the process, and registering possible improvements. In some interviews some additional follow-up questions were included. The interviews were conducted individually with each participant for about one hour remotely via Microsoft Teams or Zoom. One interviewer asked the questions, while the second interviewer observed and took notes. Each interview started by presenting information about the study's objective.

3.3   Data Analysis

Except for one interview, all the interviews were recorded and transcribed. For one interview, both the interviewer and an observer took notes. The data analysis consisted of the three steps illustrated in Fig. 2. The coding strategy was determined through pilot coding, conducted by two researchers independently and the results evaluated and discussed with all authors.

First Cycle Coding: The first cycle coding consisted of three steps: With attribute coding, meta information such as the role of the interviewees and work experiences were recorded. Descriptive coding allowed for developing codes that represent different topics of the statements given by the interviewees. Finally, initial coding, as suggested by Saldaña, was used to highlight and understand the interviewees' thoughts [25].

Second Cycle Coding: With focused coding, the initial codes from the first cycle were divided into broad categories. These broad categories were further split into subcategories. Afterwards, pattern coding was used to find emerging themes among the subcategories. Finally, each statement from the interviews were assigned to one of the created subcategories. A second independent group of three researchers validated the found themes and the assignment of both challenges and potential solutions mentioned by the interviewees to the themes. With this step, it was tried to reduce bias in the selection of the themes.

Validation of Findings: This study uses the "member checking" validation strategy as described in [5, ch. 9] to assess the validity and accuracy of the results. For this purpose, a focus group with four interviewees from the data collection phase was conducted. The session was conducted remotely using Mentimeter, a web-tool that allows for interactive questioning of the participants. The questions for the focus group were prepared a-priori. The themes related to the challenges were presented to the focus group, and the participants were asked to either agree or disagree with the challenges. Furthermore, the participants were asked to discuss the themes related to the proposed solutions of the challenges, and they were asked to rank the themes according to the participant's opinion on how important the solution of a particular challenge is.

4   Results

This section presents the results based on the data obtained through the interview sessions. The section is divided into subsections presenting each research questions individually because the research questions built upon each other.

4.1   RQ1: What Is the Current Understanding of Context Definitions?

The first 15 min of the interviews were used to establish an overview of the interviewee's understanding of the terms context and ODD.

What is Context? The interviewees were asked to elaborate on their understanding of what is meant by context definition in relation to automated driving. All interviewees were not entirely sure what context definition describes in relation to automated driving systems. Two interviewees considered the context

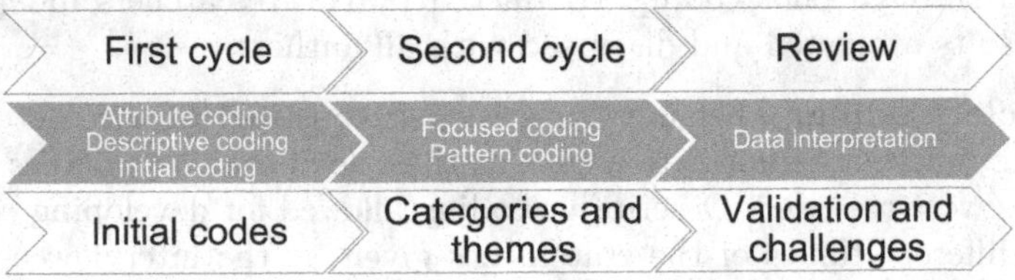

Fig. 2. Steps of the data analysis

definition and ODD to be identical in that they both describe environmental conditions in which the system is designed to operate:

> "[...] it's kind of the same things as the ODD is describing but context contains all the possible combinations, if you like, of where this is going to operate."

However, the majority of interviewees did not see context and ODD as identical definitions. Instead, they stated that the ODD is a form of representation of the context.

What Entails the Context? All interviewees describe the context as a dynamic, and rather wide entity, that should include situations, scenarios, and the environments in which a system operates.

> "But it is a way to define a situation, or define a system, or defining [...] a scenario, or an environment [...]. So that is what I would call a context."

One interviewee includes also the functional state of the vehicle in the context. All interviewees stated that knowledge and a clear description about the context is important for validation, safety, and security of the system. If assumptions about the context of a system are made, they need to be clearly communicated as assumptions, which is according to the interviewees not always the case.

What is the ODD? All interviewees agreed with the SAE J3016 definition of the ODD [24, Page 14]. Although SAE J3016 provides a definition of the ODD, all interviewees mention that there is lack of standardisation of the format of an ODD. A majority of interviewees added that a description of a design domain beyond the actual ODD, in which the system's performance is degraded but still safe, is necessary in addition to the ODD. As an example, interviewee F described the process in place for deriving the ODD: After the use case is defined, an exploratory search starts to identify the context in which "the use case is actually happening". Once they established an understanding of the context, the internal conditions of the vehicle and the external environment are analysed for the given context. The information about internal conditions of the vehicle and external environment states are what defines the ODD. In this process, the ODD is derived from the use cases via an exploratory search of the context. Interviewee K however describes the process for defining the ODD different: After an initial ODD is defined, the ODD is analysed and use cases and requirements are derived based on the initial ODD. An iterative process is started to adjust ODD and use cases "back and forth" until ODD and use cases comply with each other. This is done by first reducing the number of use cases to the most relevant ones that fit into the initial ODD. Then, they try to get a better understanding of the capabilities of the system, which allows them to widen the initial ODD and to take up more use cases gradually. In contrast to the process described by interviewee F, here they start with the ODD and derive the use cases based on the targeted ODD.

"[...] in the ODD you have to describe it as sort of a graceful degradation of the system when you go outside it's never included".

What Entails the ODD? A majority of interviewees claimed that the SAE definition is incomplete. A major missing aspect that was mentioned is the internal state of the vehicle, i.e., capability of sensors and actors. Furthermore, the drivers' behaviour in and around the vehicle should be described in the ODD (e.g. can the system operate with an intoxicated or distracted driver?). Ten interviewees reminded that the road and lane conditions should explicitly be highlighted in the ODD, as they play a major role in the correct function of automated driving systems.

What is the Difference Between Context and ODD? All interviewees associate the ODD with safety and performance guarantees. The context is associated with validity of requirements derived from a given use case. An interpretation of the interviewees' answers can be, that the ODD is an abstraction, or mode, of the context. Similar to the World-Machine Model described by Jackson in [13], the ODD can be interpreted as an abstraction of the context in which a given system can testable operate with desired characteristics, such as safety, reliability, and performance. And in some cases, as described by two of the interviewees, the ODD as abstraction and the context itself, seem identical for a given use case. This can occur, for example, if the the context derived from the use case is limited enough such that the ODD can completely embrace the operational context.

4.2 RQ2: What Are the Challenges with Deriving Context Definitions from Use Cases?

This section describes the major challenges through themes identified from the interviews. Three areas of challenges illustrated were identified from the interview sessions and validated by the focus group. They are "deriving context definitions", "process and communication of context definition", and "deriving the ODD from context definition". For each area of challenge, only the themes validated with a simple majority by the focus group members are presented in Table 2. A full list of themes can be made available upon request.

Table 2. Themes relates to challenges with deriving context definitions.

Theme	Description
Deriving context definitions	
Difficult to describe context	There is a lack of terminology for describing non-numeric parameters within the context, like the weather: It is for example not clear what "in good weather conditions" actually means. Therefore, non-numeric parameters are difficult to compare between different context descriptions. Furthermore, the environment is often dynamic and containing unknown unknowns, which can change the context of a system unpredictably

(continued)

Table 2. (*continued*)

Theme	Description
Lack of standard	A common language for context definitions is lacking, which makes it difficult to work on a system or product in different countries, companies, or even teams. Unlike requirement specification, there is no correspondent context specification, which results in ambiguities in the context in which requirements are valid
Lack of transparency	A lack of transparency in use case creation and requirement negotiation leads to challenges when defining the desired and feasible context of the system. It is seen as important that the function developers obtain more knowledge about the use case in order to understand the necessary context in which a function/system shall operate. Furthermore, it was stated that there is no good practise in determining if a system still operates within its designated context
Defining ODDs	
Lack of arguments for completeness	It is difficult to know when an ODD captures all relevant scenarios and elements, mainly because there is no standardised method or template for determining if the ODD is complete
Difficult to capture all scenarios in ODD	To enumerate all possible scenarios in the ODD is impossible. It is difficult to determine, which scenarios the ODD should entail, and which scenarios are not required to be captured by the ODD. Especially "edge case" scenarios are difficult to describe in the ODD, because many assumptions are necessary in these scenarios, which are often not well documented in the context description
Hard to understand context definitions	Function developers are not always involved in defining the context definitions, which makes it difficult for them to develop an ODD that fits the desired context
Lack of standard for ODD	ODD tends to mean different things, which makes it difficult to understand what an ODD shall entail. Different OEMs, and even different teams within an OEM, have different approaches to define the ODD, which creates confusion for Tier 1 suppliers. The lack of a standardisation has been mentioned by all interviewees as a major obstacle
Overly cautious	A consequence of not knowing the right context of the system is that the ODD will be overly cautious. Developers will start with a too strict and too limited ODD, and only expand it once safety has been proven within small extensions. This can lead to unnecessary long developing and testing times, or overly cautious systems
Process and communication	
Assumption not documented	A concern mentioned was that assumptions about the context and in the requirements are not being properly documented as such. In many cases it is necessary to make assumptions, but they must be clearly documented as such. A typical context assumption for a function is to assume a linear behaviour of some measured dynamic
Insufficient involvement of function developers	Function developers are detached from the overall picture, because they are not involved enough in defining requirements and context definitions. This makes it hard for them to understand the context in which the system is supposed to function
Lack of feedback	Sometimes changes in the context, and even requirements, of a system are only discovered during the development. A feedback loop is often missing to verify if these changes in context are acceptable
Misinterpretation of requirements	Textual requirements and context definitions can be misinterpreted by different peoples with different views on the system. Often, the person writing the requirements and context definitions has no direct contact to the person implementing them
Too difficult process	The process of deriving contextual information and requirements from use cases was described as being "blurry and unsharp by nature". It was also mentioned, that a common structured process is either missing or too complex for deriving both requirements and context definitions

4.3 RQ3: Which Support Would Be Appropriate for Deriving Context Definitions from Use Cases?

For each of the three areas of challenges described in Sect. 4.2 the interviewees were asked to suggest improvements. Out of the interviews, themes were identified and presented to the focus group for validation. All themes that achieved a simple majority vote in the focus group are presented in Table 3.

Table 3. Themes related to improvement ideas for deriving context definitions.

Theme	Description
Improvement ideas for deriving context definitions	
More diverse data	According to one interviewee, a more diverse set of sensor data of the environment allows for easier interpretation and limitation of the context in which the system operates
Standardised approach	All interviewees suggested to standardised context definition to ease cooperation between different teams and companies
Improvement ideas for defining the ODD	
Automatic tool for deriving ODD	The described improvement would encompass a tool that can take as input the context, requirements based on the context and test cases. It would then propose an appropriate ODD, that is valid in the desired context, entails all requirements, and is verified through test cases
Complete-ness criteria for ODD	One interviewee suggested that an explicit method and criteria are needed to proof that the ODD is complete and correct
Information should be described clearly	The ODD should contain more information about the context of the system. According to one interviewee, this would improve identifying wrong assumptions about the context early
Measure of exposure to a safety event	One interviewee explained that the hazard and risk assessment to evaluate the dimensions of the ODD from a safety viewpoint. The HARA includes assumptions about the context, and especially the exposure to a hazardous context can then be used to decide on the ODD
Standardised process	All interviewees suggested to improve the standardisation of processes for defining the ODD
Improvement ideas for the process and communication	
Better continuous improvement	Automated driving is a new technology, which needs to evolve continuously. The processes for deriving relevant artefacts, such as the context definition and ODD need to evolve together with the technology
Faster feedback	One suggested improvement was to derive requirements faster, and creating faster feedback loops between the stakeholders. This expedites also the definition of the context, because assumptions can be made and verified faster
Improved leveraging from other contexts	Typically, automated driving systems are developed for and tested in confined areas, such as factory areas or harbours. Lessons are learnt in these confined contexts, and it is important to be able to leverage the knowledge from these confined contexts into new contexts
Improved integration into SAFe setup	It is perceived that requirement engineering is not well integrated in scaled agile frameworks (SAFe), which hinders an efficient development and handling of requirements, and consequently context definitions
Involvement of function developers	Function developers should be more involved in the requirement engineering process, including context definition and deriving the ODD. On one hand, the function developers would get a better understanding of the requirements and context. On the other hand, they can contribute with deep knowledge about the used technologies, which eases the understanding of the technology's capability for desired contexts

5   Discussion

5.1   Triangulation with Background Literature

Already in 2001, Dey described that for computing environments there is only "an impoverished understanding of what context is and how it can be used" [14]. The results from the interviews show that although the understanding about context definitions have increased over 20 years, it is still difficult to use context definitions in practise. A main reason for this seems to be lack of standardisation and processes when dealing with context definitions, and ODDs as abstraction thereof. Some attempts for standardisation of an ODD taxonomy have been attempted recently, such as described in [12,26] or through pending standards such as ISO/TR 4804:2020 [11]. This lack of standardisation in regards to ODDs (as abstraction of context definitions) has also been described by Gyllenhammar et al. [9]. The difficulty to capture all scenarios in an ODD has also been described in [17] and arguing for completeness has been discussed in [10]. A theme mentioned by all interviewees was that the process for deriving context definitions is difficult in the sense that it contains too many uncertainties. Damak et al. identified this difficulty as well, and developed a method to adopt architectural decisions for automated driving systems to the operational context [8]. Thron et al. observed challenges in the communication of ODDs between stakeholders of a system [29]. A majority of interviewees, including all function developers, described a lack of transparency in requirement negotiations (and context definition) for desired use cases, which indicates that the communication problem is not solved.

5.2   Discussion and Main Findings

Keeping the background literature in mind, we argue for four main findings that can trigger future investigations: Firstly, we identified confusion in the definitions of context, and operational design domain. The connection between the context definition and operational design domain is ambivalent and requires more clarification, for example through standardisation. Furthermore, we identified a lack of clear processes leading to context definitions and ODDs. Although many attempts of creating some form of standard or template process exist, especially for the case of ODD, there is no clear picture in our case. Major problems are arguing for completeness and lack of stakeholder involvement. Also, we noticed problems when defining and documenting assumption about the context. Interviewees reported that assumptions about the context are not documented as such, and therefore it is difficult to differentiate assumptions about the context from facts during function development. Lastly, we observed a disconnection of the function developers from the requirement engineering, which also includes the context definition from use cases. Especially with the introduction of more agile frameworks, it is beneficial to move parts of the requirement engineering towards the function developers, including defining context from use cases and deriving of ODDs. Applying machine learning in systems for automated driving systems requires that the context of the systems can be clearly defined and described in well working processes. Machine learning is a key technology for perception systems in automated driving. Often implicitly, by selecting data sets for training and validation, machine learning models are limited to the context represented in these data sets. Specifically, a machine learning system requires not only an understanding of the desired behaviour (given through use cases, and functional requirements), but also of the context in which the system operates. The context is important, because it defines both the necessary training and necessary testing scenarios of the system. The training scenarios, and in most learning scenarios the training dataset, define the final behaviour of the machine learning system. Desired behaviour and context are therefore closely intertwined, and that might be a reason for the difficulties observed in defining the context and consequently the ODD for a machine learning system. Should the desired behaviour in form of use cases be defined first, or should the desired context be first? We saw in the answers that there is no clear picture on the order and the processes of defining use cases, context and ODD. This interlacement of use case and context, and the lack of established processes, could be the reason for the overly cautious definitions of ODDs that was reported in the interviews. We argue that a better understanding is needed how the context influences the desired behaviour of a system with machine learning components. This relation between desired behaviour and context needs to be made explicit, in order to understand the consequences on the desired behaviour of context changes. Based on the explicit definition of the context and its relation to the desired behaviour of the system, data requirements for training and validation data can be derived (see also [31]).

5.3   Threats to Validity

The study focused on context definitions for the development of automated driving systems that use machine learning for the perception system. Automated driving system are often considered context-aware systems and therefore the findings of this study could potentially be transferred to other context-aware systems. Most of the interviews were conducted at one Tier 1 supplier company with offices in Sweden and the United States. To support generalisability of the results, a sampling strategy was chosen that included different roles on different levels and at both locations of the case company. In addition, individual interviewees outside of the case company were included in the study. A threat to validity is the sole focus on the automotive industry. In order to support transferability of the results to other fields, the interview questions were formulated with the intent of being non-specific to the automotive field.

5.4   Conclusion

This case study was conducted in the setting of an automotive supplier company by collecting qualitative data through interviews with automotive experts, thematic analysis of the data, and validation of findings through a focus group and background literature triangulation. The results show a lack of standardisation of concepts and processes for defining the operational context and deriving the ODD for automated driving systems. Because of the typically distributed development of systems in the automotive industry, this creates challenges which lead to misinterpretation and slow iteration loops between the stakeholders. A major problem the study identifies are missing documentations of context assumptions. Whether a context is assumed, or explicitly given through a use case, can make a difference during the function development and testing. Furthermore, the study reveals a lack of involvement of function developers in the requirement engineering activities that lead to the context definition. As a result, function developers often misinterpret or question the defined operational context.

The study also elicited possible solutions to the challenges. Besides obvious solutions, such as more standardisation and deeper involvement of function developers in the definition of the operational context, the participants also suggested ideas such as diverse data about the context, completeness criteria for the ODD, more efficient leveraging from other contexts, and improved integration of context definitions into scaled agile frameworks. These ideas can serve future efforts and research towards a standardisation of context definitions for automated driving systems or other context-aware systems that use AI.

References

1. Brown, P.J.: The stick-e document: a framework for creating context-aware applications. Electronic Publishing-Chichester, Technical report, June 1996
2. Chen, H., Finin, T., Joshi, A.: An ontology for context-aware pervasive computing environments. Knowl. Eng. Rev. **18**(3), 197–207 (2003)
3. Cockburn, A.: Writing effective use cases. Addison-Wesley Longman, Technical report (2000)
4. Colwell, I., Phan, B., Saleem, S., Salay, R., Czarnecki, K.: An automated vehicle safety concept based on runtime restriction of the operational design domain. In: Intelligent Vehicles Symposium, Proceedings, pp. 1910–1917 (2018)
5. Creswell, J.W.: Research Design: Qualitative, Quantitative, and Mixed Methods Approaches, 4th edn. Sage Publications, Thousand Oaks (2014)
6. Creswell, J.W., Poth, C.N.: Qualitative Inquiry and Research Design Choosing Among Five Approaches. Sage Publishing, Thousand Oaks (2017)
7. Czarnecki, K.: Operational Design Domain for Automated Driving Systems - Taxonomy of Basic Terms (2018)
8. Damak, Y., Leroy, Y., Trehard, G., Jankovic, M.: Operational context-based design method of autonomous vehicles logical architectures. In: 15th International Conference of System of Systems Engineering (SoSE), pp. 439–444. IEEE (2020)
9. Gyllenhammar, M., et al.: Towards an operational design domain that supports the safety argumentation of an automated driving system. In: 10th European Congress on Embedded Real Time Systems, pp. 1–10 (2020)
10. Henricksen, K., Indulska, J.: A software engineering framework for context-aware pervasive computing. In: Proceedings of the Second Annual Conference on Pervasive Computing and Communications, pp. 77–86. IEEE (2004)

214   H.-M. Heyn et al.

11. International Organization for Standardization: ISO/TR 4804:2020 Road vehicles - Safety and cybersecurity for automated driving systems - Design, verification and validation. International Organization for Standardization, Geneva (2020). www.iso.org
12. Irvine, P., Zhang, X., Khastgir, S., Schwalb, E., Jennings, P.: A two-level abstraction odd definition language: Part i. In: 2021 IEEE International Conference on Systems, Man, and Cybernetics (SMC), pp. 2614–2621. IEEE (2021)
13. Jackson, M.: The world and the machine. In: 17th International Conference on Software Engineering (ICSE), pp. 283–283. IEEE (1995)
14. Dey, A.K.: Understanding and using context. Pers. Ubiquit. Comput. **5**, 4–7 (2001)
15. Knauss, A.: Acon: A learning-based approach to deal with uncertainty in contextual requirements at runtime. Inf. Softw. Technol. **70**, 85–99 (2016)
16. Knauss, A., Damian, D., Schneider, K.: Eliciting contextual requirements at design time: a case study. In: 4th International Workshop on Empirical Requirements Engineering (EmpiRE), pp. 56–63. IEEE (2014)
17. Koopman, P., Fratrik, F.: How many operational design domains, objects, and events? In: Proceedings of AAAI Workshop on Artificial Intelligence Safety, Honolulu, USA (2019)
18. Nemoto, Y., Uei, K., Sato, K., Shimomura, Y.: A context-based requirements analysis method for PSS design. Procedia CIRP **30**, 42–47 (2015)
19. NHTSA: Automated Driving Systems: a vision for safety (2017)
20. Palinkas, L.A., Horwitz, S.M., Green, C.A., Wisdom, J.P., Duan, N., Hoagwood, K.: Purposeful sampling for qualitative data collection and analysis in mixed method implementation research. Admin. Policy Mental Health Mental Health Serv. Res. **42**(5), 533–544 (2013). https://doi.org/10.1007/s10488-013-0528-y
21. Pfeffer, R., Basedow, G.N., Thiesen, N.R., Spadinger, M., Albers, A., Sax, E.: Automated driving - challenges for the automotive industry in product development with focus on process models and organizational structure. In: 2019 International Systems Conference (SysCon), pp. 1–6. IEEE (2019)
22. Ramirez, A.J., Jensen, A.C., Cheng, B.H.C.: A taxonomy of uncertainty for dynamically adaptive systems. In: 7th International Symposium on Software Engineering for Adaptive and Self-Managing Systems (SEAMS). pp. 99–108. IEEE (2012)
23. Reschka, A., Böhmer, J.R., Nothdurft, T., Hecker, P., Lichte, B., Maurer, M.: A surveillance and safety system based on performance criteria and functional degradation for an autonomous vehicle. In: Conference on Intelligent Transportation Systems, Proceedings (ITSC), pp. 237–242 (2012)
24. SAE: J3016B Taxonomy and Definitions for Terms Related to Driving Automation Systems for On-Road Motor Vehicles. Technical report, SAE International (2018). https://www.sae.org/standards/content/j3016_201806/
25. Saldaña, J.: The Coding Manual For Qualitative Researchers. Sage Publishing, Thousand Oaks (2013)
26. Schwalb, E., Irvine, P., Zhang, X., Khastgir, S., Jennings, P.: A two-level abstraction odd definition language: Part ii. In: 2021 IEEE International Conference on Systems, Man, and Cybernetics (SMC), pp. 1669–1676. IEEE (2021)
27. Shalev-Shwartz, S., Shammah, S., Shashua, A.: On a Formal Model of Safe and Scalable Self-driving Cars, pp. 1–37 (2017)
28. Soultana, A., Benabbou, F., Sael, N.: Context-awareness in the smart car. In: Proceedings of the 4th International Conference on Smart City Applications (SCA), pp. 1–8. ACM Press, New York, New York, USA (2019)

29. Thorn, E., Kimmel, S., Chaka, M.: A Framework for Automated Driving System Testable Cases and Scenarios (2018). https://www.nhtsa.gov/sites/nhtsa.dot.gov/files/documents/13882-automateddrivingsystems_092618_v1a_tag.pdf
30. University of Oxford: Oxford Learner's Dictionary, Entry: Context (2021). https://www.oxfordlearnersdictionaries.com/definition/english/context
31. Vogelsang, A., Borg, M.: Requirements engineering for machine learning: perspectives from data scientists. In: IEEE 27th International Requirements Engineering Conference (RE), pp. 245–251. IEEE (2019)

Cognition and Expression

Requirements Engineering for Software-Enabled Art: Challenges and Guidelines

Niklas Möller[1] and Jennifer Horkoff[1,2(✉)] (iD)

[1] University of Gothenburg, Gothenburg, Sweden
gusmolnia@student.gu.se, jennifer.horkoff@gu.se
[2] Chalmers|University of Gothenburg, Gothenburg, Sweden

Abstract. Context and motivation: With the rise of new technologies, new forms of interactive and mixed-media art are generated. Due to the technological complexity of such systems, software developers are needed to support their creation. **Question/problem:** Previous work guiding the requirements process for software-enabled art is scarce. **Principal ideas/results:** In this paper, we articulate challenges as well as guidelines in the process of requirements-finding for art-systems. We interviewed eight developers and interaction designers in a Design Science Study, leading up to the design of an artifact consisting of guidelines aimed at supporting the elicitation process of developers collaborating with artists for the first time. **Contribution:** The artifact is evaluated as useful through an online survey with experienced practitioners in the field of art and technology.

Keywords: Digital-art · Software-enabled art · Requirements guidelines

1 Introduction

During the last two decades an increase in technologies, devices and applications have challenged traditional system boundaries and produced new combinations of creative and innovative products [1]. One sector that is accelerating and taking advantage of new technologies are the creative arts, giving contemporary artists the possibility to extend and transform their practices beyond traditional forms of artmaking [2]. Technology (as well as the growing amount of data and information) generates artforms within a new and interdisciplinary horizon, fusing boundaries within arts, science and technology [3].

These artworks are often described as digital art, mixed-media art or interactive art [4]. Examples include the use of: sensor cameras and motion tracking to produce digital and interactive scenography within dance and theatre [5]; VR, AR and 360° film to produce immersive storytelling [6]; real-time data, API's and IoT to influence light and images for a museum installation [7]; and touchscreens to produce interactive films [8]. Technologically, the design and implementation

© Springer Nature Switzerland AG 2022
V. Gervasi and A. Vogelsang (Eds.): REFSQ 2022, LNCS 13216, pp. 219–234, 2022.
https://doi.org/10.1007/978-3-030-98464-9_17

of such systems are often complex which naturally calls for programmers and software engineers to work with artists towards their art realisation [9].

In order to design the right software system, the software engineering process usually starts with understanding the system requirements. For software developers who are eliciting and capturing requirements for an art-system, it can be difficult specify the requirements apriori [10]. Rather, art-systems tend to have an emergent and evolving functionality due to the exploratory and creative process of an artist. This conditions the development process and creates certain problems related to requirements finding [11]. Biswas and Singh [10] elaborate on this problem: "The artistic design can not be and should not be decided a priori, to preserve the core value of the artistic creativity. Creative artist's work processes do not necessarily follow "analyze-model-design-build" trajectories like engineers. They iteratively and intuitively generate creative ideas and evolve their design based on their perception and experience."

Although agile methods and agile requirements engineering (RE) practices may seem like a promising solution to this challenge [11], using Agile Methodologies at a broader scale in the art world would imply structuring creative processes of artists in an iterative manner suitable to engineers. The artist would need to be well informed about how to manage agile projects in order to still govern their own productions. This makes solutions like these arduous.

The motivation of this study is to further articulate and describe common challenges that arise when a software developer is working together with an artist, with emphasis on the process of requirements elicitation. Further, we aim to improve a real-world solution by developing an artefact that can support the developers in their process of requirements finding when enabling art with the use of software. This can possibly help art-projects become more successful in using technology for novel purposes, while similarly making the process of requirements elicitation less challenging for the developer.

The research questions are as follows:

RQ.1: Which specific challenges arise when eliciting and capturing requirements for software-based art systems?
RQ.2: What possible guidelines can be followed to meet these challenges?
RQ.3: Are the guidelines perceived as useful to those with experience in art and technology?

This paper is organized as follows. Section 2 summarizes related work, while Sect. 3 describes the research method. Section 4 presents the research question results and Sect. 5 discusses these findings. Finally, Sect. 6 concludes the paper.

2   Related Work

Requirements Engineering in an Art Context. Biswas and Singh describe the challenges that arise when traditional software engineering methods are applied in an art context, including the difficulties of discovering requirements apriori due to the emergent nature of artistic work, and artists' refusal of standardisation in work methods [10]. Their solution is an altered development process involving a skilled requirements engineer that is well informed about art and aesthetics, who is handed the role to translate the requirements to a developer who is quickly generating prototypes and new code. While such a solution seems possible, the researchers did not evaluate their proposition in any real world application or case study, and we note that the proposal seems to fit better within larger organisations rather than small teams. In this work we focus on evaluating guidelines aimed for smaller teams.

A Systematic Literature Review on the application of software engineering principles within an art context has been performed through the project SArt (Software and Art) at the Norwegian University of Science and Technology. The researchers assessed that requirements engineering in the arts are challenging and that it "deserves extended further research from software engineering point of view" [9]. Even though the SArt project was completed 2009, to our knowledge there is no larger study that has covered the subject more in depth.

Creative Requirements Engineering. Maiden et al. propose the application of specific creativity techniques to stimulate the requirements finding to become a more innovative process [1]. The techniques are facilitated by the Requirements Analyst through workshops with one or several participating stakeholders. These workshops seek to find incomplete ideas rather than acquire complete information and explore search spaces instead of exclusively performing requirements documentation. While this understanding of requirements finding as a creative problem solving process can be useful when exploring elicitation in the creative arts, the research assumes that the stakeholders involved need help coming up with creative ideas. This does not overlap very well with the arts, where the stakeholder (artist) has creativity as his/her profession.

Agile Methods for Art. Marchese [11] reports on the development of an interactive art installation applying Adaptive Software Development, an agile method. Here, the frequently changing and evolving requirements stabilize thanks to the iterative, feedback based process. However, requirements elicitation is performed through standard methods such as interviews and observation, without mentioning if these techniques were altered to better suit the arts.

Prototyping. Prototyping is a commonly used elicitation technique in situations with unclear requirements [12]. It allows for experimentation with different configurations and can help clarify fuzzy requirements. For a study about requirements elicitation in the arts, we investigate if prototyping is used and if so, in which way it combines with other elicitation techniques.

3   Methodology

Research Approach. The problem has been improved by applying a Design Science approach, solving problems through the creation and evaluation of artifacts [13]. Here, the artifact is a series of guidelines that software developers can follow when eliciting requirements in art-projects. Guidelines do not have a predefined structure, but they usually make suggestions about appropriate actions to perform when one encounters a particular situation [14].

Scope. The guidelines has been designed based on the assumptions that the creative team is small enough to be self-managing, and that the artwork is discovered during a shared process of creation between developer and artist. Also, the guidelines are based on the assumption that the collaboration between the developer and artist is happening for the first time.

In terms of the type of digital art covered by this study, Candy [15] describes different use cases of technology in artmaking. 1) Software as a tool: this can be a physical device such as a smartphone used to take a photo or capture a video, or a software application that helps artists to design their content (such as Adobe Photoshop or Ableton Live). Even though software is involved, we do not consider art created and expressed with such tools to be relevant, as these artworks can be created without a software developer. However, some digital tools for artmaking involve the need for computer programming, putting them in our scope. A game engine, such as Unity, would be such an example where scripting can enable graphical effects or interaction between a user and virtual objects. 2) Technology and software as an artistic medium: a good example is Augmented Reality where the software is enabling superimposed virtual images onto a real-world environment. Here, computer programming and software development is necessary in order to enable technology to be used as a medium, and, thus, such art is within our scope. 3) Technology as a mediator: here, the technology invites two or more parties to interact with one another. This can be an interaction between an environment, audience and/or practitioner-performer. If such a mediation took place through a software that has already been implemented (such as YouTube or Zoom), this would exclude the artwork from our scope. However, if the mediation is happening through a software that was programmed specifically for the purpose (such as a Media Capture and Streams API, or sensors and IoT-systems) the artwork would fall in our scope.

Design Science Steps. Design Science is performed as an iterative search process. We have performed two iterations, described in Fig. 1. These are adapting activities proposed by Peffers et al. [13] in the following manner:

Activity 1: Problem identification and motivation. The problem was identified through academic literature on the subject of Requirements Engineering for interactive art-systems. It was confirmed and further understood in a real-world context by interviewing one artist about an upcoming interactive art project.

Activity 2: Define the objectives for a solution. Our solution objectives focus on designing an artefact that shall have a practical usefulness, and were based on collected challenges (RQ1).

Activity 3: Design and development. Design and development has been performed during both iterations, creating an artefact consisting of guidelines (RQ2).

Activity 4: Evaluation. In the context of this research, the evaluation is performed

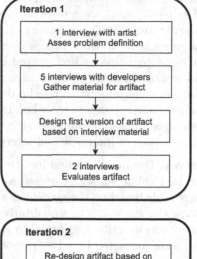

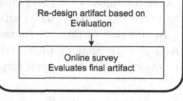

Fig. 1. Design science iterations

in relationship to the usefulness of the artefact. It was performed at the end of both iterations and has taken on the form of both interviews and a survey (RQ3).

Activity 5: Communication. Lastly, the artefact and the findings are communicated via publication.

Interviews. The major form of data collection has been semi-structured interviews [16]. The interviews were recorded and took between 30–45 min and were in all cases except one performed as video meetings over the Internet. An initial interview with an artist was performed to assess the problem definition from the artist's perspective. Although the final artifact is created for the developer perspective, we felt it was useful to understand the problems and challenges from the artist perspective as well. The second round of interviews focused on exploring challenges and guidelines for the RQ's and design of the artefact. The third round of interviews focused on evaluation of the initial design of the artefact. All interview guides can be found in our online appendix https://doi.org/10.5281/zenodo.5568964.

In total, eight different participants were contacted over email. Since the problem area involves a relatively small population of software developers who have experience of collaborating with artists, the sampling was non-probabilistic and purposive. Participant 1 was chosen as she was leading an upcoming software-enabled project, with questions focusing on anticipated challenges. All other participants were software developers, except for participant 7 who was an artist and a PhD candidate in Interaction Design. They were chosen as they had worked in at least two projects involving programming and art. Two of the eight participants had worked in more than five such projects, while three had worked in more than 10 such projects. As an example of such a project, motto.io is an interactive novella designed for smartphone-based web browsers. It allows participants to record and share video clips and narrates these together with algorithms and computer vision[1]. The mapping between the participant ID, role, purpose of interview and interview guide can be found in Table 1.

Survey. During the second iteration the evaluation was performed as an unsupervised online survey. It presented all the guidelines and evaluated these on a likert scale based on the guidelines's usefulness, and offered a possibility of evaluating the guidelines in a qualitative way, suggesting additions or changes. The survey was initially distributed to 10 participants. Five of these were developers who were contacted based on personal contacts or recommendations. The other five were the participants who participated in the second round of interviews (ID 2–6). In addition to this, we contacted Ars Electronica Futurelab, a laboratory for Arts and Technology in Austria [17], to distribute the survey internally to their developers. There were 9 responses in total.

Table 1. Participants mapped to roles and interview guides

Participant ID	Role	Purpose of interview	Interview guide
1	Artist and PhD Candidate in Contemporary Performance Practices	Assess problem definition	1
2	Software Developer and Interaction Designer	Data collection for RQ1 and RQ2	2
3	Software Developer	Data collection for RQ1 and RQ2	2
4	Software Developer	Data collection for RQ1 and RQ2	2
5	Interaction Designer, Professor and Composer of Generative Music	Data collection for RQ1 and RQ2	2
6	Software Developer	Data collection for RQ1 and RQ2	2
7	Artist and PhD candidate in Interaction Design	Evaluation of the first version of the artefact	3
8	Software Developer	Evaluation of the first version of the artefact	3

Data Analysis. Open Coding has been applied to analyze the qualitative data from the interviews and surveys [16,18]. The process started by transcribing

---

[1] https://www.nfb.ca/interactive/motto/.

the recorded interviews using a speech-to-text API. Then, each recording was listened to again and transcription errors were corrected.

The coding began by identifying relevant sentences that related to research questions and their themes of challenges and guidelines. Following Runesson and Höst [18], sentences from each interview were extracted and captured through tabulation in order to get a better overview of the data. Here, specific codes were assigned to each sentence. The tables were later rearranged where each table represented a particular challenge or guideline. Later, the codes in the tables were arranged in a hierarchy through a tree structure. To avoid coding bias, parts of the transcribed interviews together with relevant coding tables were confirmed with the second author.

4 Results

Here we present results in relationship to the research questions. Figure 2 outlines the codes generated from interviews with participants 1–6, gathering requirements for our artefact, where the codes are structured hierarchically through a tree. We share a selection of quotes adapted to written language for better readability, with the codes in bold letters.

Pre-condition. There are pre-conditions in the domain of arts that creates challenges when eliciting requirements for an art-system. Participant 3 emphasised the **lack of technical understanding** when saying that: *"They have the same problem as every other artist when we're working with digital art, they have a lot of good ideas and a lot of talent, but they don't know what they can do."* Participant 4 experienced the same issue and added that software-related artefacts generated by artist sometimes *"are pretty boring because they haven't been thinking so much of what is possible".* Participant 5 described the problem in more general terms by describing how **tools condition creativity**: *"knowledge of technology and tools are conditioning our imagination. They are part of the ideation process. If you don't know a certain concept, you can't think in those terms."* He went on describing that *"that's the danger of these artists that are too much focused on the ideas. They don't realize that the technology and their understanding of technology is conditioning their ideation, and that is a crucial thing".* He suggested that artists in general tend to focus too much on ideas by saying that *"in the fine arts circles tool is sort of a swear word, and craft is a swear word and ideas are the holy grail".*

RQ1. Which specific challenges arise when eliciting and capturing requirements for software-based art systems? We summarize our high-level resulting codes for this question in the following.

Planning. Often the **technical collaborations starts late**. This means that the ideation has already taken place, making the developer more involved in scoping rather than idea finding. As participant 3 described: *"if you arrive late, then usually they have **too big vision** for what we can actually do"* continuing saying that *"my role will be more **to cut** and that's a very frustrating role".*

Fig. 2. Challenges - Hierarchy of codes

Participant 4 encountered similar issues: *"I think the problem is that the often the technical specifications are coming into the process pretty late. It's a problem since a lot of **ideas are set**"*. He suggested that this made the quality suffer: *"if they want to have a technical process that is integrated and it feels like it's having a good purpose in the show, then they have to bring it in at the same time as they're doing the script because otherwise it will not be any good"*. Part of this problem related to funding, as participant 3 reported that *"the artists will get a little bit of money for writing, you know, and they will write a project and they will have these big ideas and they will, they will say, we can do this and this. And they will consult maybe if you're lucky a few hours with a technician"*.

Content. The artistic content seemed further to create challenges. The content that conditions the software system is unknown from the beginning and it shall ideally also be novel. It also involves many non-functional requirements such as feelings, poetic visions or envisioned experiences. Participant 1 related this to her own practice when saying that *"In an artistic idea and artistic development, often it is maybe an **experience** that you as an artist want to create. This is difficult from the very beginning to say how it is going to work"*. She admitted that *"sometimes not so easy to already have a set definitio"*. In her own vision for how to use technology in an upcoming project, she was using concepts and **non-functional requirements** such as enhancement, meta-reality and fifth dimensionality: *"the key ideas is the enhancement and being able to create a meta reality which is not visible for the audience"* and *it probably goes a little bit **feeling**-wise into this direction* and *"a possibility of having more layers where the space becomes fifth dimensional"*.

Participant 4 said that: *"the hardest thing is to make a **poetic** vision. It's really hard and they have to have some concrete examples. How should it look like, what should it look like?"*. Participant 5 described related observations from his practice as a composer saying that *"maybe the requirements are not very clear. It might be a test of an algorithm from some other domain onto generative graphics or pitch patterns or whatever. It might be an appropriation or learning of a new algorithm"*. Further, he suggested that artistic creations are novel: *"You apply it in **novel** ways because every person is different. What comes out is my music."* Speaking about this in relationship to a production process, he admitted that the content is **unknown** by saying that *"you voluntarily obey to create something that was outside of your initial prediction or beyond your horizon* *of prediction."* Finally, he went on suggesting that this is a general, maybe unconsciously, adapted attitude in arts and music: *"It's part of the definition of contemporary art and music that you want to do something that hasn't been done before. Not all artists do that consciously, but it's part of the value system of contemporary art and especially experimental art"*. This, he suggested, might be a requirement itself for contemporary art: *"the requirement may only be that it should be something that you haven't seen before or heard before"*.

Process. Finally, the challenges encountered by developers when eliciting requirements with artists seemed tied to the processes that artists employ when making artistic work. Participant 4 reported on **volatility** when describing a work with a data-driven video projection: *"It can be really frustrating doing that projection if they don't really know why. What will happen is that they will find out why they want the projection meanwhile you're doing the projection and then they are gonna change it all the time. They can say: Oh no, we don't want it like that anymore, we want to like this."* Participant 6 reported on an experienced artist duo he worked with when saying that *"They're always very quick to take new turns within their vision"* and admitted that *"it's **not going to be structured** at all. Things can change during the process"*. He suggested that *"programming this kind of stuff is really different. Let's say if you work on Spotify or if you're making a product, then you want everything super structured"*. Participant 2 suggested described the idea finding as *"more of a collaborative **exploration**. The requirements grew over time"*.

RQ.2. What possible guidelines can be followed to meet these challenges? Data from the first six interviews were also coded by searching for suggestions of possible guidelines that could be used to meet the challenges described. Further iterations were made after evaluation interviews with participants 7 and 8. The final version of the artifact is presented in Fig. 3, together with a preamble. These guidelines seeks to answer RQ.2.

Mapping Between Challenges and Guidelines. We can describe how the guidelines presented in this section meet the challenges collected as part of RQ1. The issues related to poor planning, with the developers come in late into the ideation and creation process, is meant to be solved by encouraging collaboration from the start of the creative process (Guideline 7).

The challenge related to pre-conditions where artists often have a lack of technical understanding and similarly are conditioned in their ideation through their awareness of tools is meant to be solved through a demonstration of the tools at an early state (Guideline 4) as well as making the initial prototyping into tutorial sessions (Guideline 5). Also, by showing examples of other software-enabled art (Guideline 1) a technical understanding of possibilities is cultivated.

Where Marchese [11] applied the agile methodology Adaptive Software Development when producing an interactive art installation, none of the interviewed participants described using a particular agile methodology as such. However, iterations were often a part of the process and are therefore encouraged through Guideline 10. This guideline is meant to mitigate the challenge related to a volatile process while similarly allowing explorations.

Guidelines for software developers in art projects

Today, modern computer technologies have made possible a new horizon of aesthetic expressions in the field of contemporary arts. In some cases, this is calling for software developers to engage and contribute in the creative development of such digital artworks.

The following guidelines have emerged from research with the purpose to support software developers who are engaging in a collaboration with artists. The aim is that they shall have a practical usefulness in the process of understanding and enabling the artistic vision to materialize into a concrete software implementation.

The guidelines are designed with the assumption that:

- The collaboration between the developer and the artist is happening for the first time
- The creative team is self-managing
- The artwork is original and discovered during a shared process of creation

They are ordered in a way that relates to the creative development process, starting out with activities that are encouraged in the initial creative phases.

---

1. When beginning the creative process, it can be helpful for artists who are inexperienced with software-driven art to see related examples of other digital artworks in order for them to clarify their vision and understand technical possibilities. When you as a developer are collecting and presenting such examples, keep in mind that these have to be realistic and manageable within the constraints of the project. Also, an artwork that serves as an example can be multi featured and therefore exemplify several things. In order to not confuse the artist, try showing examples that are clearly defined and take time explaining them well.

2. The examples you bring can work as a frame, but keep as well an openness about other possibilities in order to not narrow the creative thinking in a limiting way. Show only that which is required to get the point across. Also, be mindful that there are aesthetics trends in how to use software for art-purposes, and that these might not always overlap with the personal style of the artist.

3. Similarly, you as a developer can generate a deeper understanding of the artist's works and vision in the beginning of the process by exploring their portfolio and previous artworks, combined with a structured conversation.

4. In the beginning, demonstrate the software-tools that you are intending to use. The knowledge of tools will condition the imagination and creative thinking of the artist. Try therefore to encourage the artist to gain a basic understanding of how the tools you are using works. This will make it easier to discover novel requirements together. Knowing the tools will also make the chosen implementations affect the aesthetics more appropriately and help the artist to better understand and manage the processes that drive the development.

Similarly, if the artist is using certain tools and development is aimed toward a mixed-media work, this guideline also goes the other way around for you.

5. A good way to demonstrate the available tools and performing tutorials with them is through prototyping. Further, it is helpful to elicit requirements through prototypes. Start prototyping early on in the process and possibly through rapid development. Prototypes can be built to be discarded (such as wireframes or simple websites) but possibly also built in an evolutionary way where they evolve into a final design realizing the artistic vision. If this vision is hard to overview in the beginning, smaller prototypes can also be built along the way and brought together as a whole later in the process. In order to build the right prototypes, it is sometimes also appropriate to first build environments in which the prototypes later are developed.

6. Also keep in mind that artworks that involve technology sometimes only have to present an illusion that the technology is working. This is different from regular software, where the functional requirements always have to be met. This can in appropriate situations make elicitation techniques such as Wizard of Oz useful, where the responses of the system are generated by a human rather than the system itself (without the user's awareness).

7. If the budget for the project allows for it and this feels inspiring to you, collaborate with the artist right from the start of the project, possibly bringing in the technology in the writing and ideation process. This will contribute in developing a shared vision for the project as well as making the artist aware of both the technical possibilities and limitations. Since the mental imagination of what technology can do always is quicker and larger than the realistic possibilities, collaborating from the start will also enable the requirements and their scope to become more manageable and achievable.

8. If the artist welcomes it and this feels inspiring to you, try to overall see the collaboration as a distributed agency where you as a developer are a co-author of the artwork. Strive to play an active part in the ideation process by suggesting and implementing features that can contribute to the artwork and help the artist to think outside their normal idea space. Ideally, you shall be credited for these creative contributions.

9. Also, keep a constant verbal communication during the process, asking a lot of questions and having continuous stand-up meetings. If it suits both parties, it can be helpful if the development of the software happens in the same studio as the artist inhabits. Else, working in the same city would enable continuous physical meetings.

10. If you are making digital art that involves interaction, working iteratively with a lot of testing sessions will help evaluate requirements, as well as help limit the scope. When performing user testing during these iterations, welcome audience reactions but don't let these overtake or steer the vision of the artwork. In the beginning, testing with other team members might be sufficient.

Fig. 3. Guidelines for software developers in art projects

The challenge of an unstructured process was taken into account by writing the guidelines in a sequential order, beginning with activities that are encouraged at the start of the process. The intention is that the artifact will guide the process roughly sequentially, without imposing too much rigidity.

Prototyping is a well known elicitation technique from within RE [12]. It is included in the artifact (Guideline 5) to solve the challenge of having an explorative process since it allows for experimentation. Also, prototyping seems like a good way to elicit a content that is unknown because of its tangible nature. It further allows for non-functional requirements to be elicited and communicated about and it is easily integrated within an iterative process.

Easterbrook [19] mentions that prototyping can be combined with other elicitation activities. The Wizard of Oz (Guideline 6) seems to be one such activity in the field of the arts, where the functionality of a system can be faked beyond the user's awareness. This is applicable since an art-system sometimes only has to present the illusion that it works, which is different from the standards in software engineering where the functionality always has to be met.

Finally, in order to support the challenge related to producing novel content, Guideline 2 emphasizes that it is important to keep an open attitude in the beginning of a creative process as well as holding an understanding that current aesthetic trends in how to use software for art-enabling purposes don't always align with the personal style of the artist.

RQ.3. Are the guidelines perceived as useful for those with experience in art and technology? Figure 4 shows the quantitative results from the nine survey responses, including the distribution and average response for each guideline. The average ranged from 4 to 4.77 out of 5, showing that those with experience in art and technology agree on average that the guidelines are useful.

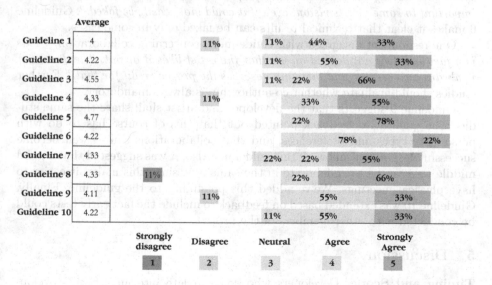

Fig. 4. Final evaluation - Survey responses

We further took into account the qualitative feedback from the survey resulting in the guidelines presented in Fig. 3. Regarding guideline 1, one respondent pointed out that examples could be confusing because an art-work with software might involve many functionalities and features. Therefore a developer who is showing examples should clearly defines them and explain them well.

Guideline 2 emphasizes that the examples shall "not narrow the creative thinking in a limiting way". Feedback was received saying that *"The risk with showing examples is that they become the milestone/pinnacle of achievements. Show only that which is required to get the point through. Otherwise, inspiration can become a guideline, or a measuring stick which everything else is measured against"* while another respondent wrote that *"showing examples of other work too early can limit creativity and prevent a fresh take on the subject"*. We have updated the guideline to indicate that the developer should show only that which is required to get the point across.

Guideline 3 received feedback *"this is a superficial understanding and requires the developer to have the tools and means to understand the artist. A structured conversation provides more powerful means of understanding, rather than observation"*. We have added this suggestion.

Guideline 5 received the feedback that *"While producing prototypes it's additionally appropriate to also prototype the prototypes"*, suggesting a need to first build environments where prototyping later is performed. This overlaps with the interview with participant 3 who stated that he was avoiding existing tools such as Unity and TouchDesigner and instead prototyped with his own tools that he had been building over several years based on top of existing Javascript libraries. These insights have been added to Guideline 5.

Guideline 6 received the feedback *"I very much agree, but keep in mind that sometimes having the artwork really perform what it claims to do can be very important to some artists vision, even if it could more easily be faked."*. Guideline 6 makes it clear that technical results can be faked only in some cases.

One respondent disagreed with Guideline 8, concerning collaboration. *"This is a fact and does not depend on whether the artist likes it or not. The developer is always a co-creator and therefore deserves the proper credit for that."* Further studies should evaluate whether co-authorship is always mandatory.

Guideline 9 suggests that the developer and artist shall share the same studio. The qualitative feedback pointed out that this of course has to do with personality types and preferences, and that collaborations can as well become successful despite not following this guideline. Also, it was suggested that a good middle way can be to collaborate in the same city, since this makes it easier to have physical meetings. We've added this possibility to the guideline. Finally, Guideline 10 was extended based on feedback to include the fact early tests could be conducted with other members of the project.

5   Discussion

Timing and Scope. Developers who come in late into an artistic development process reported that they needed to cut and make decisions rather than contributing to idea finding. Rather than weaving the artistic search process with technological development, the artistic search process seemed to happen by itself in isolation, generating visions too big to be realised or ideas that were unrealistic. Being part of the requirements finding from the start seemed the most ideal way of generating a manageable and realistic scope. It allowed for integration of prototyping in a way that links the artistic idea development to an evolutionary development process, something that many developers reported as useful.

In a situation where the developer is coming late to the process, we would argue that the developer is seen more as an assistant and engineer responsible for implementation rather than a co-creator. Participant 5 suggested that this way of treating the collaboration between an artist and engineer had historic roots, still being popular in France where they have a master and assistant culture. However, he also suggested that this view is outdated and that both sides lose in this model *"because the artist often is not aware of the extremely large amount of aesthetic implications that come from their chosen implementations"*.

Funding. Another circumstance to why developers are brought in late into the process seems to be tied to the funding and economic circumstances in art projects. Participant 7 reported that developers on average earn five times as much as an artist. This made it according to her possible to only bring in a developer for a few days. Participants 3 and 4 reported on similar circumstances, pointing out that a small budget makes it difficult to engage in a way where the possibilities of what technology can do meets the artists expectations.

However, there are funding opportunities in the art sector where longer collaborations between developer and artist are possible. Participant 3 participated in a project that was designed over several sprints during a three years period, where the length of the sprints in total added up to a year. The guidelines have been constructed based on the condition that such collaborations are possible.

Collaboration. In this process of idea finding, the developer's knowledge of tools seemed very valuable. By both proposing features that are feasible, as well as implementing these in a quick way and demonstrating for the artist, the developers help the elicitation and idea finding to become creative. In many cases the developers seemed to not wait for the artist to tell them what to do but instead took a proactive role and implemented several features that could then be evaluated and prioritized together through an iterative process. Guideline 8 seeks to encourage such an attitude among developers.

We would argue that such an attitude seems crucial if one seeks to overcome the problem defined by Biswas and Singh [10]. Where they state that "system developers need specifications to be clearly spelt out" they assume a more passive role of the developer in the process of idea finding, reducing the role to only implementation. For art-systems, being proactive and contributing in the idea finding seems crucial, and this does not always require system specifications. This is why Guideline 8 states that the developer shall be credited for creative contributions, simply since the role extends beyond bare implementation.

Such an insight points to the fact that this kind of development requires an interest in art. Participant 4 said that *"I have always been doing a lot of different art projects"* and Participant 6 said that *"I wouldn't really deep down call myself only a programmer, but I'm a bit of an artist myself"*. Participant 7 pointed out that feeling inspired and called to take part in such projects are important by saying *"ask your heart and stomach, is this a project you want to be part of"*. As such, the division between developer an artist is not strict, with many developers being artists themselves.

Future Work. We have presented an initial version of the guidelines based on an interview study and survey. The guidelines should be applied, evaluated, and revised as part of future software-enabled art projects. Furthermore, the guidelines are designed for self-managing creative teams, i.e., teams with relative flexibility working without top-down leadership, given that many independent art projects are based on funded projects. However, there are also larger arts organisations that are exploring the integration of software technologies, such as theatres and museums. Here, it would be necessary to investigate to what extent the guidelines can be scaled given that larger organisations have other constraints and ways of working.

We have investigated the problem from the developers point of view. In future studies, it might be interesting to also explore the problem from the artist point of view. Artists have the same interest since they want to make interesting art. What guidelines would artists need to follow in order to better enable art through software? Are there any particular guidelines that artists shall follow when collaborating together with a developer, conditioned by the tools and processes that enable software? We have also focused broadly on a wide set of possible art forms. Future work can look at whether work with particular media (e.g., augmented reality) needs more specific and specialized guidance.

Threats to Validity. We follow the classifications of Runeson and Höst [18] when discussing validity threats.

Construct Validity. The interview guide for interviewing the developers was based on concepts and terminologies common in Requirements Engineering. These were concepts such as *functional and non-functional requirements, scoping, scenarios, Goal-models, constraints* etc. There is a risk that these were misunderstood by the developer who were interviewed, especially since these terminologies might not suit the context of art-systems given that artists don't think or design through concepts found in Requirements Engineering. This was mitigated by explaining the terms when necessary.

Internal Validity. To avoid bias in open coding, the first authors has shared parts of the transcriptions and the coding tables with the second author. However, there is still a risk that the data is biased since not all the transcriptions were checked. The mapping done in the discussion between the challenges and the guidelines tries to assess that there is a relationship between these. However, there is still a risk that more factors are affecting and creating the challenges described, and that these are not mitigated through the guidelines.

External Validity. We have only interviewed a number of developers and artists, having experience of a particular set of projects. Thus results may not be applicable to every collaboration between a developer and an artist. However, the participants that were interviewed had many years of experience from a broad range of multiple projects. Furthermore, RE and art is an area without extensive study, so we feel data from a smaller sample is useful to report and build upon.

Reliability. The first author has previous knowledge about art. This threat has been mitigated by providing clear interview guides that other researchers can follow if they were to conduct the same study.

6   Conclusion

In this Design Science Study, we have described and articulated specific challenges that arise when eliciting and capturing requirements for a software-based art-system. We have designed an artifact consisting of guidelines that is intended to be used by developers in a real-world context when beginning a collaboration with an artist. The guidelines are structured in relationship to the development process, beginning with activities that are useful at the start of the collaboration. They try to mitigate or solve the challenges that were found by suggesting elicitation techniques such as prototyping and Wizard of Oz, as well as describing specific recommendations for elicitation of art systems. The guideline also promotes elicitation as a process of creative problem solving and idea finding, encouraging the developer to be a co-author of the artwork, and taking an active role in helping the artist cultivate an understanding of software tools which are crucial in their own ideation.

The guidelines have been evaluated through an online survey based on their usefulness. The results show that all guidelines can be considered useful for software developers eliciting requirements for art-systems and suggest ways for further improvements. A future artifact can investigate guidelines that are designed for artists who are working with software developers, describing the constraints and possibilities that exist when embarking on an artistic search process for novel requirements in collaboration with a developer.

Acknowledgements. We wish to express my thanks to all artists and developers who participated in the interviews. You brought valuable insights with your real-world perspectives.

References

1. Maiden, N., Jones, S., Karlsen, K., Neill, R., Zachos, K., Milne, A.: Requirements engineering as creative problem solving: a research agenda for idea finding. In: 2010 18th IEEE International Requirements Engineering Conference, pp. 57–66. IEEE (2010)
2. Salter, C.: Entangled: Technology and the Transformation of Performance, 1st edn. The MIT Press, Cambridge (2010)

3. Miller, A.I.: Colliding Worlds: How Cutting Edge Science is Redefining Contemporary Art, 1st edn. W. W. Northon & Company Ltd., London (2014)
4. Giannini, T., Bowen, J.: Of museums and digital culture: a landscape view. In: Proceedings of EVA London 2018. BCS Learning and Development Ltd. (2018)
5. Mitsi, M.: How digital scenography and images affect the visual spectacle in a site-specific choreographic installation (2018)
6. Theatre, N.: About the studio (2021). https://www.nationaltheatre.org.uk/immersive/studio
7. Postscape: IoT art - real time networked art installations (2020). https://www.postscapes.com/networked-art/
8. NFB of Canada: Motto: A behind-the-scenes look at the making of Vincent Morisset's latest adventure (2020). https://blog.nfb.ca/blog/2020/11/30/motto-case-study/
9. Trifonova, A., Jaccheri, L., Bergaust, K.: Software engineering issues in interactive installation art. Int. J. Arts Technol. 1(1), 43–65 (2008)
10. Biswas, A., Singh, J.: Software engineering challenges in new media applications. In: Software Engineering Applications (SEA 2006) (2006)
11. Marchese, F.T.: The making of trigger and the agile engineering of artist-scientist collaboration. In: Tenth International Conference on Information Visualisation (IV 2006), pp. 839–844. IEEE (2006)
12. Alavi, M.: An assessment of the prototyping approach to information systems development. Commun. ACM 27(6), 556–563 (1984)
13. Peffers, K., Tuunanen, T., Rothenberger, M.A., Chatterjee, S.: A design science research methodology for information systems research. J. Manage. Inf. Syst. 24(3), 45–77 (2007)
14. Offermann, P., Blom, S., Schönherr, M., Bub, U.: Artifact types in information systems design science – a literature review. In: Winter, R., Zhao, J.L., Aier, S. (eds.) DESRIST 2010. LNCS, vol. 6105, pp. 77–92. Springer, Heidelberg (2010). https://doi.org/10.1007/978-3-642-13335-0_6
15. Candy, L.: Creating with the digital: tool, medium, mediator, partner. In: Brooks, A., Brooks, E.I. (eds.) ArtsIT/DLI -2019. LNICST, vol. 328, pp. 13–28. Springer, Cham (2020). https://doi.org/10.1007/978-3-030-53294-9_2
16. Seaman, C.B.: Qualitative methods in empirical studies of software engineering. IEEE Trans. Softw. Eng. 25(4), 557–572 (1999)
17. A. Electronica: Laboratory and atelier for future systems (2021). https://ars.electronica.art/futurelab/en/
18. Runeson, P., Höst, M.: Guidelines for conducting and reporting case study research in software engineering. Empirical Softw. Eng. 14(2), 131–164 (2009)
19. Nuseibeh, B., Easterbrook, S.: Requirements engineering: a roadmap. In: Proceedings of the Conference on the Future of Software Engineering, pp. 35–46 (2000)

A Study on the Mental Models of Users Concerning Existing Software

Michael Anders[1]([✉]) [iD], Martin Obaidi[2] [iD], Barbara Paech[1],
and Kurt Schneider[2] [iD]

[1] Heidelberg University, Im Neuenheimer Feld 205, 69190 Heidelberg, Germany
{michael.anders,paech}@informatik.uni-heidelberg.de
[2] Leibniz University Hannover, Welfengarten 1, 30167 Hannover, Germany
{martin.obaidi,kurt.schneider}@inf.uni-hannover.de

Abstract. Context and Motivation: Software users describe requirements for new software and give feedback to existing software. Both are well studied in requirements engineering research. However, both are also heavily influenced by the users' comprehension of existing software. We do not know which aspects of software users have in mind when they talk about it. While their mental model is interesting in itself, knowing this mental model could be helpful both, during requirements elicitation and validation-whenever user statements need to be understood.

Problem: There is no standard methodology to study mental models and existing mental model studies mostly focus on specific elements of a specific software.

Principal results: We have asked students to describe and draw a certain software. We coded the answers to understand the abstraction levels and the software aspects mentioned. We also analyzed differences. Our results showed a strong focus on the interaction and domain level. The users' drawings primarily represented the user interface. We found only small differences between participants with a computer science background compared to those without one.

Contribution: This paper presents initial insights on the software aspects in the mental model of users concerning existing software. It also describes our method to study this model and ideas for future studies.

Keywords: Mental model · User understanding · Software aspects · User language analysis

1 Introduction

Software users make statements about requirements for new software and give feedback to existing software. Requirements engineering (RE) research and practice has engineered techniques to capture these statements informally, e.g. in interviews, and to represent them in a structured form, e.g. in user stories or

Supported by the Deutsche Forschungsgemeinschaft (DFG) - 433661943.

V. Gervasi and A. Vogelsang (Eds.): REFSQ 2022, LNCS 13216, pp. 235–250, 2022.
https://doi.org/10.1007/978-3-030-98464-9_18

goal models [7,13]. Furthermore, user feedback is captured in social media or user forums in terms of users' opinions, complaints, questions and requested features regarding a software they are using. RE research has devised techniques to classify this feedback into these categories [18]. However, we know very little about how users *comprehend* an existing software. What do they know about this software, what do they not know? What have they learned about the software? How would they explain the software to other people? We call this comprehension the *user view* or synonymously the *outside view* of software. It most probably refers to software facets that are visible to the user, such as the user interface (UI) or the features offered. This is in contrast to the *inside view* of software which encompasses the components and their composite behavior.

In psychology and human-computer-interaction, this comprehension is called *mental model*. Jones et al. state "Mental models are conceived of as a cognitive structure that forms the basis of reasoning, decision making, and, with the limitations also observed in the attitudes literature, behavior. They are constructed by individuals based on their personal life experiences, perceptions, and understandings of the world. They provide the mechanism through which new information is filtered and stored" [10]. Thus, also user requirements and user feedback are influenced heavily by the users' comprehension of existing software. We do not know which aspects of software users have in mind when they talk about it. While the mental model is interesting in itself, knowing this mental model could be helpful both, during requirements elicitation and validation. Requirements engineers could better understand user requirements and feedback and respond to it.

In this paper, we report on an exploratory study of mental models of users concerning existing software. We are interested in the software aspects comprised by this mental model and their expression by·the users, not in the specifics of a certain software. We cannot use user statements from social media and user forums as they mostly focus on individual software features. Furthermore, they are by nature short and often without adequate context to provide comprehensive information. Along the same lines, requirements interviews are not suited as they only describe new features. Requirements documents are not adequate either, since they are not original user statements. We therefore conducted interviews with 17 students about the e-learning software that they are currently using (Moodle and Stud.IP).

In search of a research method to frame the interviews, we resorted to related work in the area of mental models. Mental models are studied in the area of human-computer-interaction in order to understand whether the mental representation of a particular software helps to explain its behavior. This goal is obviously different from our goal. However, as discussed in Sect. 2, there are some studies that try to characterize the mental model [4,5,16]. Based on these, we asked the students to explain the software and to draw their comprehension thereof. We used ideas from qualitative analysis for coding texts [17].

This paper offers three contributions: (1) We describe a method to study the characteristics of a mental model, (2) we report on first insights into the users' mental models and (3) we reflect on the usefulness of this method, the results we obtained, and the consequences for future studies.

The paper is structured as follows: In Sect. 2 we present background and related work. Section 3 reports on the study design and Sect. 4 on the results. In this section we also reflect on the results. In the next section we discuss the threats of validity. The final section concludes and presents ideas for future studies.

2 Background and Related Work

In this section, we first introduce some related work in the field of mental models and then discuss the task-oriented requirements engineering (TORE) framework [15] which we later use to categorize the software aspects mentioned by users.

2.1 Mental Model

The general concept of a mental model has been adapted for technical systems in the context of human-computer-interaction (HCI). In 1983, Norman [14] stipulated that when a person interacts with a software, they form an internal mental representation of themselves and the things they interact with, called a *mental model*. He distinguished between the *target system*, the *conceptual model* of the target system as a reference model described by target system experts, the *mental model* of the user and the *scientist's conceptualization* of the mental model of the user. In our research, the target system is an existing software. Norman's conceptual model corresponds to all models developed during software engineering by the developers. The aim of this paper is to contribute to the scientists' conceptualization of the mental model of software users. A user builds a mental model in order to operate software [11]. By applying this mental model, a person is able to mentally simulate, understand, and predict the behavior of software. Such a model resides in the brain of the user and is out of reach for software engineers. By making mental models explicit, the view and expectations of a person related to software can be better understood [2].

The GOMS (Goal-Operator-Method-Selection) model was developed as a conceptualization of the mental model in HCI [9]. It describes the relationship between operator goals, such as moving a piece of text, and the operations that the software offers to do so. The mental model is thus described primarily by the handling of functions on the user interface (UI). Several research studies have been conducted in the past to elicit mental models. Some use conceptualizations of specific software, e.g. processing components for a search engine such as indexing and searching of specific systems [4]. Others are interested in the general approach underlying a mental model. For example Hofer et al. [5] distinguish 9 different ideas including behavior, structure, and purpose of a system, while Rieh et al. [16] distinguish processing model, global-view model, interface model, and interactivity model.

Results of these mental model studies looking for a general approach vary. For example, Zhang et al. [19] found that the majority of students describing the Web used the connection-view (focusing on the communication in the Web) followed by the functional view (focusing on the tasks to be supported by the Web) and less students used the process view (focusing on the search engine) or the technical view (focusing on the components). Rieh et al. [16] wanted to use the same categories, but they were not suitable for describing a repository. They found that most students use the processing model (focusing on operations and algorithms) followed by the interaction model (focusing on the UI) and few students use the global-view model (focusing on the context of the repository) or the interactivity model (focusing on the interaction steps with the repository). Reasons could be that Zhang's students knew the system well, while Rieh's students just had a short introduction to the system. Both had to execute tasks before describing the mental model. Clearly, also the system type differs.

For our purposes, specific concepts are not suitable as we are interested in aspects of software in general. The general approach categories are not suitable, as they are too coarse-grained and, as discussed above, system dependent. GOMS includes general aspects, but is too limited, and therefore, we base our conceptualization on TORE (see Sect. 2.2).

A major challenge for mental model studies is the question of how to access a user's mental model. These models cannot be accessed directly, but only through representations created by the users. As stated by Zhang [19], some methods of accessing mental models are limited because they focus on a single representation. Therefore, she recommends combining representations like oral interviews, drawings, and solving tasks related to the software. We combined two representations: oral explanations of the software to another person and a drawing together with a drawing description as both can easily be created during an interview.

2.2 TORE

We base our analysis of the users' statements on the TORE framework introduced in [15]. TORE has been applied in different development projects in the past [1] to guide requirements engineers in their communication and decisions while eliciting and specifying requirements. It originally consists of 18 decision points (which will be capitalized in this work, to highlight them). For each decision point a part of the requirements is specified. These partial requirements are called decisions as requirements engineers make decisions while crafting the requirements together with the users. TORE does not prescribe a specific template, but gives some recommendations. The decision points are grouped into four abstraction levels as can be seen in Fig. 1. The *Goal* and *Task Level* and the *Domain Level* capture the system context. The *Interaction Level* captures decisions on how the software supports the users' tasks and activities. On the *System Level*, the UI is described by refining the *Interaction Level*. Furthermore, details of the application core are determined. Thus, TORE comprises decisions, and thus requirements, ranging from the context through interaction to the level

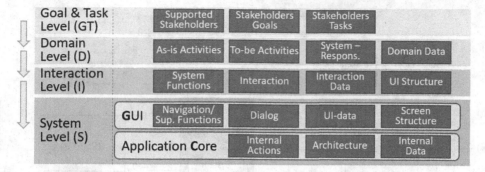

Fig. 1. TORE levels and their individual categories

Table 1. TORE categories and their definitions

Goal, Task, and Domain Level	
Stakeholders	Roles supported by or influencing the developed software
Stakeholders' Goals	Goals the software should fulfill
Stakeholders' Tasks	Responsibilities of the Stakeholder as part of larger processes in the domain
Activities	Steps in the Stakeholder Tasks
Domain Data	Data relevant to some activity
Interaction Level	
Interaction	The interaction between a user and the software Includes in addition the *Dialog* as a refinement of the Interactions into screen sequences
System Functions	Functions executed by the software that consume, manipulate or produce data Includes in addition the *Navigation and Support Functions* needed for the data related functions
Interaction Data	Data relevant for the System Functions Includes the *UI-Data* which refines the Interaction Data
UI Structure (Workspace)	Grouping of Interaction Data and System Functions which are relevant for one Task into so-called Workspaces Includes *Screen Structure* as a refinement of the Workspaces
System Level	
Internal Actions	Steps needed to realize the Interaction Level
Architecture (Software)	Components of the software and their relationships
Internal Data	Data processed by Internal Actions

of an object-oriented design. In the following, we call decision points *categories*, as we use them as coding categories.

A detailed description of the categories we used in the coding can be found in Table 1. We selected TORE for our analysis as it offers a rich framework for different abstraction levels of software and different kinds of requirements.

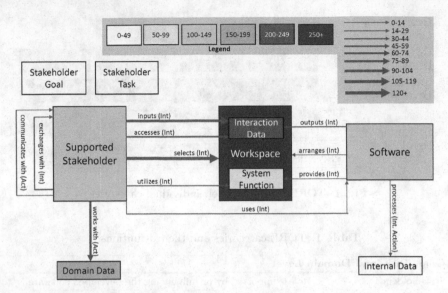

Fig. 2. TORE model including relationships as a heat map

Goal models also provide a rich framework to elicit and specify requirements [6]. However, they focus on agents, their intentions, resources, and dependencies and do not include means to talk about the software design, e.g. in terms of data and interaction.

For our purposes, we simplified TORE to include less categories, but kept the abstraction levels (see Table 1). Since we analysed user statements about existing software, we did not make use of *To-Be Activities*. We omit the *System-Responsibilities*, as they are part of *As-Is Activities* (from here on simplified as *Activities*) and refined into *System Functions*. We omit the GUI-categories as they are refinements of *Interaction Level* categories.

The TORE categories *Activities, Interaction* and *Internal Actions* correspond to actions executed by the user or the system. As such, they establish relationships between an actor and an object. Because these actions are of great importance in the behaviour of the users to the system, we further refined these relationships. In our case, the actors are the supported stakeholders (users) of the software or the software itself, and the objects are the other categories. This enables us to more closely analyse how the users describe the actions between them and the system and to better analyse who the actor and the object of a certain action are. These refined relationships can be seen from the arrows in Fig. 2 (colors and thickness to be ignored here). *Activity* is refined into relationships *"works with"* with regard to *Domain Data* and *"communicates with"* with regard to *Stakeholders. Interactions* relate *Stakeholders* to *Interaction Data* (*"inputs or accesses"*), *Workspaces* (*"selects"*), *System functions* (*"utilizes"*) or *Stakeholders* themselves (*"exchanges with"*). *Internal Actions* relate *Software* and *Internal Data* (*"processes"*).

As TORE does not cover non-functional requirements (NFR), we also used codes for the NFRs mentioned in the ISO 25010 standard [8].

3   Study Design

3.1   Research Questions

We want to understand the mental model from different perspectives: We look at two representations, namely text and drawings, as will be explained in Sect. 3.2. Our assumption is that we can gain a deeper understanding of the users' mental models by analyzing which aspects of the software they mention in the text. Regarding the drawings, we are interested in the overall understanding of the software conveyed by the drawing, which we call the *fundamental idea*. Through the analysis of the number of different words used by the users, we also want to understand how the aspects are described and how uniform these descriptions are across users. We additionally analyze the differences between the two representations (and the corresponding interview task) and the influence of software variants as well as knowledge backgrounds. This leads to the following research questions:

RQ1: Which mental model of existing software do users have?
RQ1.1: Which software aspects do users discuss in how many different words?
RQ1.2: Which fundamental ideas do users express in their drawings?
RQ1.3: What influence does the interview task have?
RQ1.4: What influence does experience with software development have?
RQ1.5: What influence does the software variant have?

3.2   Data Collection

We conducted exploratory interviews with 17 students from different fields at two universities. We recruited them through personal contacts and in our lectures. For diverse views, we included 9 students from fields unrelated to computer science, such as biology, language studies, metals technology, urban design, and teaching. They did not possess any advanced programming skills. The other 8 students came from computer science or other related fields with profound programming experience. The software we selected for this study were two e-learning platforms widely used at the participating universities: Stud.IP[1] and Moodle[2]. Interviews were conducted online.

The first task for the participants was to give an *oral explanation* of what the software is and what it does. We asked them to imagine that they were explaining the software to their grandparents to motivate them to give a thorough explanation and not assume anything as too basic to explain. We intentionally did not present them any uses cases or specific parts of the software to discuss because

---

[1] https://studip.de/.
[2] https://moodle.org/.

any use case created by us could influence their mental model and invalidate our later analysis. In the following, we abbreviate the documents of this task with (E). The second task for the participants was to *draw* their inner picture of the software on a plain sheet of paper and to *describe* what they were drawing. The description helps us to avoid misinterpretation of the participants' intentions. In the following, we abbreviate the documents of this task with (D). Participants were not given any time constraint for either task and were allowed to restart their drawings at any point, though only one participant used this possibility.

All interviews were conducted in the students' native language of German, to allow them to express themselves as fluently as possible and to ensure that they could express themselves without being hindered by language barriers. The interviews were then transcribed manually by two German native speakers. Then the transcripts were translated into English. The translations were done by a trained translator and additionally double checked with the original German sentences during coding. The focus of the translation was to maintain the original structure and the used wording as much as possible.

In total, the collected data set contains about 7600 words and 464 sentences. The average interview contained 447 words (221 in E & 226 in D) and 27 sentences.

3.3 Data Analysis

We used manual coding with the help of MAXQDA[3]. While (E) could be coded individually without further context, coding of (D) had to take both the description and the user's drawing into account. Examples of this were statements about the position of certain objects (e.g. "Here on the left you have this thing"), where annotators had to decide if certain statements were about the discussed software itself or merely statements about the drawing process. Each textual document (of both E and D) and each drawing was coded individually by the first two authors and then discussed to ensure the correctness of the assigned codes. In the following definitions, we explain the codes, the coding steps, and the inter-rater agreement.

Codes and Coding Steps. We assigned codes to sub-phrases where a *phrase* is defined as a linguistic entity of any length made up of a whole or parts of a sentence and a *sub-phrase* is a distinct, relevant part of a phrase (from one to several words), distinguished from neighboring parts.

We used the codes explained below. Note, that while we set out with an initial set of coding rules, these were refined iteratively throughout the coding process. Table 2 gives an example of the resulting codes when applying the rules to sentences.

- **TORE-Codes** (RQ1, RQ3, RQ4, RQ5): Each relevant sub-phrase is assigned to a distinct TORE category according to the definitions of Table 1.

---

[3] https://www.maxqda.de/.

- **Word-Codes** (RQ1): Relevant words in coded sub-phrases are additionally used as Word-Codes in their lemmatized form where Word-Codes for verbs include a "to".
- **Relationship-Codes** (RQ1, RQ3, RQ4, RQ5): Each sub-phrase coded with *Activity, Interaction,* or *Internal Action* is coded with its relationship introduced in Fig. 2.
- **NFR-Codes** (RQ1, RQ3, RQ4, RQ5): One or more consecutive sub-phrases containing a judgement relating to an NFR mentioned in the ISO 25010 standard [8], are coded with the NFR.
- **Drawing-Codes** (RQ2, RQ3, RQ4, RQ5): The codes for the fundamental ideas of the drawings emerged when looking at the drawing. We distinguish drawings mainly showing the UI or parts of it (*UI*), drawings using a metaphor as a central graphical element (*Analogy*), drawings providing different user steps in the drawing (e.g. through arrows) and corresponding explanations (*Process*), and finally drawings with a general mind-map or connections between parts and features (*Structure*).

The codes were assigned in the order listed above, where TORE-Codes and Word-Codes were assigned in parallel.

Table 2. Coding examples

Sentence:	*Lecturers can upload exercises and pictures*			
Sub-Phrases:	*Lecturers*	*upload*	*exercises*	*pictures*
Word-Codes:	lecturer	to upload	exercise	picture
TORE-Codes:	Stakeholder	Interaction	Interaction Data	Interaction Data
Rel-Codes:		inputs		

Sentence:	*It's a pity that there is no uniform setup*
NFR-Codes:	Usability

Inter-rater Agreement. The inter-rater agreement was captured in each of the textual coding steps to fulfill multiple purposes. The first purpose was to guarantee the correctness of the coding process as especially Word-Codes and Relationship-Codes depend on the assigned TORE-Codes. Secondly, it was measured to improve the definitions and rules of the individual codes. After each step, both coders discussed every single disagreement to come to a definitive understanding. Afterwards, the main causes of disagreement between the coders were captured and the coding rules were adapted accordingly.

The agreement and values were measured using MAXQDA's own "Intercoder Agreement" functionality using the Brennan and Perediger [3] Kappa. TORE-Codes were the most difficult to assign with a Kappa value of *0.66*. The main cause for disagreement was the classification into the individual TORE categories. Our rules of assignment proved more comprehensive and clear for

244 M. Anders et al.

some categories than for others. Specifically the judgement between whether a segment was part of the *Interaction Data* or the *Workspace* category posed a challenge for the coders. Of all disagreements, 22.2% could be traced back to this classification problem alone. We clarified our definition subsequently, which should drastically reduce this problem in the future. Relationship- and NFR-Codes showed a higher agreement between the annotators with values of *0.75* and *0.77* respectively. Word-Code agreement was not measured, as their position (i.e. the relevant sub-phrases) was defined by TORE-Codes and their label was defined by the lemmatized word.

4 Results and Discussion

In this section, we present the results of our analysis and discuss insights following from them. We have made the data set publicly available online[4].

4.1 Answering the Research Questions

In the following, we distinguish two kinds of numbers: (i) The *appearance* of a code in an interview and (ii) the *occurrence* of a code in an interview. If a code is used in an interview several times, it has several occurrences, but only one appearance. The latter thus abstracts from particularities of interviews where people use words repeatedly.

RQ1.1: Which software aspects do users discuss in how many different words?

Table 3 presents the occurrences in percentages (Occ) and appearances (App) of TORE-Codes for explanations, drawings, and overall interviews. Of the overall 1431 occurrences of TORE-Codes, almost two thirds focus on the *Interaction Level*, primarily *Workspaces* (21.7%) and *Interactions* (23.9%). *System Functions* were rarely mentioned (4.5%). More than a quarter (26.1%) of all occurrences are on the *Goal, Task, and Domain Level*, half of them *Domain Data*. Only 8.2% (mostly *Software* with 7.7%) of the occurrences relate to the *System Level*.

Figure 2 visually represents the occurrences of TORE- and Relationship-Codes as a heat map. The colors and width of the arrows indicate the magnitude of the occurrences. For *Activity* relationships (5.7%), users primarily focus on "works with". Of all *Interaction* relationships (23.9%), "selects" is used most often, followed by "inputs." All other Relationship-Codes occur, but much more rarely.

NFRs were also used only sparsely (26 occurrences with mostly usability and functional suitability). Only 12 of the 17 interviews mentioned an NFR.

Figure 3 shows the variation of occurrences between the interviews. The most often used categories *Workspace* and *Interaction* also show the highest variation. Both have a median of 19 occurrences per interview with high outliers at 43

---

[4] https://doi.org/10.5281/zenodo.5910981.

Table 3. TORE occurrences and appearances

TORE	Explanation text		Drawing text		Total	
	Occ	App	Occ	App	Occ	App
Goal	0.1%	1	0.3%	1	0.2%	1
Task	1.1%	8	0.2%	1	0.7%	8
Stakeholder	9.2%	17	4.2%	7	7.2%	17
Activity	8.7%	16	1.7%	7	5.7%	16
Domain Data	15.7%	16	7.8%	11	12.4%	16
Domain Level	**34.7%**	**17**	**14.2%**	**11**	**26.1%**	**17**
Interaction	27.4%	17	19.1%	14	23.9%	17
System Function	4.7%	12	4.3%	11	4.5%	14
Interaction Data	15.8%	17	15.5%	13	15.7%	17
Workspace	8%	14	40.6%	15	21.7%	17
Interaction Level	**55.8%**	**17**	**79.5%**	**15**	**65.7%**	**17**
Software	9%	17	5.8%	10	7.7%	17
Internal Action	0.2%	2	0.5%	2	0.4%	4
Internal Data	0.2%	2	0%	0	0.1%	2
System Level	**9.5%**	**17**	**6.3%**	**10**	**8.2%**	**17**
Total	**830** (100%)	**Avg. 9**	**601** (100%)	**Avg. 6**	**1431** (100%)	**Avg. 10**

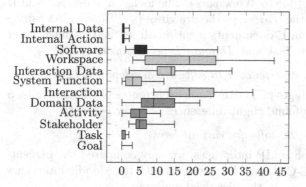

Fig. 3. Variation of TORE occurrences

Table 4. Mental model ideas

Idea	Interviews
UI	11
Analogy	1
Structure	3
Process	2
Total	**17**

and 37 respectively. *Interaction Data* has the next highest median at 14 with significantly lower variation.

Table 5 shows the number of Word-Codes for each TORE category. The number of occurrences of a category does not determine the number of words for the category. For example, *Domain Data* occurs only half as often as *Interaction*, but has only 12 fewer words (84 to 72). However, comparing the three levels, the number of words is roughly proportional to the number of occurrences.

Table 5. Word-Codes per TORE category

Domain Level		Interaction Level		System Level	
Category	Nr.	Category	Nr.	Category	Nr.
Goal	1	Interaction	84	Software	24
Task	6	System Function	31	Internal Action	5
Stakeholder	17	Interaction Data	73	Internal Data	2
Activity	49	Workspace	82		
Domain Data	72				
Total	**145**	**Total**	**270**	**Total**	**31**

RQ1.2: Which fundamental ideas do users express in their drawings?

As shown in Table 4, UI is the idea used most often (11 of 17 drawings). Only a single drawing is based on an Analogy (a chest of drawers). Even Process is used only twice despite the focus of users on *Interactions* in their statements.

RQ1.3: What influence does the interview task have?

Table 3 also shows the differences between E and D. The *Domain Level* is much more prevalent in E (34.7%) than it is in D (14.2%). The *Interaction Level* is more prevalent in D (due to *Workspace*). The focus on *Workspaces* in D correlates with the focus on the UI-idea in the drawings (see Table 4). As can be seen from the appearances, all E-documents mention all levels, but much fewer D-documents mention *Goals, Task and, Domain Level* or *System Level*.

RQ1.4: What influence does experience with software development have?

We compared the percentages of TORE-Code occurrences of CS and Non-CS student interviews, but only found slight differences of a few percent.

RQ1.5: What influence does the software variant have?

As there are much fewer Stud.IP-interviews, we only compared the percentages of occurrences of TORE-Codes in all interviews with the Moodle-interviews and found almost no differences in the discussed aspects.

4.2 Discussion and Future Work

In the following, we discuss the insights we draw from this study.

Preliminary Insights on the Users' Mental Models. The heat map in Fig. 2 visualizes the most prominent aspects in the users' mental models. We found that overall the text focuses on the *Interaction Level*, mainly on *Workspaces* and *Interactions*, and less on *System Functions*. This is confirmed by the drawings which mainly base on the UI-idea. It is well known that during RE the UI (or an abstraction like the workspace) is important for the users [12]. Our research shows that this is also the case for the mental model of existing software.

Similarly, from the use case description technique, it is well known that users prefer requirements which describe what they can do with the software over pure system functions. Again, this is confirmed in our study for the mental model. However, this might also be influenced by our type of application, which does not have complex system functions. Figure 2 shows that *Interaction*-relationships relating to *Interaction Data* and *Workspaces* are equally prominent. Therefore, during interaction the whole UI as well as the data are equally important. This insight needs to be confirmed in future studies and can be used to improve the communication with users. Also for the *System Level* in terms of *Internal Data* and *Software*, our research confirms experiences from RE that they are not important for the mental models of users.

It is important to note that during the analysis we discovered that users often use the same words on the *Domain* and *Interaction Level*. They use domain-specific terms to describe different *Interaction Data* elements (e.g. "Assignment" instead of "File"). We want to study this phenomenon further, as we believe it to be a source of ambiguity in understanding the user.

NFRs are often neglected during RE. They are frequent in the statements of users in terms of user feedback. Our research shows that they are not prominent in the mental model when giving explanations.

While our research shows that the *Goal, Task* and *Domain Level* is important in the mental model, it seems surprising that *Stakeholder Goals* and *Tasks* were mentioned only very rarely. In our coding, both are very far from the actual software use (e.g. *"to keep track of university courses"*). The type of application might have an influence here. The users might relate our type of application more to small-grained interactions (save a file, register for a class, broadcast a message), rather than an overarching vision or goal. For other applications (e.g., a Corona Pass App) the final user goal (e.g. get access to restaurants) might be more prominent in the mental model than any interaction details. In goal-oriented languages, goals are often also low-level operational goals. In TORE, an overarching goal such as exchanging information with peers is a *Goal* or *Task*, whereas a low-level goal such as making a file available to students is an *Interaction*. Thus, low-level goals are prominently represented in the mental models. We want to study the role of goals in the mental models in more depth, as this is a frequent concept in the communication with users.

As Fig. 3 and Table 5 show, the aspects discussed and the number of words used to express them can vary significantly, both between different users and TORE categories. Also, these differences might hinder the communication with users and should be studied in the future.

The similarity of CS and Non-CS students needs to be studied with a higher number of participants.

Preliminary Insights on the Study Design. Through our study method, we could derive first results on the users' mental models of existing software. As discussed in Sect. 5, the scenario used in the interviews might pose a threat to construct validity. Therefore, in the future, we will ensure a study setting where participants describe software on a detailed level, while focusing on their own mental model. Very likely, the complexity of software has an influence on the ideas and aspects discussed by users. We will study more complex software in future studies. Using different representations is very important. Drawings make the user focus on the UI. Our research showed that textual explanations are much richer (in terms of appearances) than textual explanations of drawings. Thus, it might suffice to use textual explanations and drawings without text.

5   Threats to Validity

We categorize the threats to validity for our study according to the guidelines from Runeson et al. [17].

Construct Validity: To ensure that the statements of the participants were as generic and basic as possible, we created a scenario in which the users had to explain the software to their grandparents. However, a possible side effect of this scenario might be that the expressed mental model is not that of the participant itself, but rather the assumed mental model of their grandparents. This might significantly change the aspects discussed. It is, however, difficult to avoid this effect, as we wanted the participants to describe the software in fine detail, without assumptions as to what is common knowledge and thus not worth expressing. Furthermore, we specifically asked the participants not to consider the grandparent-scenario for their drawings and the results for the drawings have many similarities to the explanations.

Internal Validity: The user interface layout of Moodle has changed significantly within the last year. The effect this has on the mental models of users, especially those users that expressed general ideas in the UI category, is impossible to measure without detailed studies about their mental model prior to the changes.

Another threat we encountered while conducting the interviews is the participants' uncertainty about their drawing skills. Many participants explicitly mentioned their - in their own opinion - insufficient drawing skills. This might affect the extent to which they are able to express their mental model in the drawing. We aimed to counter this uncertainty by ensuring the participants, that their artistic talent is of no concern and that we would use the description of the drawing to clarify any ambiguities resulting from a lack of drawing skills.

External Validity: We cannot claim any external validity as this was only an exploratory study with a limited data set focusing on a particular type of system with a particular group of users (namely students), which are inherently native to the use of computers. Many other mental model studies have students as subjects and focus on specific systems such as search engine, Web, technical systems or repositories [4,5,16,19]. Still, despite the difficulties of acquiring participants completely unfamiliar with the use of modern technology, future studies should also look into the mental models of these kinds of users, to draw more meaningful conclusions on the differences between different user types. Additionally, employing students as participants poses another threat. Some of them depend on the researchers in their classes or potential thesis papers. This might affect their behaviour and consequently their expressions towards the interviewer. However, this effect should be minimal as none of the participants were actually dependent on the interviewers at the time of the interview. Lastly, the use of only one specific software could have a significant influence on the reported results. We do not yet know how a specific software affects the discussed software aspects and other parts of our analysis. We want to analyze different software systems in future studies in order to investigate the effect that a specific software or domain in which it is used has on the results of our analysis.

Reliability: A threat for reliability is the fact that both coders also drafted the coding rules, as they were part of the research team. In addition, both coders have a computer science background, which may have had an influence on their coding. Future work should employ independent coders to check the quality of our developed coding rules.

6   Conclusion

In this paper, we introduce an approach for the analysis of users' mental models regarding existing software. The approach is based on the manual analysis of users' statements and focused on extracting the software aspects that users discuss when explaining a software and drawing their own mental model of it. We present results from the application of this method in an exploratory study. We show which aspects users focus on in their oral statements and which ideas they use in their drawings. We also analyze the effects of different interview tasks, software systems, and computer science backgrounds. The study confirms the usefulness of our method. It also allows us to derive first insights into the mental models and gives us hints for future studies. We are encouraged to design larger studies where we capture user statements from more participants regarding more complex software.

References

1. Adam, S., Doerr, J., Eisenbarth, M., Gross, A.: Using task-oriented requirements engineering in different domains - experiences with application in research and industry. In: 17th IEEE Requirements Engineering Conference, pp. 267–272 (2009)
2. Banovic, N., Buzali, T., Chevalier, F., Mankoff, J., et al.: Modeling and understanding human routine behavior. In: CHI Conference on Human Factors in Computing Systems, pp. 248–260 (2016)
3. Brennan, R.L., Prediger, D.J.: Coefficient kappa: some uses, misuses, and alternatives. Educ. Psychol. Meas. **41**(3), 687–699 (1981)
4. Hendry, D.G., Efthimiadis, E.N.: Conceptual models for search engines. In: Spink, A., Zimmer, M. (eds.) Web Search. ISKM, vol. 14, pp. 277–307. Springer, Heidelberg (2008). https://doi.org/10.1007/978-3-540-75829-7_15
5. Hofer, S.I., Reinhold, F., Loch, F., Vogel-Heuser, B.: Engineering students' thinking about technical systems: an ontological categories approach. Front. Educ. **5**, 66 (2020)

6. Horkoff, J., Yu, E.: Analyzing goal models: different approaches and how to choose among them. In: ACM Symposium on Applied Computing, pp. 675–682 (2011)
7. Horkoff, J., Yu, E.: Interactive goal model analysis for early requirements engineering. Requirements Eng. **21**(1), 29–61 (2014). https://doi.org/10.1007/s00766-014-0209-8
8. ISO/IEC: ISO/IEC 25010 system and software quality models. Technical Report (2010)
9. John, B.E., Kieras, D.E.: The GOMS family of user interface analysis techniques: comparison and contrast. ACM Trans. Comput. Hum. Interact. **3**(4), 320–351 (1996)
10. Jones, N., Ross, H., Lynam, T., Perez, P., et al.: Mental models: an interdisciplinary synthesis of theory and methods. Technical Report (2011)
11. Kieras, D.E., Bovair, S.: The role of a mental model in learning to operate a device. Cogn. Sci. **8**(3), 255–273 (1984)
12. Lauesen, S., Harning, M.B.: Virtual windows: linking user tasks, data models, and interface design. IEEE Softw. **18**(4), 67–75 (2001)
13. Lucassen, G., Dalpiaz, F., Werf, J.M.E.M., Brinkkemper, S.: The use and effectiveness of user stories in practice. In: Daneva, M., Pastor, O. (eds.) REFSQ 2016. LNCS, vol. 9619, pp. 205–222. Springer, Cham (2016). https://doi.org/10.1007/978-3-319-30282-9_14
14. Norman, D.A.: Some observations on mental models. In: Mental Models, pp. 7–14. Psychology Press, Hove (2014)
15. Paech, B., Kohler, K.: Task-driven requirements in object-oriented development. In: do Prado Leite, J.C.S., Doorn, J.H. (eds.) Perspectives on Software Requirements. SECS, vol. 753, pp. 45–67. Springer, Boston (2004). https://doi.org/10.1007/978-1-4615-0465-8_3
16. Rieh, S.Y., Yang, J.Y., Yakel, E., Markey, K.: Conceptualizing institutional repositories: using co-discovery to uncover mental models. In: 3rd Symposium on Information Interaction in Context, pp. 165–174. ACM (2010)
17. Runeson, P., Host, M., Rainer, A., Regnell, B.: Case Study Research in Software Engineering: Guidelines and Examples, 1st edn. John Wiley & Sons, New York (2012)
18. Santos, R., Groen, E.C., Villela, K.: A taxonomy for user feedback classifications. In: REFSQ Workshops, vol. 2376. CEUR-WS (2019)
19. Zhang, Y.: The influence of mental models on undergraduate students' searching behavior on the web. Inf. Process. Manage. **44**(3), 1330–1345 (2008)

Vision Video Making with Novices:
A Research Preview

Melanie Busch[1]([⊠]), Jianwei Shi[1], Lukas Nagel[1], Johann Sell[2],
and Kurt Schneider[1]

[1] Software Engineering Group, Leibniz Universität Hannover,
Welfengarten 1, 30167 Hannover, Germany
{melanie.busch,jianwei.shi,lukas.nagel,
kurt.schneider}@inf.uni-hannover.de
[2] Didaktik der Informatik/Informatik und Gesellschaft, Humboldt-Universität zu
Berlin, Rudower Chaussee 25, 12489 Berlin, Germany
sell@informatik.hu-berlin.de

Abstract. [**Context and motivation**] It is crucial to develop a vision of what a new piece of software will do and how it will affect personal tasks, processes, and the environment. Vision videos have been proposed for visualizing a tentative vision very early in a project, long before prototypes are in reach. Such a video can support the elicitation and validation of (software) product visions. [**Question/problem**] However, vision videos often have to be produced by people without prior knowledge in video production. Can video novices be adequately supported through an adapted vision video creation process? What materials, documents, and steps are crucial for planning, recording, and finalizing a video? [**Principal ideas/results**] We derived recommendations for *Affordable Vision Videos*. In this paper, we describe how the recommended process and techniques performed when we created a vision video with the "Viva con Agua" (VcA) NGO. [**Contribution**] The lessons learned from this case study helped us improve our recommendations for requirements engineers who are not proficient in directing videos but consider using them as a good medium for expressing visions and soliciting rich feedback.

Keywords: Requirements engineering · Vision · Video · Video making

1 Introduction

Nowadays, countless different software systems exist in our everyday life. To name just a few examples: The day begins with the use of a smartphone alarm clock, followed by the preparation of a coffee with a fully automatic coffee machine and the drive to the office with a smart car. The creation of software systems like these require a *vision* at the very beginning of the development process [2]. But how can a vision be communicated clearly and simply? One possible solution for conveying a vision that appeals to both the visual and the auditory channels is to use video, so-called *Vision Video*. According to Schneider et al. [9], vision videos generally present the underlying problem, a solution illustrated

V. Gervasi and A. Vogelsang (Eds.): REFSQ 2022, LNCS 13216, pp. 251–258, 2022.
https://doi.org/10.1007/978-3-030-98464-9_19

by the future software system, and the added value associated with it. Before a
vision video can be used for requirements engineering, it has to be produced. As
this aspect is only rarely covered by research [3,5,6], in this paper, we focus on
the vision video making process.

In our research, we take the position that vision videos must be easy to
produce, with little effort and without additional costs. This approach is called
Affordable Video Approach [9]. Karras and Schneider [4] found that software professionals without prior knowledge in video production need guidance for producing vision videos. In a subsequent publication, Karras and Schneider compiled
guidelines for vision video production [5]. Based on our previous work in the field
of vision videos [1,4,5,8,9], we have gained experience in preproduction, shooting and editing of vision videos. We now derived a step by step process of vision
video creation, which we tested in the case study with novices without prior
knowledge of vision videos. We supported the novices in the phase of preproduction through recurring exchanges, guiding documents and materials so they
could shoot the vision video on their own. After the vision video was finalized,
we conducted an interview with the two vision holders about their experience
and opinion on making a vision video.

The paper is structured as follows: Sect. 2 describes the case study. Section 3
presents the results. Section 4 includes the discussion, lessons learned and threats
to validity. The paper is concluded in Sect. 5.

2   Case Study: A Vision Video for Viva con Agua e.V.

The goal of this research is to *review and improve the existing vision video creation process and techniques*. In particular, we wanted to figure out whether
vision video novices could be adequately supported by an adapted video creation process. We supported and guided such novices as part of our case study.
Afterwards we conducted interviews with the two involved vision holders.

2.1   Case Organization

We performed a case study with members of the non-governmental organization Viva con Agua de St. Pauli e.V. (VcA)[1], who were interested in spread-
ing the vision of a software pool architecture among their volunteers. VcA has
more than 15000 volunteers. The volunteers of the association collect donations
to support Water, Sanitation, and Hygiene (WASH) projects worldwide. Since
volunteering is a free time activity and VcA applies the principle of open participation, the organization faces challenges regarding the coordination that have
been addressed by the self-implemented computer-supported cooperative work
tool *Pool*[2] in 2011. After the introduction of the Pool, a socio-technical organization [7] and thus, also a structural coupling between the Pool and the social
system of the organization arose.

---

[1] VcA, https://www.vivaconagua.org/, accessed 2021-09-21.
[2] https://pool2.vivaconagua.org/, accessed 2021-09-21.

2.2   Process and Materials Used

Four roles from two participating organizations took part in the video-making process. On the side of the vision holder (VcA), three lay actors played the scenes in the video. To keep the effort for vision videos low, scenes are often played by the requirements engineers themselves as in Schneider et al. [9]. In addition, two vision holders communicated with RE-Coaches. The RE-Coaches (instantiated by researchers of the Leibniz Universität Hannover), are the authors of this paper and one vision holder is a co-author. In addition, a video expert (one student assistant) was in close dialogue with the RE-Coaches. All exchanges between vision holders and RE-Coaches took place online via conferencing tools or email.

The RE-Coaches participated actively in the preproduction and postproduction, whereas the vision holders were active in the sections of preproduction and shooting. In the following, we describe the sequence of exchange in chronological order. First, exchanges between vision holders and RE-Coaches took place. The product vision was identified. In the next step, one of the vision holders created a short written draft of the vision. Since the RE-Coaches are familiar with the creation of vision videos, they prepared the necessary materials and documents in consultation with the vision holders during the preproduction phase. The following materials and documents were created specifically to support novices:

- **storyboard:** hand-drawn pictures next to short descriptions of the scenes
- **emotion graph:** shows the development of emotion through the scenes
- **key video shooting recommendations for novices**
- **material list:** tabular listing of materials, quantity, scene, source
- **scene list:** tabular listing of location and time, scene, actor, material

Figure 1 shows the adapted process of vision video making which based on the guidelines of Karras and Schneider [5]. In the preproduction phase, after the step of planning the shots, the step "Create Vision Video of Vision Video" was added. This novel additional step is inserted to convey the main idea of the video's content concretely, e.g. to possible actors or other persons on the side of the vision holders who did not take part in the preproduction phase. Based on the storyboard, the RE-Coaches developed a simple low-effort orientation video to help vision holders produce the real vision video. This **"vision video of the vision video"** consists of a montage of the hand-drawn storyboard images with an audio track of the dialogues. In the preproduction phase, we selected key video shooting recommendations from existing guidelines [5] we deemed most relevant to novices. These guidelines are documented on one-page as a quick reference for vision holders during the shooting. The green colored boxes with dashed lines indicate the steps which the vision holders performed by themselves without any further support of the RE-Coaches.

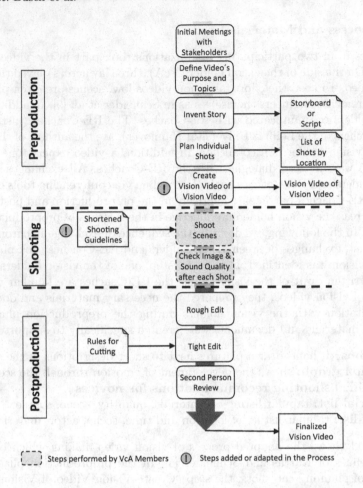

Fig. 1. Adapted process of vision video making according to [5]

2.3 Empirical Investigation: Interviews

We interviewed two vision holders from VcA who had a vision in mind and wanted to communicate it through a vision video. The interviews were semi-structured, as an interview guide was used, but we also asked situational follow-up questions. Due to the pandemic the interviews were held online via BigBlue-Button[3], a conferencing system. During the interviews, the audio was recorded with the consent of the interviewees and then transcribed for the analysis. The interviews took place after the video shoot and took 18 and 37 min respectively. One interview participant answered in much more detail, hence the different interview duration. Each interview was divided into three sections: **(1)** The

---

[3] https://bigbluebutton.org/.

experience of creating a vision video **(2)** The use of materials and documents **(3)** Rating of the final vision video.

3 Results

Experiences of Making a Vision Video
Both interviewees were very positively surprised that the video shoot worked so well considering that they had no prior knowledge regarding vision video creation. One of them stated that they did not expect the shooting to be completed in just one day. Another positive statement was that the video quality was surprisingly good, even though only smartphone cameras were used to film the scenes. The filming of the video took place using several smartphones partly from different angles.

Helpful Materials for Novice (Vision) Video Makers
Both interviewees said that the **material list** was used and one stated that the list was important. One interviewee said that the **discussions** with the RE-Coaches prior to the actual shooting were very supportive in clarifying the vision more and more. Opinions are divided on the "**vision video of the vision video**". One interviewee stated that they remember the "vision video of the vision video" most closely of all the support materials they were given. On a scale from 0 (not helpful at all) to 5 (totally helpful) they rated the video with a 4. One interviewee said the hand-drawn pictures and the spoken dialogues were very illustrative. According to the other interviewee, the video was shown to the actors too late. For this reason, the respondent rated the helpfulness of the "vision video of the vision video" with a 3. Another document that was considered important by one of the interviewees was the **storyboard**. The sequence of the scenes and images included in the storyboard were perceived as relevant. The **scene list** had also been considered, as mentioned by one interviewee. The scene list showed that double casting of a role was possible, so the scene list was explicitly mentioned by one interviewee. The **emotion graph** and the **key video shooting recommendations for novices** were consulted before the shooting but not used during the shoot.

Rating of the Final Vision Video
One question in the interview asked about the rating of the finished vision video on a 6-point Likert-scale from 0 (not at all satisfied) to 5 (completely satisfied). Both interviewees were satisfied with the vision video and rated it a 4. In the interview, the respondents were asked whether they would use vision videos in the future, and if so, for what purpose or in which context. One interviewee stated that a future use of vision videos in the context of workshops could be well imagined. To detail the previous statement, they mentioned contexts where it is necessary to present things under time pressure and without much effort. The other interviewee issued a similar statement and noted that vision videos could be seen as a kind of workshop result.

4 Discussion

Vision videos provide a good way to convey a vision among stakeholders in the early phases of a project. In this paper, we focus on how to best support novices during vision video making. An important point to emphasize is that all scenes for the vision video were shot by novices during only one day. This result is comforting, as even novices can make vision videos in a moderate amount of time. The required time of only one day and the exclusive use of smartphones for filming further underline the principles of the *Affordable Video Approach* proposed by Schneider et al. [9].

4.1 Lessons Learned

The order of the lessons corresponds to the sequence of steps or the used materials in the video making process:

- The purpose of using vision videos is to elicit, visualize, and validate visions about software and its use. Discussions between vision holders and RE-Coaches are an important step in evolving and sharpening the vision.
- The "vision video of the vision video" was a fast and inexpensive way of providing a first version of a vision video with sound. It is recommended to benefit from such a rich-media shortcut before filming all scenes with real people.
- We propose using the emotion graph as an orientation in the preproduction phase.
- The items on the material list have to be reviewed in terms of availability by participants of the video shoot.
- Ways to ensure a good sound quality for outdoor recordings are required.

4.2 Threats to Validity

Despite careful design and execution, there are some limitations to our work which we discuss in the following section. We classify threats according to Wohlin et al. [10]. **Construct Validity**: A threat to the construct validity is that the process has only been practically implemented on the example of one case, which resulted in only one vision video. **Internal Validity**: One of the vision holders interviewed is also a co-author of this paper, as they assisted us with their knowledge of VcA during the writing process. The impact of this limitation was mitigated by interviewing the other vision holder as well. Furthermore, the mentioned co-author was strictly separated from the preparation and evaluation of the interviews. These tasks were only performed by the RE-Coaches. **Conclusion Validity**: The conclusion validity concerning the evaluation of the vision video creation process could be subjectively impacted, as the analysis was primarily performed by a single author. However, the other authors participating as RE-Coaches reviewed the transcripts and the derived findings and came to the same results. **External Validity**: An important threat to the external validity is that a replication of the case study is not possible. Our adapted process of vision video making requires replication in other case studies to support our findings and gain generalizability.

5 Conclusion

In the case study reported in this paper, the authors supported novices in creating a vision video using an adapted vision video making process. Novices with no previous experience were able to shoot the scenes for a vision video in just one day. In the end, the vision holders were satisfied with the final vision video. In addition, the case study showed once again that no expensive camera equipment is needed for filming; all scenes were shot with smartphones.

Evaluation Plan: Our results indicate that further research on the creation of vision videos with novices is necessary and promising. In the short term, we plan to interview the vision holders once the created video has been distributed to the target audience. We also look to give out questionnaires to audience members. In the long term, we plan workshops for novices with a focus on creating vision videos. Workshop participants might be able to create videos with little effort by following a process influenced by the results of this paper.

Acknowledgement. This work was supported by the Deutsche Forschungsgemeinschaft (DFG) under Grant No.: 289386339, project ViViUse.

References

1. Busch, M., Karras, O., Schneider, K., Ahrens, M.: Vision meets visualization: are animated videos an alternative? In: Madhavji, N., Pasquale, L., Ferrari, A., Gnesi, S. (eds.) REFSQ 2020. LNCS, vol. 12045, pp. 277–292. Springer, Cham (2020). https://doi.org/10.1007/978-3-030-44429-7_19
2. Creighton, O., Ott, M., Bruegge, B.: Software cinema-video-based requirements engineering. In: 14th IEEE International Requirements Engineering Conference (RE 2006), pp. 109–118. IEEE, September 2006
3. Karras, O.: Supporting Requirements Communication for Shared Understanding by Applying Vision Videos in Requirements Engineering. Logos Verlag Berlin GmbH (2021)
4. Karras, O., Schneider, K.: Software professionals are not directors: what constitutes a good video? In: 2018 1st International Workshop on Learning from other Disciplines for Requirements Engineering (D4RE), pp. 18–21. IEEE (2018)
5. Karras, O., Schneider, K.: An interdisciplinary guideline for the production of videos and vision videos by software professionals. Technical Report, Software Engineering Group, Leibniz Universität Hannover (2021). https://arxiv.org/abs/2001.06675v2
6. Karras, O., Schneider, K., Fricker, S.A.: Representing software project vision by means of video: a quality model for vision videos. J. Syst. Softw. **162**, 110479 (2020)

7. Kunau, G.: Facilitating computer supported cooperative work with socio-technical self-descriptions. Ph.D. thesis, Technische Universität Dortmund (2006)
8. Nagel, L., Shi, J., Busch, M.: Viewing vision videos online: opportunities for distributed stakeholders. In: 2021 IEEE 29th International Requirements Engineering Conference Workshops (REW), pp. 306–312 (2021)
9. Schneider, K., Busch, M., Karras, O., Schrapel, M., Rohs, M.: Refining vision videos. In: Knauss, E., Goedicke, M. (eds.) REFSQ 2019. LNCS, vol. 11412, pp. 135–150. Springer, Cham (2019). https://doi.org/10.1007/978-3-030-15538-4_10
10. Wohlin, C., Runeson, P., Höst, M., Ohlsson, M.C., Regnell, B., Wesslén, A.: Experimentation in Software Engineering. Springer, Heidelberg (2012). https://doi.org/10.1007/978-3-642-29044-2

Author Index

Printed in the United States
by Baker & Taylor Publisher Services

Printed in the United States
by Baker & Taylor Publisher Services